The Future of Sterling
as an International Currency

By the same author

The Future of Sterling as an International Currency

BENJAMIN J. COHEN
Department of Economics
Princeton University

MACMILLAN
ST MARTIN'S PRESS

First published 1971 by
THE MACMILLAN PRESS LTD
London and Basingstoke
Associated companies in New York Toronto
Dublin Melbourne Johannesburg and Madras

Library of Congress catalog card no. 75–148463

SBN 333 12189 9 (hard cover)

Printed in Great Britain by
R. & R. CLARK LTD
Edinburgh

For Peter Kenen

Contents

List of Tables and Figures

It's a shame to see what has happened to sterling. Once, a note issued by the Bank of England proudly read: 'I promise to pay the bearer on demand the sum of one pound.' Now it simply reads: WATCH THIS SPACE.

David Frost

We do not rule out some further changes in the reserve role of sterling in future.

Roy Jenkins

Acknowledgements

MORE debts of gratitude were accumulated in the writing of this book than can possibly be acknowledged in the space of a few paragraphs.

In particular, I wish to thank the following friends and colleagues who all gave graciously of their time and patience to comment on various drafts of my manuscript: Professor Harry G. Johnson of the London School of Economics and the University of Chicago; Professor John Spraos of University College, London; Professor John H. Williamson of Warwick University; Professor John Knapp of Manchester University; Mrs Susan Strange of the Royal Institute of International Affairs (Chatham House); Mr W. S. Ryrie of Her Majesty's Treasury; Mr Stephen J. Canner of the American Embassy in London; Mr Ernest H. Preeg of the United States Department of State; Mr John R. Karlik of the Joint Economic Committee of the Congress; Mr Anthony M. Lanyi of the International Monetary Fund; Mr William Diebold, Jr, of the Council on Foreign Relations; Professor Raymond F. Mikesell of the University of Oregon; and, last but no by means least, Professor Fritz Machlup of Princeton University. Of course, I alone remain responsible for all errors of fact or interpretation which may still remain.

I also received considerable assistance and encouragement from a number of persons in the City of London, including especially Mr William M. Clarke and Mr W. A. P. Manser of the Committee on Invisible Exports; Mr John Cooper of J. H. Schroder Wagg & Company Ltd; Mr J. P. MacArthur and Mr George K. Young of Kleinwort Benson Ltd; and Mr V. R. A. Baillie, Mr David Huelin and Mr A. J. Ponte of the Bank of London and South America.

The bulk of this study was carried out during the academic year 1968–9, while I was on leave of absence from my teaching duties in the Department of Economics of Princteon University. The leave was made possible by the Council on Foreign Relations, by granting me an International Affairs Fellowship for the year. I am particularly indebted to the programme director, Mr John T. Swing, for his aid and advice, and to the Rockefeller Brothers Fund, which financed the fellowship. The Department of Political Economy of University College, London, enabled me to do my research on the scene by kindly providing me with office space and secretarial assistance. I also benefited from discussion and comment by the other members of the Department.

Several portions of this study have already appeared in preliminary and abbreviated form elsewhere. The principal findings of Part Two concerning the benefits and costs of sterling as an international currency were summarised in two articles in *Euromoney* in September 1969 and April 1970. An earlier version of the major part of Chapter 6 was published in an article in *The Banker* for February 1970. And a condensed version of Part Three appeared as a Princeton Essay in International Finance in December 1969 under the title 'The Reform of Sterling'. I am grateful to the publishers of *Euromoney* and *The Banker*, and to the International Finance Section of Princeton University, for permission to use portions of this earlier material in the present book.

The book is dedicated to Professor Peter B. Kenen, of Columbia University, who as teacher, as adviser and as close personal friend during my years as a student at Columbia, by encouragement and by personal example, gave me the confidence I needed to complete my formal studies. In the deepest possible sense, this book could never have been written without him.

BENJAMIN J. COHEN

Introduction

WHAT is the future of sterling? At present the pound is a great international currency – not so great as it used to be perhaps, but still second only to the dollar. At the level of private international transactions it functions globally as a vehicle, or trading, currency. At least a fifth of world trade is still invoiced and settled in sterling; in addition, a considerable amount of private wealth is still held in the form of sterling assets in London. The pound also functions as a reserve currency, albeit today largely on a regional rather than a genuinely global scale. Since the Second World War the use of sterling as an official intervention and reserve medium has been confined almost entirely to the countries of the sterling area.

Should sterling be reformed – and if so, then to what extent and by what means? Should the pound continue to function as international money at both the private and official levels of international transactions, or should one or both of these roles be eliminated? Should the currency serve on a global scale or a regional scale? Should reform be unilateral or multilateral? These are the questions we are concerned with in the present book.

Essentially, this is a book about structural financial *arrangements*. Our objective is to evaluate alternative reforms of sterling as an international currency – to find, in the apt words of one writer, 'a long-term solution to the tangled problem of the short-term sterling liabilities'.[1] The following chapters therefore touch only quite peripherally on the problem of present British policy affecting the balance of payments. Though highly important and closely related, current financial *management* is not our concern here; that problem is analytically distinct.

The approach of this book is frankly national rather than cosmopolitan in outlook. The problem of the pound's position as an international currency is treated as an exercise in foreign economic policy.

[1] Malcolm Crawford, 'Funding the Sterling Balances', *The Banker*, CXVIII 509 (July 1968) 607.

The desirability of any reform is considered strictly from the point of view of the national interest of the United Kingdom – not from the point of view of the world as a whole.

From this national point of view, many observers conclude that reform of sterling would in fact be desirable. In their opinion, an intolerable burden is imposed on the British economy by the continuing use of the pound for international purposes. This burden includes of course the payment of interest to foreigners on the huge 'overhang' of short-term sterling liabilities abroad. Even more importantly, it includes the constraint imposed by that overhang – that is, the constraint imposed by the threat of reduction or withdrawal of liabilities – on the nature and timing of domestic full-employment policies. Whenever a 'run' on the pound develops, additional measures of domestic deflation, or trade or capital restriction, are required to protect the nation's gold and dollar reserves. In the words of Andrew Shonfield:

> The more extensively sterling is used in international trade and payments, the more Britain is exposed to speculative flurries of this kind. . . . In retrospect, the enormous effort made by the British authorities since the war to encourage the ever wider use of sterling in international trade and payments appears an extraordinarily hazardous venture.[1]

Accordingly, many alternative reforms of sterling have been proposed by all kinds of experts. Yet for all the wealth of ideas expressed, there has been remarkably little consensus of judgement. If all the experts on sterling were laid end to end, they would still not reach agreement.

Why this lack of agreement? A principal reason is that no one really is quite sure just how serious the burden of the sterling balances happens to be. Another reason is that many experts overlook the substantial benefits of sterling which happen also to accrue to the United Kingdom. As Maxwell Stamp has written:

> Many people . . . regard the sterling balances as a 'burden', which we ought to get rid of. Of course, it is always nice to have the assets without the liabilities, but having had the money and the resources which that represents it is not too reasonable to complain about the debt. By and large, as anyone in the banking business knows, it is a 'good thing' to have deposits, and provided one makes proper use of the resources they represent it is a profitable thing. Britain has, in fact, gained from having had the use of the resources, and from the use of

[1] Andrew Shonfield, *British Economic Policy since the War* (London: Penguin Books, 1958) p. 151.

sterling as a reserve and trading currency; this must be taken into account when we consider what could or should happen to sterling. . . .[1]

I concur: to evaluate alternative reforms of sterling, it is necessary to take into account not only costs but also benefits as well. 'The economic value of the international role of sterling is very much a two-sided question', as a former high Treasury official noted recently.[2] Yet in fact few systematic attempts have ever been made to measure the economic gains and losses resulting from the pound's use, past or present, for international purposes.[3] No wonder, then, that there has been so little consensus of judgement among the experts. They have not had sufficient data. This is a deficiency that the present book aims to remedy. The following chapters will present, for the first time, a full and comprehensive analysis of every one of the major economic benefits and costs of sterling.

In order to be able to analyse the benefits and costs of an international currency, it is necessary, first of all, to have a proper analytical framework. That is, it is necessary to understand what all the functions are of an international currency and how they are interrelated; in addition, it is necessary to understand what the benefits and costs are of each of these functions. Unfortunately, a coherent theory of international currencies cannot be found in contemporary international monetary literature. This also helps to account for the lack of consensus among experts on the sterling problem. The present book aims to remedy this deficiency as well.

The plan of organisation of the book is as follows. Part One is devoted to the development of a coherent theory of international currencies. The first chapter works through the logic of the evolution of international money; the second enumerates and attributes international money's separate potential gains and losses. The result of this discussion is a proper analytical framework, which is then used in Part Two to measure (as closely as possible) the various benefits and costs of sterling. The main body of the empirical analysis is contained in Chapters 5–8. Chapter 4, which briefly recounts the history of sterling as an

---

[1] Maxwell Stamp, 'Sterling and the Common Market', *The Banker*, CXVI 490 (Dec 1966) 846.

[2] Harold Lever, 'Conditions for Sterling Reform', in *Sterling: European Monetary Co-operation and World Monetary Reform* (London: Federal Trust for Education and Research, 1968) p. 8.

[3] The most detailed attempt along these lines was by Alan P. Kirman and Wilson E. Schmidt, 'Key Currency Burdens: The U.K. Case', *National Banking Review*, III 1 (Sep 1965) 101–2.

international currency, represents something of a digression. The methodology and assumptions of the analysis are introduced in Chapter 3; the principal results of the analysis are summarised in Chapter 9. These data are then used to approach our main objective – an evaluation of alternative reforms of sterling – in Part Three (Chapters 10–12). The conclusions of the examination are summarised at the end of Chapter 12.

The essence of the book is concentrated in the latter half of Chapter 1 and in Chapters 2, 3, 9, 11 and 12. These are recommended for the reader lacking sufficient time – or patience – to work through all twelve of the chapters from start to finish. The reader really in a hurry can pick up the basic ideas of the study by glancing at Tables 2.2 and 9.1 together with the final section of Chapter 12.

PART ONE

A Theory of International Currencies

1 The Roles of an International Currency

INTERNATIONAL monetary economics still has no adequate theory of international currencies. Sir John Hicks wrote: 'One of the chief things which monetary theory ought to explain is the evolution of money.'[1] Likewise, one of the chief things which international monetary theory ought to explain is the evolution of international money. (Throughout this study the terms 'international money' and 'international currency' will be used interchangeably.) What is international money? What needs does it serve? And why do just certain national currencies come to perform its various functions?

I. DOMESTIC MONEY

The roles of money

We can approach the answers to these questions about international money by beginning with identical questions about the money circulating within each country – 'domestic' money. First, what is money? The answer to that question is not so simple as it might appear. In fact, money can only be defined in terms of the functions it performs; that is, by the needs it fulfils. 'Money is one of those concepts which, like a teaspoon or an umbrella, but unlike an earthquake or a buttercup, are definable primarily by the use or purpose which they serve.'[2] Money is anything, regardless of its physical or legal characteristics, that customarily and principally performs certain special functions.

These functions are usually specified as being three in number. They correspond to the three basic needs served by money – the need for a *medium of exchange*, the need for a *unit of account*, and the need for a

---

[1] Sir John Hicks, *Critical Essays in Monetary Theory* (London: Oxford University Press, 1967) p. 2.

[2] Sir Ralph Hawtrey, *Currency and Credit*, 3rd ed. (New York: Longmans, Green, 1928) p. 1.

store of value. Obviously these three functions are closely interrelated, as we shall be continually reminded as our analysis proceeds. Nevertheless it is useful to distinguish among them. Most familiar is the first, the function of medium of exchange, whereby goods and services are paid for and contractual obligations discharged. In performing this role the key attribute of money is general acceptability in the settlement of debt. The second function of money is to act as a unit of account – the common denominator or *numéraire* in which goods and services are valued and debts expressed. In performing this role, money is said on the one hand (in valuing goods and services) to be a 'standard of value' or 'measure of value', and on the other hand (in expressing debts) to be a 'standard of deferred payment'. The third function of money is to act as a store of value – a means of holding wealth.

For many economists, the medium-of-exchange function of money is paramount: money is defined simply as being synonymous with the circulating means of payment. In effect, the medium-of-exchange function is said to be not only necessary but sufficient. 'The essential function, the performance of which enables us to identify money, is very simple: it is that of acting as a medium of exchange.'[1] However, this approach is not entirely satisfactory. Indeed, for our analytical purposes it could be downright misleading, as we shall shortly see. A preferable analytical approach, I am about to argue, is to distinguish between *partial* moneys and *fully developed* moneys.[2] Partial moneys are defined as having one or two monetary functions, but not all three; they possess only some of the attributes of money. Fully developed moneys are defined as performing all three roles.

Not that I would attempt to deny the paramount importance of the medium-of-exchange function in the *evolution* of money. But this should not lead us astray in defining for analytical purposes the *attributes* of money. It is quite likely that money did begin, first of all, as a means of payment. Before money there was only simple barter, the archetypical economic transaction, which required an inverse double coincidence of wants if exchange was ever to occur. The two parties to any transaction each had to desire what the other was prepared to offer.

[1] W. T. Newlyn, *Theory of Money* (London: Oxford University Press, 1962) p. 1. See also Basil J. Moore, *An Introduction to the Theory of Finance* (New York: The Free Press, 1968) chap. 6; Boris P. Pesek and Thomas R. Saving, *The Foundations of Money and Banking* (New York: Macmillan, 1968) chap. 1; and Leland B. Yeager, 'Essential Properties of the Medium of Exchange', *Kyklos*, xxi (1968) fasc. 1, pp. 45–69.

[2] Hicks, op. cit., p. 2.

This was an obviously inefficient system of exchange, since under even the most elemental circumstances it was unlikely to exhaust all opportunities for advantageous trade:

> Bartering is costly in ways too numerous to discuss. Among others, bartering requires an expenditure of time and the use of specialised skills necessary for judging the commodities that are being exchanged. The more advanced the specialization in production and the more complex the economy, the costlier it will be to undertake all the transactions necessary to make any given good reach its ultimate user by using barter.[1]

The invention of generalised exchange intermediaries cut the Gordian knot of barter by decomposing the single transaction of barter into separate transactions of sale and purchase, thereby obviating the need for a double coincidence of wants. This served to facilitate multilateral exchange since, with costs of transaction minimised, exchange ratios could more efficiently equate the demand and supply of goods and services. Consequently, specialisation in production was promoted and the advantages of economic division of labour became attainable – all because of the invention of a generally acceptable means of payment.

It is clear that this was one of the most important steps in the evolution of human society, 'comparable', in the words of one writer, 'with the domestication of animals, the cultivation of the land, and the harnessing of power'.[2] No wonder that so many monetary theorists stress this particular function of money.

But can this particular function suffice to define money – fully developed money, that is? Certainly the medium-of-exchange function is a necessary condition: no one would argue with that proposition. Nothing is fully developed money that does not serve as a generalised means of payment. But it is a sufficient condition as well? That proposition is more dubious. Fully developed money performs three functions. If the single function of exchange intermediary is to suffice to define money, then it must follow that any medium of exchange automatically, and *simply by virtue of its being a medium of exchange*, functions also as a unit of account and as a store of value. In other words, as a logical necessity any exchange intermediary – *qua* exchange intermediary – performs all the three roles of money. Let us call this the

[1] Boris P. Pesek and Thomas R. Saving, *Money, Wealth, and Economic Theory* (New York: Macmillan, 1967) p. 47.

[2] E. Victor Morgan, *A History of Money* (Baltimore: Penguin Books, 1965) p. 11.

'sufficiency implication' of the medium-of-exchange function. I shall now argue that while there are some grains of truth in the sufficiency implication, they are neither numerous nor powerful enough to carry the full weight of analysis. This will be particularly evident at the level of analysis of international money, where a number of national currencies do fulfil the role of an international exchange intermediary but do not serve as unit of account; and where a number of currencies do fulfil the role of store of value, but do not serve as medium of exchange.

Consider first the relationship between the medium-of-exchange and unit-of-account functions. These two roles of money have always been closely linked together, for there are obvious practical advantages in using the same unit both for reckoning values and for making payments. But by the same token it should be noted that there is no logical *necessity* for the two functions to be shared by the same unit. Indeed, even when unit of account and medium of exchange are called by the same name, they remain quite distinct, one an accounting abstraction, the other a concrete object that happens to serve as a means of payment. The distinction between them is only emphasised all the more when the two are called by different names, as has occurred from time to time throughout monetary history. In medieval Europe, for example, the lira was the conventional unit of account, though never coined, at the same time that a variety of other moneys were employed as means of payment; and even until very recently in twentieth-century England many prices were traditionally quoted in guineas, even though these no longer circulated alongside the familiar – and colourful – array of pennies, florins, half-crowns, etc. Similarly, in the United States today some states and local governments express their tax rates in terms of the mill, equal to one-tenth of a cent, whereas the penny (equal to one cent) happens to be the smallest coin actually in circulation.

To be sure, whether unit of account and medium of exchange are called by the same name or by different names, the distinction between them makes little difference for analysis so long as the relationship between them remains fixed. And the fact is that in examples such as the three just cited, the mutual relationship does happen to be a constant one. This, of course, is the real point of the sufficiency implication in so far as the unit-of-account function is concerned: monetary theorists simply assume that they can ignore, as for instance Leland Yeager has insisted, 'the far-fetched . . . concept of a system in which the two functions are split, with the actual medium of exchange fluctuating in price in terms of the separate unit in which ordinary goods and services are also priced'.[1] But is the concept so far-fetched? Surely, so long as the possibility exists, monetary thought ought to be general enough to include it. At the level of domestic money, one is reminded of the 'wildcat' banking era of the United States, when the note issues of many private banks were quoted daily in the newspapers at fluctuating values in terms of the national dollar. One is also reminded that even today in the United States there are still well over 750 so-called 'non-par' banks, clinging to their right to honour cheques drawn on them and cleared through the Federal Reserve clearing system at a discount from face value – in effect creating a network of variable exchange rates between the national dollar and various local dollars. And likewise, at the level of international money, one is reminded of such a widely circulated exchange intermediary as the pound sterling, whose price twice in the last generation has been altered in terms of both gold and the U.S. dollar, the standard international accounting units. At this level of analysis the potentially variable price relationship between medium of exchange and unit of account is crucial. Here the sufficiency implication can only mislead the monetary analyst.

Now consider the relationship between the medium-of-exchange and store-of-value functions. Here the sufficiency implication is perfectly valid: logically, an exchange intermediary must function also as a means of holding wealth (at least temporarily). Yet here too the implication can mislead the monetary analyst – if he is not careful. For the reverse correlation is not valid at all: there is absolutely no logical necessity for a store of value to take on as well the function of payments medium. The line of causation necessarily works in one direction, but not in the other.

If people are willing to use an asset as an exchange intermediary, by definition this means that they are willing to use it also as a store of value. This is a logical necessity of the notion of general acceptability. For in separating the single transaction of barter into two distinct transactions of purchase and sale, the introduction of an exchange intermediary also necessarily separates the transactions in time: an interval is created between the sale of goods and services and the subsequent use of money. Consequently, to that extent at least, the means of payment must necessarily be held as a temporary reserve of ready purchasing power. People must be willing to hold it; otherwise it could not function as exchange intermediary. As Professor Newlyn has

[1] Yeager, op. cit., p. 61, n. 21.

argued: 'The general acceptability of anything as a medium of exchange implies that, to some extent, it will be held over time.'[1]

On the other hand, if people are willing to use an asset as a store of value, this does *not* mean that they must also be willing to accept it regularly in payment. Any marketable asset appropriately appearing in the balance sheet – land, an insurance policy, even an automobile – may be regarded as a means of holding wealth. In this sense, all marketable assets are partial moneys.[2] But partial moneys are not fully developed moneys. Stores of value do not automatically become generally acceptable in settlement of debt, even though the quality of value-storage can enhance the attractiveness of assets for transactions purposes. In fact, relatively few stores of value are ever chosen to be used as exchange intermediaries.

To explain why this should be so, we shall have to examine more closely the notion of general acceptability. But before we get to that (in the following section, entitled 'The Choice of Moneys'), it would be appropriate to examine briefly a different notion first – the notion of a store of value itself. Why are certain assets more attractive than others as means of holding wealth? Fully developed money is, for most purposes, the most attractive store of value of all. The reason for this is that fully developed money offers two distinct advantages over other kinds of assets. The first is *exchange convenience*, owing to money's low transfer costs in the exercise of purchasing power; and the second is *capital certainty*, owing to the high short-run predictability of money's future value.[3] Other assets are more likely to be used for store-of-value purposes to the extent that they are capable of approximating these two advantages.

The exchange convenience of money is a direct consequence of its function as medium of exchange. By definition, a means of payment

---

[1] Newlyn, op. cit., p. 1. See also Moore, op. cit., p. 155; and J. C. Gilbert, 'The Demand for Money: The Development of an Economic Concept', *Journal of Political Economy*, LXI 2 (Apr 1953) 147. Note that in a system in which exchanges are instantaneous – the interval between the sale of goods and services and the subsequent use of money being reduced to zero – the medium of exchange would become redundant: there would be no need for a unique means of payment. Consequently there would be no need for a temporary reserve of ready purchasing power either. But it would still be convenient to have a unit of account in which to calculate the exchange ratios of all commodities. This provides an additional argument for the logical separability of the medium-of-exchange and unit-of-account functions I have insisted upon. See Gilbert, op. cit., p. 150.

[2] Cf. Hicks, op. cit., chap. 2, esp. pp. 17–18.

[3] Moore, op. cit., chap. 6.

is generally acceptable at zero or near-zero transactions cost in exchange for other economic goods. Indeed, one way of defining a means of payment is by describing it as the asset with lowest transactions costs.[1] Consequently, exchange intermediaries are the most *marketable* of all assets, in the sense that the market for them is the broadest and most efficient. They are also the most *reversible* of all assets, in the sense that they tend to have the smallest difference between buying and selling price (realisable value) at an instant of time. These characteristics confer on monetary assets a differential cost advantage over other highly realisable assets which alternatively might be held as a temporary reverse of ready purchasing power.[2]

The capital certainty of money is a direct consequence of its function as unit of account. This refers of course to real-value certainty, not money-value certainty. By definition, since a unit of account is a *numéraire*, it must have absolute money-value certainty. Indeed, one way of defining a unit of account is by describing it as the only asset with absolute money-value certainty at all points of time.[3] However, what really matters here is that monetary assets also have a higher certainty of real value, in the short run at least, because capital loss can occur only as a result of changes in the general price level. Such changes are ordinarily smaller and more predictable than changes in the price of other individual assets which might be held as a store of value.

The choice of moneys

In a simple barter economy, nearly every commodity may be a 'money'. Any durable good could conceivably serve as a unit of account and store of value, and all commodities are, by definition,

---

[1] Yeager, op. cit., p. 67. Yeager points out that ambiguity about the lowest transactions costs could explain the coexistence of two or more varieties of medium of exchange. Each might have the lowest transactions costs in some types of transactions (p. 67, n. 28).

[2] These characteristics are often lumped together under the notion of 'liquidity'. However, this is such an elusive concept, and means so many different things to different people, that it seems best not to introduce it in the present context. But, see Newlyn, op. cit., chap. 10; and H. Laurence Miller, Jr, 'On "Liquidity" and "Transaction Costs" ', *Southern Economic Journal*, II 1 (July 1965) 43–8.

[3] Newlyn, op. cit., pp. 51–4. Bonds also have absolute money-value certainty, but only at time of maturity (unless the government intervenes as a matter of policy to support their price); money has zero time to maturity.

means of payment for all other commodities. Yet in fact we observe in even the most elemental economic circumstances a historical tendency to limit the number of moneys. In every economy and in every epoch, just a few select commodities have come to play a special role as exchange intermediaries – commodities as diverse as cattle, cloth, cereals, shells, stones, ornaments, ceremonial objects, etc., as well as precious metals like silver and gold.[1] What accounts for this historical tendency, and what determines the choice of moneys? These are the questions to which we now turn.

I have suggested that one way of defining a means of payment is by describing it as the asset with lowest transactions costs. In barter economies these costs tend to be high because of the practical problem of achieving the required double coincidence of wants: much time must be devoted to search and bargaining. But waiting time can be substantially diminished for an individual if, by observing the mix and amount of commodities traded in the community, he adapts his own commodity mix to that of other individuals – that is, if he begins to hold for specific use as exchange intermediaries inventories of those commodities that are most widely demanded by other individuals, whether or not these commodities are of any use to him directly. True, in one respect the individual's waiting time is thereby increased, for certain commodities will now be stocked that were formerly ignored. But in a much more important respect his waiting time is significantly decreased, for owing to his increased assurance that desired purchases can be carried out expeditiously, he will now require much smaller total inventories of all commodities. We may be quite certain, therefore, that on balance transactions costs can be significantly reduced in a barter setting by the practice of holding commodity-exchange intermediaries. And consequently we may be equally certain that this accounts for the origin in all barter economies of the historical tendency to limit the number of moneys.[2]

Professor Hicks has written that 'one way of looking at monetary evolution is to regard it as the development of ever more sophisticated ways of reducing transaction costs'.[3] And indeed the facts of monetary history do confirm what the logic of economies of scale would lead us to expect: that once the historical tendency to limit the number of

[1] Morgan, op. cit., chap. 1.

[2] Hicks, op. cit., chap. 1; and Robert Clower, 'Barter Exchange and Monetary Theory' (mimeographed) pp. 1–9.

[3] Hicks, op. cit., p. 7.

moneys began, the process was inevitably pursued to its logical conclusion. Societies tended to standardise upon just one commodity-exchange intermediary, or on just a small group of them. Usually the commodities eliminated as exchange intermediaries were the intrinsically useful, such as cattle, cloth, etc. Those that remained were the intrinsically useless, commonly weights of metal, since apart from their lower opportunity costs these had certain transactions-cost advantages as money. In the first place, they were durable, not much affected by storage or frequent use. Second, they were easy to grade and easy to divide. And third, most importantly of all, those selected tended to have a 'reasonable price per unit'. That is, they tended to have an economic value such that a 'reasonable' quantity of goods could be bought with a non-microscopic amount of it, and high-valued goods could be bought with a manageable amount of it. In short, they were scarce – but not too scarce.

Over time the commodity aspects of money were further suppressed, first by a transition from the tangible (coins) to the intangible (paper certificates), and later by a transition from asset money to debt money. For the most part, the evolution was haphazard and accidental – a classic example of the time-honoured process of trial and error. Only one element remained constant throughout: each society's willingness to endow one or a few commodities and/or tokens with the attribute of general acceptability in the settlement of debt. Given this willingness, they were able continually to reduce overall costs of transactions to the low level characteristic of money economies today.

What it is that accounts for the phenomenon of general acceptability is not easy to say. As Professor Newlyn has written, 'it falls within that perplexing but fascinating group of phenomena which is affected by self-justifying beliefs. If the members of a community think that money will be generally acceptable, then it will be; otherwise not.'[1] For this reason it is commonly thought that the explanation lies more within the province of the social psychologist than within that of the political economist. That may be correct. But it would be a mistake to conclude thereby that economic analysis has nothing at all to contribute to an understanding of the subject. In fact, economic analysis can contribute significantly, as we shall see – indeed, as we have already seen, in tracing the historical origin of acceptability in the usefulness of certain commodities as exchange intermediaries.

Probably one of the most important factors helping to establish the

[1] Newlyn, op. cit., p. 2. See also Moore, op. cit., p. 155.

acceptability of money is its legal status. Specific kinds of money are made legal tender – that is to say, payment in these moneys is deemed by the courts to be full satisfaction to debts. Usually these comprise the note issues and coinage of the national government. But what accounts, then, for the continued circulation alongside legal tender of what is called 'customary' money[1] – privately issued moneys which, even though lacking in legal-tender status, are nevertheless generally acceptable in the settlement of debt? Usually these comprise the demand-deposit accounts of the commercial banking system, and sometimes other obligations of financial institutions as well.

There is no mistaking the incentive of financial institutions to issue some kind of money. Being a resource-cheap product, money can in effect be 'sold' to the public in exchange for real resources (or command over real resources) capable of earning an income. But it does not necessarily follow, therefore, that the issues of financial institutions will begin automatically to circulate as customary money alongside legal tender. The public must be persuaded to buy the product: they must be persuaded to endow it as a medium of exchange with the attribute of general acceptability. They will not do so unless the issuers are capable of satisfying two very rigorous requirements – the requirements of *convertibility* and *attractiveness*.[2]

In the first place, issuers must be able to assure the public that by buying and using customary money rather than legal tender, individuals will not be exposing themselves to an economic loss. The best way to accomplish this, of course, is to promise that any holdings of customary money will always be convertible into legal tender at a fixed (presumably one-to-one) rate of exchange. That is, issuers can pledge to repurchase the customary money, on demand of the initial buyer or any subsequent holders, at its original sale price. This, it should be noted, in turn logically imposes two significant operating constraints on the issuers of customary money. A pledge of convertibility demands, first, that issuers remain *solvent* at all times, in order to be able to cope with the possibility (however remote) of a sudden conversion of their entire issue. In addition, a pledge of convertibility demands that issuers remain highly *liquid* at all times, in order to be able to avoid any risk of temporary insolvency in meeting short-term repurchase obligations. Solvency and liquidity are essential if the pledge of convertibility is to have credibility.

[1] Newlyn, op. cit., pp. 2–3.
[2] Pesek and Saving, *Foundations*, chap. 7; and *Money, Wealth*, chap. 4.

The second requirement of issuers of customary money is that they offer a type of exchange medium that is for at least some types of transactions more attractive than legal tender. This can be accomplished basically in three ways. First, the product can be differentiated. Relative to commodity money, for example, commercial banks can offer paper money which is easy to store and carry about. Similarly, relative to government paper money, they can offer the medium of the cheque, which is effectively a generalised variable-denomination banknote that the owner himself may print, provided he does not exceed the size of his ownership of this money as shown by his demand-deposit account. Second, issuers can invent better merchandising techniques. Typically these consist of better instalment plans. Governments as a rule issue money only for cash or for delivery of goods or services. Commercial banks, by contrast, can offer credit facilities to induce the public to use customary money. This certainly ensures that for at least some purposes bank money will become more attractive to potential users than legal tender.

Third, issuers can make customary money more attractive as a means of holding wealth: by enhancing its store-of-value quality, they may thereby succeed in making bank money more generally acceptable in settlement of debt. A direct approach would be to offer a discount on the price of customary money relative to legal tender; but given the convertibility requirement, this is really out of the question. Bankruptcy would quickly follow if money were sold at a lower value and then returned for repurchase at a higher value. However, an effect comparable to a more attractive price can be achieved indirectly by offering to share the income to be earned on the resources exchanged by the public for customary money – in other words, by offering to pay a rate of interest. This certainly ensures that for at least some purposes bank money will become more attractive as a store of value than legal tender.

II. INTERNATIONAL MONEY

The roles of international money

We may now return to the three questions with which this chapter began. The first two are considered together in this section; the following section addresses itself to the third. To begin with, what is international money? Like domestic money, international money can only be defined in terms of the functions it performs. And like the functions performed by domestic money, these correspond to the three basic needs for medium of exchange, unit of account and store of value. One difference from domestic money, however, is that international money is not always used in all international monetary transactions, whereas domestic money is always used in all domestic monetary transactions.

Many international purchases and sales and many foreign loans and investments are made without any international money being used at all. Transactions are consummated simply by converting one domestic money into another through the foreign-exchange market. A purchaser (borrower) discharges his contract in the national currency of the seller (lender), after acquiring it in return for his own national currency; in this case, from the seller's (lender's) point of view, no international exchange medium is involved. An international exchange medium *is* involved, however, if the seller (lender) accepts payment in the purchaser's (borrower's) national currency – or in any other national currency, for that matter – for by this act he endow the foreign currency with the attribute of acceptability beyond the borders of the nation issuing it. This is true even if the seller (lender) holds the foreign currency no longer than is absolutely necessary to convert it into domestic currency. By the same token, an international exchange medium is involved whenever a borrower accepts a loan in any currency other than that of his own country, no matter how short the time before he disposes of it.

By similar reasoning, we may conclude that an international store of value is involved whenever assets are held denominated in a currency other than that of the country of the holder. An international unit of account is involved, on the other hand, *whenever* foreign transactions are made, whether the exchange medium used is international or not. By definition, foreign transactions involve at least two domestic currencies. But also by definition, contracts must be quoted in terms of just one currency; some common denominator is necessary.[1] Therefore, either one of the domestic currencies concerned, or else some third currency, must be employed in order to value goods and services or express debts. Whichever currency it is, it is in that use an international unit of account.

A second difference of international money from domestic money is

---

[1] Occasionally, contracts do happen to be quoted in terms of more than one domestic currency. But then an exchange rate must be specified between them.

that international money is used at two distinctly different levels – at the level of private international transactions, and at the level of official international transactions. Analytically, the distinction is crucial, even though its source is admittedly systemic rather than economic. The necessity for insisting on the distinction arises solely from the fact that under present international monetary arrangements, exchange rates are not free to move without limitation. Governments are obliged by the Articles of Agreement of the International Monetary Fund to limit rate movements to a range not wider than 1 per cent on either side of a declared par value.[1] They accomplish this by intervening in the foreign-exchange market to offset discrepancies between demand and supply of their own currency, functioning in effect as residual buyer and seller. To effect these purchases and sales, governments need international money – exchange media that can be used to support currency parities. This is a logical requirement of the system of pegged rates. Exchange media in so far as they are used for this purpose have been called *intervention currencies*.[2]

It is clear that if present monetary arrangements were to be replaced by a system of totally flexible exchange rates, there would then be no need for intervention currencies, since governments would by definition no longer have any motivation to intervene in the foreign-exchange market.[3] But so long as they are motivated to do so, it becomes important for analytical purposes to separate out the role played by intervention currencies, and to distinguish that role from the conventional medium-of-exchange role played by money at the level of ordinary international transactions. Motivations are quite different when money is used merely to pay for goods or services or to discharge contractual obligations. For convenience, we may refer to this level of operation as that of private international transactions, even though it includes as well all official transactions other than those

[1] In fact, the maxima and minima for exchange transactions are usually set even closer to parity: rates generally are allowed to differ from the declared par value by no more than roughly 0·75 per cent in most cases – a total spread of just 1·5 per cent. The only significant exception is Switzerland, not a member of the Fund, which maintains margins of 1½ per cent in either direction.

[2] Richard N. Cooper, *The Economics of Interdependence: Economic Policy in the Atlantic Community* (New York: McGraw-Hill, for the Council on Foreign Relations, 1968) pp. 52–4; and Robert A. Mundell, 'The Dollar and Gold', Republican Balance of Payments Seminar, *Congressional Record*, 5 Feb 1968, p. E474.

[3] This is not necessarily an argument either for or against flexible exchange rates.

FS B

related directly or indirectly to intervention in the exchange market; we may simply assume that the motivations of governments in transactions of a commercial or capital nature are not essentially different from those of private international traders or investors. To keep the distinction clear, let us call national currencies in so far as they are used as exchange media at this level *transactions currencies*.

Another logical requirement of a system of pegged rates is that governments hedge against possible future deficiences in the demand for their currency in exchange markets. In other words, governments must stockpile some kind of a reserve of international assets. Usually, we find that these reserves tend to include gold plus certain national currencies deemed useful for store-of-value purposes. However, non-liquid assets are not usually found in official reserves;[1] governments ordinarily prefer to compose their reserves exclusively of assets that can, if necessary, be directly transferred in settlement of net payments deficits with other countries. In a sense, therefore, all reserve assets might be regarded as exchange media at this level of analysis. Such a procedure, however, would be misleading. On the one hand, lump-sum settlement of outstanding payments debits is not significantly different from the discharging of contracts at the private level. On the other hand, it *is* significantly different from intervention on a regular and continuous basis in the foreign-exchange market. The latter is the truly unique medium-of-exchange function of money at the level of official international transactions – and not all reserve assets are useful for this purpose. Assets that are useful for this purpose have already been described by the term 'intervention currency'. It would clarify matters to have a separate term for describing assets that are useful for a store-of-value purpose in official reserves, whether or not they also happen to serve as intervention currencies. These we shall call *reserve currencies*.[2]

The role of reserve currencies is distinct not only from the interven-

---

[1] One important recent exception was the United Kingdom. For years, the British Government maintained a substantial secondary reserve of non-liquid external assets. However, the circumstances of the creation of this portfolio were unusual, to say the least: the reserve resulted from the nationalisation of external assets at the outset of the Second World War. In any event, the secondary reserve was completely liquidated after 1964.

[2] Usually, only the national currencies held in official reserves are described as reserve currencies. However, for our purposes, it will be useful to extend the label to gold as well, in so far as gold performs this particular role of international money.

tion-currency role played by money at the level of private international transactions. It is also distinct from the conventional store-of-value role played by money at the level of private international transactions. Both kinds of assets are means of holding wealth, to be sure; but once again, the motivations involved are very different. To keep the distinction clear, let us call national currencies in so far as they are used for private store-of-value purposes *asset currencies*.

Finally, it is manifest that in any system in which par value must be declared, a third logical requirement is that there be at least one unit of account in which parities may be expressed. Not that there need be *only* one unit of account. There may be many, as many in fact as there are national currencies, since any national currency (or gold or any other asset) may be used as a standard of value for any other national currency, so long as cross-rates are consistent. However, it is surely practical to have fewer rather than many denominators, and in practice governments have always relied upon just one or two. Let us call these (including gold in so far as it performs this particular role) *unit-of-account currencies*. Analytically, of course, these are very different from national currencies used as accounting units for quoting exchange rates or denominating international contracts at the level of private international transactions. Currencies performing this function we may call *quotation currencies*.[1]

I have now distinguished six separate role of international money – three different functions operating at two different levels. These may be arranged for illustrative purposes in a 3×2 matrix, as in Table 1.1. In the table I also indicate which of the functions are performed today by each of the major national currencies and by gold. What is immediately apparent from the listing is that there are in fact very few fully developed international moneys. A fully developed international money may be defined, by analogy with domestic money, as one that performs all monetary roles. The roles may be performed on a global scale, or they may be confined largely to a monetary region. As it happens, only the dollar performs all the six roles of international money on a global scale – and even the dollar's status as a universal, fully developed international money is not altogether unambiguous, as I shall suggest immediately below. Two or three other currencies are fully developed international moneys within specific regions; most prominent among these, of course, is sterling. All other international moneys are just partial.

[1] Mundell, loc. cit.

Table 1.1

The Roles of International Money

	MEDIUM OF EXCHANGE	UNIT OF ACCOUNT	STORE OF VALUE
PRIVATE TRANSACTIONS	Transactions currencies:	Quotation currencies:	Asset currencies:
	Major: Dollar Sterling	Major: Dollar Sterling	Major: Dollar Sterling Gold
	Minor: Deutschmark, Swiss franc, French franc, etc.	Minor: Deutschmark, Swiss franc, French franc, etc.	Minor: Swiss franc, Deutschmark, French franc, etc.
OFFICIAL TRANSACTIONS	Intervention currencies:	Unit-of-account currencies:	Reserve currencies:
	Major: Dollar	Major: Dollar Gold	Major: Gold Dollar I.M.F. reserve positions S.D.R.s
	Minor: Sterling French franc, Portuguese escudo	Minor: Sterling, French franc, Portuguese escudo	Minor: Sterling, French franc, Portuguese escudo

At the level of private international transactions, there are a number of national currencies that do serve all three monetary functions. These are fully developed international moneys at this level of analysis. The most important are plainly the dollar and sterling. At least one-third of world trade is thought to be invoiced and transacted in dollars, and probably 20 to 25 per cent in sterling. These two are also the most widely held currencies in foreign-asset balances. However, some trade is also invoiced and transacted, and some balances are also held, in other currencies as well, such as the Deutschmark, the francs (Swiss, French and Belgian), and the guilder, lira, yen, and Canadian, Hong Kong and Malaysian dollars. Gold on the other hand has only a partial monetary quality at the private level. True, it is widely held by individuals as a store of value for speculative or long-term precautionary purposes. But among private transactors gold does not have any other monetary functions. It does not serve as either medium of exchange or unit of account: gold coins and gold clauses have disappeared since the days of the Great Depression.

At the level of official international transactions, there is just one international money that performs all three monetary functions on a global scale – the dollar. Three currencies – sterling, of course, and also to a more limited extent the French franc and the Portuguese escudo – perform all three functions on a regional scale. All other moneys, including gold, are just partial. What sets the dollar apart is that it is the only money that serves universally as an intervention currency: in practice, all governments outside of specific monetary groupings peg their currencies by buying and selling in the dollar-exchange market. Moreover, the dollar also serves, along with gold and S.D.R.s, as the principal reserve currency for all governments outside of specific monetary regions. The total of sterling reserve balances is smaller than that of dollar reserve balances, and sterling reserve balances are confined almost entirely to the sterling area. Likewise the relatively small amounts of francs and escudos held as reserve currencies are confined to their colonial and post-colonial monetary blocs. Finally, the dollar serves universally as a unit of account for the purpose of expressing the par values of currencies. Sterling, the French franc and the escudo also serve as units of account, but they do so only for the purpose of expressing par values within their respective monetary groupings.

However, in so far as the dollar does serve universally as a unit-of-account currency, it does so on a *de facto* rather than on a *de jure* basis. Here is the source of the ambiguity regarding the dollar's status as fully developed international money. Legally, the only unit of account for the purpose of expressing par values is gold. True, the Articles of Agreement of the International Monetary Fund do appear to sanction use of the dollar for this purpose as well. Specifically, Article IV does read that par values are to be expressed 'in terms of gold as a common denominator or in terms of the United States dollar of the weight and fineness in effect on July 1, 1944'.[1] But appearances can be misleading.

---

[1] *Articles of Agreement of the International Monetary Fund*, Article IV, section 1(*a*).

In fact, Article IV does *not* make the dollar a legal unit of account for the system co-equal with gold. What it does do is endow legal status on the gold value of the dollar of 1 July 1944 – to be precise, on 0·888671 grams of fine gold. In effect, therefore, the Article is redundant: par values are to be expressed in terms of gold or in terms of gold. The dollar – the contemporary dollar – is conspicuously absent.[1]

The ambiguity of the dollar's status as fully developed international money is camouflaged so long as its price in terms of gold remains fixed. Then no choice between accounting units need be made. But suppose the weight and fineness of the contemporary dollar were to be altered – that is, suppose the contemporary dollar were to be devalued in terms of gold (and, *pari passu*, in terms of the weight and fineness of the dollar of 1 July 1944). Governments would then have to decide whether they are more concerned about the *de jure* price relationship of their currency vis-à-vis gold, or about the *de facto* price relationship of their currency vis-à-vis the dollar. Some governments would undoubtedly choose to maintain the relationship of their currency vis-à-vis the contemporary dollar rather than vis-à-vis gold. Some, however, would probably prefer to treat gold as the ultimate unit of account, breaking their link with the dollar instead.[2]

It is precisely because there would be such governments that we cannot be absolutely certain about the status of the dollar as fully developed international money. This point is often missed. Ronald McKinnon, for instance, has argued that the dollar is '*the* dominant international money'.[3] However, the argument he uses is based on a fundamental confusion. McKinnon fails to distinguish adequately between the official medium-of-exchange function of the dollar and its unit-of-account function. He simply assumes that because the dollar is used so widely as an intervention currency, by extension it must function as unit-of-account currency as well. But this does not follow

---

[1] The contemporary dollar is also conspicuously absent from other international monetary agreements specifying units of account. Gold was the basis of the unit of account of the European Payments Union in the 1950s, for instance, just as it still is the basis of the accounting units of the European Monetary Agreement, the Common Agricultural Policy of the European Economic Community, and the new I.M.F. arrangement for special drawing rights (S.D.R.s).

[2] See, e.g., C. Fred Bergsten, 'Taking the Monetary Initiative', *Foreign Affairs*, XLVI 4 (July 1968) 713–32.

[3] Ronald I. McKinnon, *Private and Official International Money: The Case for the Dollar*, Essays in International Finance, No. 74 (Princeton: International Finance Section, 1969) p. 4. Italics in the original.

at all. In fact, the dollar is *not* used universally as the basic accounting unit for expressing par values – and to the extent that it is not so used, it is not a fully developed money at all. It is only a partial money, a medium of exchange and store of value whose potentially variable price relationship with the ultimate unit of account must be a matter of concern for analysts and policy-makers. On the other hand, if all governments could be persuaded to treat the dollar as their basic unit of account, then the currency's status would be unambiguous: it would be the one universal, fully developed money in the system.[1]

The importance of distinguishing carefully among the six separate roles of international money should be obvious. Serious analysis is impossible unless we first know what we are talking about. Yet in the international monetary literature, until quite recently, few distinctions of this kind were ever made. Theorists seemed to prefer to lump the various functions of money together under rather general headings – even occasionally at the cost of some ambiguity in analysis.

Early in the post-war period, for instance, John Williams introduced the notion of the 'key currency'.[2] This was a notably imprecise label. For Williams the key currencies were the 'principal currencies' (p. 156), the only 'truly international currencies' (p. 151), important because they were the 'chief means of international payment' (pp. 123, 333), the 'currencies most essential for world trade' (p. 183). By these various phrases we can probably assume that he was referring primarily to the transactions-currency function of international money, though it is possible that the quotation and asset functions may have been implied as well. But Williams also occasionally described the key currencies as those that were 'central for an area of trade' (p. 156), implying by context the reserve-currency function as well. In fact, the key-currency notion was not much more than a catch-all phrase, a rather crude synonym for international money in general. For Williams, there were only two truly international moneys – the dollar and sterling.[3]

Writing a decade after Williams, Robert Triffin popularised the notion of the 'reserve currency', but he used it interchangeably with the notion of key currency and apparently meant the same thing by it.[4]

[1] This is not necessarily an argument either for or against demonetising gold and replacing it with a world dollar standard.

[2] John H. Williams, *Post-War Monetary Plans* (Oxford: Basil Blackwell, 1949) esp. pts iii, and iv and Appendix I.

[3] Ibid., p. 349.

[4] Robert Triffin, *Gold and the Dollar Crisis* (New Haven: Yale University Press, 1960) esp. pt i, chap. 7; and pt ii, chap. 2.

However, a useful step forward was taken a few years later when Robert Roosa divided the key- or reserve-currency notion in two, distinguishing between the 'reserve-currency' and the 'vehicle-currency' functions of international money.[1] Reserve currencies were those moneys that could be held by governments as part of their reserves and could be used by them to support their currency parities in the exchange markets. In other words, reserve currencies combined what I have called the reserve and intervention functions of international money. Vehicle currencies, on the other hand, were those moneys that could be used by private traders and investors as a vehicle in ordinary foreign transactions: they were 'widely known and generally acceptable', they were useful in invoicing, and they were held in liquid balances. They were, in short, capable of performing all the roles of international money at the level of private international transactions. For Roosa, the number of reserve currencies was severely limited, including really just two, the dollar and sterling.[2] The number of vehicle currencies, on the other hand, was considerably larger, though never specified.

The distinction between reserve currencies and vehicle currencies has by now become customary: no serious discussion of the roles of international money fails to make reference to it, except that one often finds the expression 'trading currency' substituted for 'vehicle currency.' Only two international monetary theorists have attempted to add any further precision to these discussions. One, Richard Cooper, has suggested that in discussing reserve currencies it is important to sharpen the distinction between the intervention and reserve functions.[3] Robert Mundell agrees, and adds that it would be useful to separate out the unit-of-account function of reserve currencies as well, although in his taxonomy he specifically uses the term 'key currency' to describe it.[4] Likewise, Mundell also proposes separating out the quotation

---

[1] Robert V. Roosa, *Monetary Reform for the World Economy* (New York: Harper & Row, for the Council on Foreign Relations, 1965) pp. 8–9.

[2] Robert V. Roosa and Fred Hirsch, *Reserves, Reserve Currencies, and Vehicle Currencies: An Argument*, Essays in International Finance, No. 54 (Princeton: International Finance Section, 1966) *passim*.

[3] Cooper, loc. cit.

[4] Mundell, loc. cit. Lately, Raymond Mikesell has also specifically used the term 'key currency', but he says he means by it the same thing that Robert Roosa did by the term 'vehicle currency' – any currency 'used widely as a means of payment and for invoicing in international trade'. Raymond F. Mikesell, *Financing World Trade* (New York: Thomas Y. Crowell, 1969) p. 2, n. 1. M. June

function of vehicle currencies. But even he fails to distinguish between the transactions and asset functions of vehicle currencies.

The choice of international moneys

We observed earlier that within all domestic economies there has been a clear historical tendency to limit the number of moneys. From the evidence of the previous section, it would appear that the same has been true of the international economy as well. Only a few of the world's several score national currencies (along with gold) function as international moneys. The problem we now want to consider is what accounts for this historical tendency, and what determines which national currencies will be chosen to perform international roles. In short, what explains the evolution of international money?

Gold, of course, has been the international money *par excellence*. Over the last century or more, this one metal, of all the variety of commodities ever employed as money, has played a unique role as the most generally acceptable of all international means of payments.[1] What the explanation of this is we are unable to say with any degree of assurance; here the economist must surely yield to the social psychologist and the anthropologist. All we can do is simply acknowledge gold's special status. It is still the *de jure* unit of account for the purpose of expressing currency values; it is still quantitatively the single most important component of official reserves; and it is still regarded as the ultimate means of settling intergovernmental debts (even though it does not serve *per se* as an intervention currency). It may be only a partial money today, but in the sense that all other international moneys are really just *national* currencies writ large, it is still the only truly *international* money in the system. It is *sui generis*. Indeed, in the absence of a world government or monetary authority, gold is the closest approximation we have to some form of 'legal tender'.

However, the fact that gold does serve as a kind of international legal

---

Flanders has lately used the term 'international money' to mean specifically what Robert Roosa did by the term 'reserve currency' – '*not* that which finances international trade or international payments. It is that which finances international payments *imbalances*.' M. June Flanders, 'International Liquidity is Always Inadequate', *Kyklos*, XXII (1969) fasc. 3, p. 520. Italics in the original.

[1] Morgan, op. cit., chap. 7; and Paul Einzig, *The History of Foreign Exchange*, 2nd ed. (London: Macmillan, 1970) *passim*.

tender is, for our purposes, less important than the fact that alongside gold certain national currencies have also come to be endowed with the attributes of general acceptability as international means of payment. In other words, certain national currencies have, analogously, come to serve as a kind of 'customary money'. What the explanation of this is we *are* able to say with some degree of assurance. It happened because these currencies, like domestic customary moneys, were capable of satisfying the two requirements of convertibility and attractiveness.

Convertibility into the ultimate reserve asset of the system at a fixed rate of exchange is a necessary condition for any national currency to begin serving as an international exchange medium. Since historically gold has been regarded universally as the ultimate reserve currency, this has meant that in practice convertibility has had to be into gold. However, even at the level of official international transactions, the right of convertibility has not always been direct; today, for instance, only the dollar is nominally convertible directly into gold among central banks – and the exercise of even that privilege has been limited since the establishment of the two-tier gold system in March 1968. But for other currencies there has been at least the right to convert into dollars; indirect convertibility into 'gold-exchange' will do, so long as the route to gold is not too roundabout. Not that governments necessarily insist on converting the foreign currencies they use or hold into gold. It is only that they insist on the nominal right to do so should the desire ever come upon them.

At the level of private international transactions, of course, no currency today is officially convertible into gold, either directly or indirectly. Yet gold is still widely held by individuals as a store of value, and unofficially currencies are still gold-convertible in the private gold markets of London, Zürich, etc. Gold has always had the mystique of a legal tender, even if it happens no longer to function today as a private medium of exchange. Even at this level, therefore, the right of convertibility into gold or gold-exchange would have to be assured before international transactors would begin to accept a national currency to any significant extent.

The mere *right* of convertibility, however, would probably not be enough: the right would also have to be *credible*. Transactors would not be likely to begin using just any convertible currency. They would first have to be convinced that the rate of convertibility would remain fixed (no devaluation) and that the right of convertibility would remain unqualified (no restrictions on use). This would require confidence in both the solvency and the liquidity of the nation issuing it. Thus the same operating constraints presumably apply here as apply with respect to the issuers of domestic customary money within each country. Solvency in this context probably has both stock and flow dimensions. That is, not only would the country presumably have to show a positive balance of international indebtedness, an excess of foreign assets over foreign liabilities. More importantly, it probably would also have to be a capital exporter on a fairly large scale, with a corresponding tendency toward surplus on current account of the balance of payments, in order to assure potential users of its currency that solvency would be maintained into the future. Liquidity in this context is especially essential because of the absence of a lender of last resort. The condition presumably requires a visibly high ratio of gold and gold-exchange (and/or access to gold and gold-exchange) to liquid foreign liabilities.

Historically, there have been a fairly large number of currencies that have credibly satisfied the requirements of convertibility. Yet only a few of them have ever come to be used to any significant extent as international exchange media. That is because only a few of them have been capable, in addition, of satisfying the requirement of attractiveness.

Recall for a moment the simple barter economy and the evolution of commodity moneys. An international economy with only national moneys is like a barter economy. Currencies must be exchanged before purchases of goods and services can be effected. Individuals with the currency of country A and desiring to buy goods from country B must search out other individuals holding the currency of country B and desiring to buy in country A; and then they must bargain until they reach agreement on a rate of exchange. Transactions costs are high because of the practical problem of achieving the required double coincidence of wants in the foreign-exchange market. However, as in a barter economy, transactions costs can be substantially diminished for an individual if he adapts his own currency mix to that of other individuals, holding for specific use as international exchange intermediaries inventories of the most widely demanded foreign currencies.[1] These are of course the currencies of the countries that are predominant

[1] Cooper, loc. cit.; and Alexander S. Swoboda, *The Euro-Dollar Market: An Interpretation*, Essays in International Finance, No. 64 (Princeton: International Finance Section, 1968) pp. 7–9.

in world trade – the countries that account for the largest proportion of international transactions. It follows that the currencies of such countries will come finally to predominate as international exchange media, because they are the most attractive for transactions purposes.

The transactions attractiveness of such currencies derives initially from their differentially broader purchasing power which reflects the importance in world trade of the countries issuing them. Their attractiveness grows as they become acceptable elsewhere as well. And economies of scale dictate that, eventually, those that are most attractive for this purpose will come to circulate almost universally as transactions currencies. The rise to pre-eminence of sterling in the nineteenth century, for instance, resulted from just such an importance in world trade; and so did the rise of the dollar early in the twentieth century. In both cases the transactions attractiveness of the currencies was enhanced by the availability as well of relatively cheap credit facilities for borrowers, and of relatively high rates of interest for lenders. As mentioned earlier, these two currencies are today still the only ones used widely for transactions purposes. Others (the mark, the francs, etc.) are used to a much more limited extent.

Because the dollar and sterling are the most widely used currencies for transactions purposes, they tend also to be the most extensively employed for quotation purposes. It is practical after all to invoice trade and express debts in the currency in which settlements are expected. But it is not necessary. Any currency might conceivably do for this purpose. Contracts frequently are quoted in currencies other than those used as part of the transaction itself, or even in artificial accounting units.[1] As in the domestic monetary system, the potentially variable price relationship between medium of exchange and unit of account must be acknowledged.

Likewise, because the dollar and sterling are the most widely used currencies for transactions purposes, they tend also to be most extensively held for asset purposes. All transactions currencies are held as stores of value to some extent, but none so extensively as the American and British currencies. This is because these two offer, more than other

---

[1] For example, since 1960 a number of bond issues have been floated in European capital markets denominated in 'European units of account' – accounting units that are absolutely artificial. Though gold-based, their value is also linked in a complex way to the parities of seventeen European reference currencies. See Claudio Segre, 'Foreign Bond Issues in European Markets', *Banca Nazionale del Lavoro Quarterly Review*, no. 68 (Mar 1964) 63–7.

currencies, in addition to reasonably attractive interest rates, the two advantages of exchange convenience and capital certainty.[1]

Exchange convenience tends to correlate highly with the transactions attractiveness of a currency. A currency has exchange convenience to the extent that it is both marketable and reversible. Marketability means low costs in exercise of purchasing power: if it is not possible to use the currency directly in acquiring goods and services or in making loans and investments, then it must be possible to convert it into whatever currency is required for such purposes at a very low cost. Reversibility means a very small difference between the buying and selling prices (realisable value) of the currency at an instant of time. Both marketability and reversibility are a function of the size of the market for the currency. The most exchange-convenient currencies tend to be those that either are or could be used widely for transactions purposes.

On the other hand, there is no necessary correlation at all between the transactions attractiveness of a currency and capital certainty. A currency has capital certainty to the extent that the issuing country's financial markets exhibit the favourable characteristics of depth, breadth and resiliency. Capital certainty here does not refer to the price of the currency *per se* – that is what exchange convenience and convertibility are all about – rather it refers to the price of assets denominated in such a currency. Potential store-of-value holders do not usually hold much cash. They prefer to hold interest-earning assets. But they also want to minimise the possibility of capital loss should such assets have to be sold off at short notice in order to honour commitments. Consequently, to the extent that they find it convenient to hold international assets in their reserve balances, investors prefer to acquire them in the countries with the best-organised and most efficient financial institutions and markets. These are the countries with the most capital-certain currencies.

Because the dollar and sterling are the only currencies with a truly high degree of both attributes – exchange convenience and capital certainty – and because in addition both currencies offer reasonably attractive interest rates to potential holders, these two are the most widely held national currencies for asset purposes. Other currencies are less frequently held, often despite relatively high interest rates, either because their exchange markets are comparatively narrow, or because their financial institutions are comparatively inefficient, or both. The Deutschmark, for instance, is a widely traded currency, more widely

[1] See above, pp. 8–9, and Swoboda, op. cit., p. 10.

traded, in fact, than any currency other than sterling or the dollar. But because German financial markets were until recently still quite rudimentary and underdeveloped, the DM. for a long time was not a relatively popular asset currency. On the other hand, neither are the Dutch guilder or the Swiss franc so widely used as the dollar or sterling for asset purposes, despite highly developed financial markets; for these, the exchange markets are still too narrow.

Note, however, that it is not necessary that a currency actually be used for transactions purposes in order that it be held extensively for asset purposes. Like domestic money, an international money may be held as a store of value whether or not it serves also as a medium of exchange. Today a prime example of this is gold, no longer functioning as a transactions currency, yet still being used widely as an asset currency. But note also that the attractiveness of gold as a store of value has tended to diminish somewhat: the fading of its function as a private exchange intermediary has tended to reduce its exchange convenience, at least marginally. As a rule, this is likely to be the fate of any international money that loses its transactions function: the currency may well continue to be used widely for asset purposes, but holders may not find it necessary, or be willing, to accumulate balances to the same extent as before. This has been the fate, for instance, of sterling outside of the sterling area.

At the level of official international transactions, governments prefer to use for intervention purposes fewer rather than many currencies. They could of course hold an inventory of all convertible currencies, buying or selling in each separate exchange market as required to support their own currency parities. But essentially the same results can be achieved at considerably less expense if instead they buy and sell in just the broadest exchange markets, relying on arbitrage to generalise the price effects of their interventions to all other currencies. Like private transactors, governments can substantially diminish transactions costs by adapting their own foreign-currency mix to the demands of others. In practice, this means that governments will adapt to the market's selection of transaction currencies. No currency is likely to be used for intervention purposes that is not widely used for transactions purposes. The choice of intervention currencies will be made from within the range of transactions currencies. Under the gold standard the principal intervention currencies were first gold, later sterling. Today, outside of specific monetary groupings, the preferred intervention currency is the dollar.

As it happens, all three of these (past or present) intervention currencies are also preferred today, to a greater or lesser extent, as reserve currencies. They predominate in official reserves (sterling mainly within the sterling area). As far as the dollar and sterling are concerned, this is because they are, in addition to being gold- or gold-exchange convertible, also exchange-convenient and reasonably capital-certain; and because they offer reasonably attractive interest rates to holders. Gold no longer actually serves as an intervention currency. Nevertheless, it is attractive as a reserve currency, because it can be converted into intervention currencies at low cost, and because it offers a relatively small chance of capital loss in the event that assets have to be sold off at short notice. But at the same time it must be admitted that gold is less attractive as a reserve currency than it would be were it still being used for intervention purposes. Moreover, it is a relatively expensive reserve currency to hold, because of storage costs and forgone interest.

We have noted that gold is the international money *par excellence*, the ultimate reserve asset of present monetary arrangements and the system's *de jure* unit of account for the purpose of expressing par values. This status originated during the gold-standard era, presumably owing to the practicality of expressing currency parities in terms of the most widely circulated means of payment. However, once again, it must be emphasised that like the quotation function of currencies at the level of private international transactions, the unit-of-account function at the official level is not a *necessary* concomitant of the medium-of-exchange function. The two roles might be independent: an intervention currency might not serve universally as a unit-of-account currency; and a currency used as a unit of account might not be a preferred intervention currency. The ambiguous status of the dollar in this connection has already been discussed.

The logic of the evolution of international money, then, is fairly clear (albeit complex). It may be illustrated diagrammatically by means of a flow chart, as in Fig. 1.1. International money, like domestic money, probably begins as a means of payment. Certain currencies are singled out for a medium-of-exchange function because they are both credibly gold-convertible and attractive as a means of reducing transactions costs. They become widely used as transactions currencies. *Ipso facto*, they may also become extensively employed as quotation currencies, in so far as it is practical, and as asset currencies, in so far as they are also exchange-convenient and reasonably capital-certain (and in so far as attractive interest rates are available as well). But the process

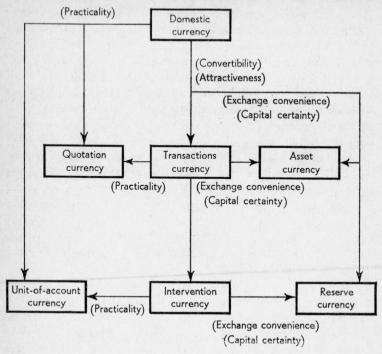

Fig. 1.1

is not inevitable: transactions currencies may not come to play the additional role of quotation currency at all, while on the other hand some currencies may come to be employed extensively for unit-of-account or store-of-value purposes even if they do not serve as transactions currencies. By contrast, widespread use for transactions purposes is a necessary condition for a currency to be used widely for intervention purposes, since governments can minimise the transactions costs of intervention only by confining their support operations to the broadest of all currency markets. In turn, use as an intervention currency may lead to extensive employment as a unit of account, in so far as it is practical, and as a reserve currency, in so far as the currency is exchange-convenient and reasonably capital-certain (and in so far as attractive interest rates are available). But again, the process is not inevitable. Intervention currencies need not be used for the former of these purposes at all, and currencies that are not used for intervention purposes may nevertheless play either of these roles.

Some interesting conclusions follow from the logic of evolution outlined here. For it appears that only one of the six roles of international money is uniquely dependent on another as a necessary condition. That is the intervention function which, as has been emphasised, is unlikely to be served by any national currency that is not used widely for transactions purposes. This point has been recognised by many monetary theorists. Robert Triffin, for example, has argued regarding the dollar: 'The role of the dollar as the main medium for central banks' operations in the exchange markets is an ineluctable and durable by-product of its continued use as the major key currency in private trade and finance.'[1] Likewise, Maxwell Stamp has argued regarding sterling: 'It is because sterling is a great trading currency that it remains a reserve currency.'[2] Both are right. Neither the pound (within the sterling area) nor the dollar could continue serving as intervention currencies if they were to cease being used widely for transactions purposes.

Note, however, that the reverse is not necessarily true. Currencies like the dollar or the pound could continue to be used widely for transactions purposes whether or not they also happen to be serving as an intervention currency. More importantly, they could continue to be used widely for transactions purposes even if they were to *discontinue* serving as an intervention currency. This point has not always been recognised by international monetary theorists. Robert Roosa, for instance, has asserted: 'The function of the dollar as a trading currency would be impaired if the option of its use as a reserve currency were to be denied or denigrated.'[3] On this, clearly, he is wrong. In fact, it is all a matter of maintaining the necessary conditions of an exchange intermediary, namely transactions attractiveness and credible gold- or gold-exchange convertibility. Significantly, Roosa himself offers no evidence for his opinion, apart from his 'own feeling' that 'separation

[1] Robert Triffin, 'Guidelines for International Monetary Reform', in *Guidelines for International Monetary Reform*, Hearings before the Sub-committee on International Exchange and Payments of the Joint Economic Committee, pt i (Washington, 1965) p. 172.

[2] Maxwell Stamp, 'Sterling and the Common Market', *The Banker*, cxvi 490 (Dec 1966) 845. For 'trading currency' read 'transactions currency'; for 'reserve currency' read 'intervention currency'.

[3] Roosa and Hirsch, op. cit., p. 4.

would be as delicate as operating on Siamese twins.'[1] I agree that the operation would be delicate, but on the evidence of the considerations discussed in this chapter, I would argue that it is more in the nature of a Caesarian section than a bifurcation. The intervention–offspring may survive or succumb, but there is no reason that I can see why, if the necessary conditions are maintained, the transactions–mother should not be able to endure and flourish. Sterling, for instance, still serves as a transactions currency outside the sterling area, even though it is no longer used for intervention purposes by other than sterling-area countries.

None of the other roles of international money is so dependent on the endurance of the transactions function. For these, other conditions suffice. If it is practical, a currency may continue to be used for quotation purposes, whether or not it discontinues serving as a transactions currency; likewise, a currency may continue to be used for unit-of-account purposes, whether or not it discontinues serving as an intervention currency. Gold, for example, functioned in gold clauses long after it ceased to be a major transactions currency, and still functions as *de jure* unit of account for expressing par values even though it is used less and less in the settlement of intergovernmental debts. By the same token, a currency may continue to be used for asset (reserve) purposes, whether or not it discontinues serving as a transactions (intervention) currency, so long as it manages to remain exchange-convenient and reasonably capital-certain, and so long as interest rates remain attractive. True, exchange convenience does tend to be closely correlated with the transactions attractiveness of a currency; use as an asset (reserve) currency is therefore likely to be reduced somewhat. But the correlation is not perfect. All that is necessary is that the currency still be convertible into the primary transactions (intervention) currencies at low cost. Sterling, for instance, is still an important component of the reserves of sterling-area countries, even of those which no longer use the pound much as an intervention currency. And the use of gold as a medium of exchange has shrunken even more than that of sterling, yet in value terms gold is still the most important single component of world reserves.

So far I have omitted from the logic of evolution outlined here any discussion of the part played by official policy in the process. It is manifest that a government cannot easily promote an international role for its currency, except to the extent that it can improve the credi-

[1] Roosa and Hirsch op. cit., p. 5.

bility of its convertibility pledge or enhance its currency's attractiveness, exchange convenience and capital certainty. In fact, the extent to which these can be done is quite restricted. These conditions are basically a function of the size of a country, the structure and magnitude of its trade, the efficiency of its financial institutions, and so on. They can be affected only marginally by official policy. In recent years, the French, Russian and Chinese Governments have all discovered to their regret that it is not so easy to build up the international roles of their national currencies.

However, this does not mean that official policy has no part at all in the process. On the contrary, there is one point at which official policy is crucial. That is when a currency first begins to be used to a significant extent as a transactions and asset currency, perhaps concurrently as an intervention and reserve currency as well. At this point a decision must be made: the government must either ratify or veto the 'verdict of the market'. A veto requires action: if the authorities are determined to stop the process, they must actually take steps to restrict the use of their currency for various purposes. This has been the traditional posture of the German and Swiss authorities, for example, who have always been impressed more by the risks than by the gains of running an international currency. Ratification, on the other hand, requires no action at all. There is no need actively to promote the process, as the British Government sometimes tried to do for sterling toward the end of the nineteenth century.[1] It is enough just to acquiesce in the process, simply doing nothing to counteract the development, like the American Government during the inter-war period. The logic of evolution gives the process, once begun, a cumulative life of its own.

In turn, this implies that once a decision has been made to ratify rather than veto the verdict of the market, whether explicitly or by acquiescence, the reversibility of the process rapidly diminishes. That is, as the international roles of a currency accumulate and grow, the government's ability to reduce or eliminate these roles unilaterally gradually declines to the point where such action appears unfeasible in the absence of an international co-operative effort. This is the position that both the United States and Britain find themselves in today. Sterling, of course, is the much more critical of the two cases.

[1] See, e.g., Herbert Feis, *Europe, the World's Banker: 1870–1914* (New York: W. W. Norton, 1965) chap. 4.

2 The Benefits and Costs of an International Currency

ONCE a currency begins to be used as an international money, substantial benefits can be expected to accrue to the country issuing it. But the international use of a currency may prove to be costly, too. For the economist, the fundamental empirical problem is to estimate which on balance are the greater – the social gains or the social losses. However, even before empirical analysis can begin, the economist must face two theoretical problems – the problems of enumeration and attribution. First, what actually are the potential gains or losses of the international use of a currency? And second, to what extent is it possible to attribute the separate gains or losses to each of the currency's specific functions? These two questions of theory will occupy us in the present chapter.

I. ENUMERATION

Let us begin with the first question. In economic theory, social benefits and costs may both be identified in terms of changes of real national income. The benefits of the use of a currency for some international purpose are the gains of income, costs the losses of income, relative to what national income would have been had the currency not been used for that particular purpose. Both benefits and costs may be either direct or indirect. That is to say, they may accrue directly – gains as the yields of, losses as the opportunities forgone because of, the international use of the currency – or they may accrue indirectly. Effects which are indirect may operate through private economic units, or they may operate through public policy. Examples of all these may be cited.

There are two potential direct benefits of the international use of a currency, one accruing to the economy generally, one to a specific sector. The first is the expansionary income effect of being able to run greater balance-of-payments deficits than would otherwise be possible. The second is the income gain from increased foreign demand for national banking services.

The former benefit derives from the fact that when a currency begins to be used internationally, the country issuing it may be able to finance payments deficits (on an exchange-market basis)[1] through voluntary accumulations of liabilities abroad rather than through losses of gold or gold-exchange. This means that with a given reserve of gold and gold-exchange, the country over time may be able to run a greater *cumulative* deficit than would otherwise be possible. In effect, the country obtains a kind of 'free' command over real resources which can be used to enlarge its purchases of foreign goods, services and assets (including interest-paying reserves). This benefit has been described elsewhere as the gain from 'seigniorage'.[2]

Originally, 'seigniorage' referred to the difference between the circulating value of a coin and the cost of bullion and minting, involving a once-for-all gain to the coin's issuer. Later the term was extended to describe the gain, over and above costs of production, to the issuer of any kind of money – including also international money. It costs nothing to produce an international money: the issuing country need only run a cumulative deficit in its balance of payments. But by so doing it increases its real national absorption (of foreign goods, services and assets) relative to real national income, and this in turn leads to a multiple expansion of income at home (assuming there is some margin

[1] By 'exchange-market basis', I mean deficits (or surpluses) measured by the discrepancy at a given exchange rate between autonomous demand and supply of foreign exchange in the foreign-exchange market. This discrepancy may or may not correspond to any observed accounting measure of deficit (or surplus). See Benjamin J. Cohen, *Balance-of-Payments Policy* (London: Penguin Books, 1969) chap. 1.
[2] Robert Z. Aliber, 'The Costs and Benefits of the U.S. Role as a Reserve Currency Country', *Quarterly Journal of Economics*, LXXVIII 3 (Aug 1964) 446. This article appears in revised and condensed form as chap. iii in Aliber's recent book, *The Future of the Dollar as an International Currency* (New York: Frederick A. Praeger, 1966). See also Alexander K. Swoboda, *The Euro-Dollar Market: An Interpretation*, Essays in International Finance, No. 64 (Princeton: International Finance Section, 1968) pp. 11–13; Ronald I. McKinnon, *Private and Official International Money: The Case for the Dollar*, Essays in International Finance, No. 74 (Princeton: International Finance Section, 1969) pp. 17–23; and Robert A. Mundell and Alexander K. Swoboda (eds), *Monetary Problems of the International Economy* (Chicago: University of Chicago Press, 1969) pt 5.

for expansion of domestic output). In effect, therefore, foreigners extend 'credit' to the issuing country. Moreover, the credit is in a sense 'free', because the acquisition of balances ordinarily is voluntary: there is no explicit obligation attached to it to repay.

There are two parts to this benefit from seigniorage – what we may call its 'current' and 'capital' portions.[1] The former consists of the current increase of real absorption made possible by the cumulative deficit in the balance of payments. This is somewhat akin to the notion of 'living beyond one's means'. The current gain ceases to accrue, of course, as soon as foreigners leave off acquiring additional balances of the issuing country's currency. The capital portion of the seigniorage benefit consists of the yield on the additional investment of resources abroad made possible by the cumulative deficit in the balance of payments. This additional investment need not occur concurrently with the deficit in the balance of payments; in fact, the resources involved may actually have been invested in a much earlier period of the country's economic history. The main point is, simply, that given the structure of the country's overall balance of payments, these investments can be maintained currently only *because* of the cumulative external deficit. This is more akin to the notion of portfolio management. Foreign acquisition of balances represents capital borrowed from abroad; and on the basis of this borrowed capital, *so long as it is not repatriated*, the issuing country can maintain a larger portfolio of assets overseas than would otherwise be possible given current levels of domestic income and absorption. And thus, unlike the current portion of the seigniorage benefit, the capital portion does not cease to accrue when foreign acquisition of balances ceases. On the contrary, even after the deficit ends the stock of foreign assets remains. Real national income therefore will continue to be augmented, so long as these assets continue to yield a rate of return in excess of what the same capital would earn if it were invested at home rather than abroad. The capital seigniorage gain will cease to accrue only if foreign balances of the international currency are withdrawn, forcing the issuing country to liquidate a portion of its portfolio of assets overseas.

I have said that the benefit from seigniorage is, in a sense, 'free'. It should be noted that this is so only in the sense that it is larger than would otherwise be possible if the country's currency were not used

[1] See Harry G. Johnson, 'Appendix: A Note on Seigniorage and the Social Saving from Substituting Credit for Commodity Money', in Mundell and Swoboda (eds), op. cit., p. 325.

internationally on a voluntary basis. The benefit is certainly not 'free' in the sense of absence of price. In fact, there is most definitely a price attached to this benefit – the cost of interest paid to foreigners on their accumulated past balances. This is a potential direct cost of the international use of a currency. Usually it is reckoned independently, as an offset to the gross expansionary income effect resulting from the seigniorage benefit. The magnitude of the interest offset to seigniorage will depend on the degree of monopoly enjoyed by the issuing country as a source of international money. If that degree of monopoly is considerable, the offsetting cost will be small. But if, on the other hand, there are a number of other internationally acceptable moneys competing with the issuing country's currency, then correspondingly higher payments of interest will be necessary to retain accumulated past balances. Under conditions of perfect competition, in fact, we would expect the gross seigniorage gain of an international currency to be largely, if not entirely, offset by the necessity to pay interest on foreign liabilities.[1]

The second direct benefit of an international currency derives from the fact that when a currency begins to be used internationally, purchases and sales, and loans and investments, will most likely have to be executed through banks or brokers in the issuing country.[2] Consequently, the earnings of the banking sector and its ancillary activities, including the foreign-exchange market, are likely to rise. These extra earnings will include not only the commissions charged for the increased volume of foreign-exchange transactions, but also the fees charged for investment services, such as the placement of foreign securities and the purchase of domestic financial assets for foreign accounts. In addition, they will include the interest earned on the higher total of foreign loans and investments.

However, as with the seigniorage benefit, there is an offset to this gain too. Unless the gross increase of banking earnings can be gained

---

[1] See McKinnon, op. cit., pp. 17–23; Herbert G. Grubel, 'The Distribution of Seigniorage from International Liquidity Creation', in Mundell and Swoboda (eds), op. cit., pp. 269–72; and below, chap. 5.

[2] All purchases and sales, and all loans and investments, would have to be executed through the issuing country if its banking system had an effective monopoly over both the issue of monetary liabilities denominated in local currency, and the exchange market for the currency. In fact, no national banking system has such monopolies, owing to the existence of the Euro-currency and world-wide foreign-exchange markets. Therefore, at least some transactions – though certainly not all – are likely to take place elsewhere.

at zero marginal cost, some income loss is necessarily implied. Zero marginal cost would imply that there is no useful alternative domestic use for the resources allocated to providing these services to foreigners – which is unlikely. What is more likely is that most if not all of the resources used in the supply of services could profitably be employed domestically. It is most proper, therefore, to reckon the second direct benefit on a net basis, equal to the difference between the gross earnings on additional banking services provided to foreigners and what the earnings on these services would be in their next-best alternative domestic use.

Once demand begins to increase for national banking services, gross earnings of other financial and commercial services are likely to rise as well, as foreigners become more aware of what facilities are available. These include the services of commodity and transport exchanges, brokerage houses and insurance companies. The additional earnings of these services together represent an important potential indirect benefit of the international use of a currency – one operating through private economic units. However, this benefit too is most properly reckoned on a net basis, since these services too are unlikely to be supplied at zero marginal cost. It represents the difference between the gross earnings on additional financial and commercial services provided to foreigners and what the earnings on these services would be in their next-best alternative domestic use.

One important potential benefit of the international use of a currency is an indirect one that operates through public policy. This is often described as the advantage of 'flexibility' in dealing with payments imbalances.[1] The notion of flexibility suggests the property of the repeated reversibility of a process. The ability of the country issuing an international currency to finance payments deficits through accumulation of liabilities abroad rather than through reserve losses has already been referred to. In addition to the cumulative direct benefit already mentioned ('seigniorage'), this means as well that a *given* deficit may be associated with a smaller loss of reserves than would otherwise be the case. In other words, in any given situation the issuing country may have more time and scope to deal with a payments deficit, and thus

---

[1] See Aliber, op. cit., pp. 445–6; William A. Salant, 'The Reserve Currency Role of the Dollar: Blessing or Burden to the United States?', *Review of Economics and Statistics*, XLVI 2 (May 1964) 165–6; and Herbert G. Grubel, 'The Benefits and Costs of Being World Banker', *National Banking Review*, II 2 (Dec 1964) 197–9.

enjoy greater freedom to resort to slower-acting remedies rather than to harsh and restrictive ones. Indeed, in some situations the country may not have to take any action to adjust at all. Use of a currency for international purposes gives the public authorities much greater latitude in their policy options than they would otherwise enjoy when dealing with temporary balance-of-payments difficulties.

There is also one important potential indirect cost that operates through public policy. This is often described as the disadvantage of 'constraint' on the nature and timing of domestic full-employment policies.[1] Of course, every country is subject to an independent balance-of-payments constraint on its domestic policies. But only a country issuing an international currency is subject to the additional constraint which results from the threat of reduction or withdrawal of past foreign accumulations of its money. This is the threat of the so-called 'overhang' of liabilities. Sometimes this threat is said to limit the government's ability to use domestic monetary and fiscal policies freely to maintain the optimal level of resource utilisation. At other times, emphasis is laid rather on the limited ability to use exchange controls or devaluation. And at yet other times, it is the necessity to acquire and hold larger gold stocks than would otherwise be required that is stressed,[2] or the necessity to extend formal or informal exchange guarantees.

Chapter 1 has explained the conditions necessary for a currency to be used for international purposes. These were exchange convertibility, transactions attractiveness, exchange convenience and capital certainty. No currency will begin to be used internationally that does not begin to satisfy these conditions. Conversely, no currency will long continue to be used internationally that begins to fail these conditions. However, suppose that the authorities are determined to maintain the international status of their currency. They may be able to do so, perhaps only briefly, perhaps indefinitely, but only in so far as they can manipulate

[1] See Aliber, op. cit., pp. 447–52; Salant, op. cit., pp. 166–7; Grubel, op. cit., pp. 200–5; and John R. Karlik, 'The Costs and Benefits of Being a Reserve-Currency Country: A Theoretical Approach Applied to the United States', in Peter B. Kenen and Roger Lawrence (eds), *The Open Economy: Essays on International Trade and Finance* (New York: Columbia University Press, 1968) pp. 320–2.

[2] Grubel and Karlik in fact stress this particular necessity as a cost *separate* from the general constraint disadvantage; however, as the text will explain, there really is no reason for treating the two as distinct. See Grubel, op. cit., pp. 199–20; an Karlik, op. cit., pp. 316–17.

public policies to prevent the failure of the necessary conditions. The cost of these policies is the extent of departure required from other public policy objectives; the economic cost may be measured in terms of the national income forgone in order to preserve the necessary conditions. That is what is meant by the constraint disadvantage.

For example, suppose that the issuing country begins to experience serious payments deficits at a time of less-than-full employment at home. Foreign users and holders may begin to doubt the government's ability or willingness to maintain the convertibility of its currency at a fixed rate of exchange. If the government is determined to prevent reduction or withdrawal of accumulated balances, it will have to enhance the credibility of its convertibility pledge; in other words, it will have to enhance foreign confidence in national solvency and, especially, in national liquidity. The first step, clearly, is to eliminate the deficit in the balance of payments. Exchange controls or devaluation, however, are out of the question. (The objective is to preserve, not alter, the terms of convertibility.) Therefore, full weight will have to be placed on deflationary monetary and fiscal policies, or on distortionary trade and capital restrictions – each potentially at the expense of domestic income and employment levels. In addition, the government may feel obliged to acquire additional gold stocks (or, what is the same thing, to prevent losses from its existing gold stock). Or the government may feel obliged to extend formal exchange guarantees to some or all foreign balances of its currency; or at least to intervene in the forward market to cheapen artificially the cost of forward cover for private transactions in the currency (an informal exchange guarantee that takes the form of a kind of officially subsidised insurance). These policies too, or others like them, either are or could be at the expense of domestic income and employment levels.

Likewise, the policies that would be required to preserve any of the other necessary conditions of an international currency also either are or could be at the expense of domestic income and employment levels. The whole variety of such policies are implied by the notion of constraint – just as a whole variety of policies are implied by the notion of flexibility. Both of these indirect effects are *contingent* effects of the international use of a currency. They are measured in terms of the gain or loss of degrees of freedom experienced by the authorities in dealing with the balance of payments and related policy problems.

This raises an interesting question: can the authorities both gain *and* lose degrees of freedom in dealing with the balance of payments and related policy problems? In other words, can the advantage of flexibility and the disadvantage of constraint be consistent with one another? They would appear to be incompatible. As William Salant has written, referring specifically to the dollar:

> The contention that the reserve currency role of the dollar imposes a constraint on the United States appears to clash head on with the claim that it provides the United States with flexibility by giving it more time to deal with deficits and thus greater latitude in its policy options. It would appear that, if one argument is right, the other must be wrong.[1]

Salant himself suggests the most reasonable way of resolving the apparent incompatibility: 'either can be valid depending on the time'.[2] In other words, the flexibility benefit and the constraint cost tend to apply sequentially rather than simultaneously. Early in the evolution of an international currency, when potential holders have no doubts about its soundness, the flexibility advantage is likely to predominate; later on, when liabilities and consequently doubts accumulate, the constraint disadvantage is likely to predominate:

> If a country performs international banking functions and its debt takes the form of deposits payable on demand, its customers' decisions whether to increase or decrease their deposits may determine whether it borrows or repays short-term debt. These decisions depend largely on the depositors' views as to the attractiveness of the reserve currency as compared with alternative reserve assets.[3]

Finally, there are two effects of the international use of a currency which may prove to be either benefit or cost for the issuing country – both indirect, contingent effects operating through public policy. One is the income effect of supplying reserves to the rest of the world.[4] Apart from acquisition costs, an increase of official reserves enables foreign nations to attain higher levels of real national income and capital formation than if reserve levels were constant; it permits them to finance subsequent balance-of-payments deficits that would otherwise force income losses on them. In turn, the income of the issuing country may be raised or lowered. As one writer has pointed out, expansion of foreign incomes permitted by additions to foreign reserves

> may or may not redound to the advantage of the reserve-currency country. Faster economic growth abroad may enhance or worsen the terms of trade of

---

[1] Salant, op. cit., p. 167.   [2] Ibid.
[3] Ibid.   [4] See Karlik, op. cit., pp. 317–18.

the center country, depending on the production and expenditure biases associated with increments in foreign income. The net effect of these biases cannot be presumed to favor trade expansion or the terms of trade of the center country. Hence, the subsequent income effect of supplying reserves may constitute either a gain or loss.[1]

The other indirect effect which may prove to be either benefit or cost is the income effect of supplying a unit of account for the purpose of expressing par values of other countries' currencies. When a money is used as unit of account, the issuing country loses effective control over its own exchange rate. For example, the government might decide that its currency should be devalued. However, whether it can make a devaluation effective or not depends on the decisions of others, not on its own decisions. If some other countries elect to maintain the relationship of their own currencies vis-à-vis the unit of account (because it *is* unit of account), there is nothing the issuing country can do about it. Likewise, a decision to revalue also depends on the decisions of others. The country thus loses an option in dealing with the balance of payments and related policy problems. Whether this is apt to result in income gains or income losses depends on the same sorts of variables as determine the net benefit or cost of the previous indirect effect. In particular, it depends on how many other countries elect to peg their own currencies to the unit of account.

Though they appear similar, this last effect is really quite different from the disadvantage of constraint. The latter refers to the inability of the government to *choose* devaluation as a policy, owing to the need to maintain the credibility of its convertibility pledge. The former refers, contrastingly, to the government's inability to *implement* devaluation as a policy – to make it 'stick' – should it be chosen. This effect has nothing to do with the convertibility pledge; it is a consequence of an international currency entirely independent of whether or not the money serves also as medium of exchange or store of value. It is strictly a consequence of the unit-of-account function of money at the level of official international transactions.

The potential benefits and costs of the international use of a currency are summarised in outline form in Table 2.1. For reasons of convenience already cited, the income gains from increased foreign demand for national banking services and for other national financial and commercial services are included in the enumeration on a net basis. All other gains and losses are included on a gross basis. The income

---

[1] Karlik, op. cit., p. 318.

effects of supplying global reserves and a unit of account for par values
are listed potentially as either benefit or cost.

Table 2.1

An Enumeration of the Potential Benefits and Costs of an International Currency

I. *Direct*
    A. Benefits:
        1. 'Seigniorage.'
            (*a*) Current portion.
            (*b*) Capital portion.
        2. Net income gain from increased foreign demand for national
           banking services.
    B. Cost: interest payments on foreign balances.

II. *Indirect via private economic units*
    A. Benefit: net income gain from increased foreign demand for other
        national financial and commercial services.

III. *Indirect via public policy*
    A. Benefit: flexibility in dealing with payments imbalances.
    B. Cost: constraint on full-employment policies.
    C. Either benefit or cost:
        1. Income effect of supplying global reserves.
        2. Income effect of supplying a unit of account for par values.

II. ATTRIBUTION

A methodological issue

We must now consider the question of the extent to which it is possible
to attribute the separate benefits or costs among the specific functions
of an international currency. To begin with, this involves a fundamental methodological issue. To some extent, all benefits and costs are
interrelated. Is it legitimate, therefore, to enumerate and attribute them
as if they were independent of one another?

Several years ago, within months of one another, four different
essays appeared comparing the benefits and costs of international currencies. Three of these, by Robert Aliber, Herbert Grubel and William
Salant, were concerned specifically with the dollar; the fourth, by Alan

Kirman and Wilson Schmidt, was concerned with sterling.[1] Each analysis was based on its own analytical taxonomy of gains and losses.[2] More significantly, each analysis proceeded as if in fact the separate effects of an international currency were genuinely independent of one another. Specific benefits and costs were enumerated; estimates for each were derived individually;[3] and then they were all totalled and compared.

More recently, one further comparison of the benefits and costs of an international currency has appeared. This essay, by John Karlik, also is concerned specifically with the dollar, and also employs its own analytical taxonomy of gains and losses.[4] But Karlik severely criticises the analytical procedures of the earlier studies. They are illegitimate, he argues, because they ignore the fundamental links between gains and losses. Consequently, the separate estimates almost always tend to be mutually inconsistent:

> . . . the gains and losses from reserve-currency status are not independent of one another; on the contrary, the magnitudes of various costs and benefits are inter-related. Thus, costs and benefits cannot be estimated individually (as if they were independent) and totaled. Instead, starting with the date when the nation in question became a reserve-currency country, one must construct a hypothetical non-reserve-currency growth path. This alternative path must be traced using an assumed set of plausible, consistent policies that do not involve reserve-currency status. The sign of the compounded difference between the actual and hypothetical real national income streams can then be used to determine whether reserve-currency status has resulted in a net gain or loss.[5]

[1] Aliber, op. cit.; Grubel, op. cit.; Salant, op. cit.; and Alan P. Kirman and Wilson E. Schmidt, 'Key Currency Burdens: The U.K. Case', *National Banking Review*, III 1 (Sep 1965) 101–2.

[2] Interestingly, not one of these four analyses includes all of the potential benefits and costs enumerated in Table 2.1. All fail to recognise the two possible income effects of supplying either global reserves or a unit of account for par values. In addition, for reasons that are not altogether clear, Aliber chooses to ignore the income gain from increased foreign demand for national banking and other financial and commercial services. Salant makes no pretence of designing an exhaustive taxonomy: he includes only the single benefit and single cost he considers most important – the flexibility advantage and the constraint disadvantage.

[3] Salant's estimates were roughly qualitative rather than quantitative like the others.

[4] Karlik, op. cit. Karlik's taxonomy is also less exhaustive than the enumeration in Table 2.1: he omits both the flexibility advantage and the possible income effect of supplying a unit of account for par values.

[5] Ibid., p. 314.

Now, no informed economist would deny that there are links between the various gains or losses of an international currency; nor would one deny that where such interdependencies exist, some degree of accuracy is sacrificed if the separate effects are estimated individually and then added together. Strictly speaking, Karlik is absolutely right. But all that is really beside the point: ultimately there are links between all the variables of economic analysis, and ultimately all analysis must sacrifice some degree of accuracy. The main point is not so strict. It is a question, rather, of how *strong* the interdependencies are, and therefore how *much* accuracy is lost if for analytical purposes the links are ignored. We have already confronted this problem in considering the different functions of money, and I concluded then that even though the different functions are closely interrelated, for the purposes of this study they can be analysed separately *as if* they were independent of one another. I submit that for the same purposes, the potential benefits and costs too can be analysed *as if* they were independent (just as they were analysed in the four earlier cost–benefit studies of international currencies).

To be sure, the analytical procedure I am proposing to use is less sophisticated, technically, than Karlik's. But I truly doubt that any higher degree of sophistication is necessary here. This study is conceived as an exercise in foreign economic policy. Our purpose is to evaluate alternative proposals for reform of the international roles of sterling, in terms of the net benefit or cost for Britain implied by each monetary function. For such a purpose, all that policy-makers really need is some rough idea of rank order of magnitude – and this much, at least, the procedure I am proposing to use can surely provide. That is why I believe that for such a purpose, it will be legitimate simply to analyse the separate effects as if they were independent. The technique may be relatively simple-minded, but as we shall see, it will not prevent us from deriving some quite powerful results.

Tactically, the procedure I am proposing to use differs only slightly from Karlik's. He insists that the benefits or costs of an international currency can be analysed only by comparing them with what economic welfare would be if the currency were not used for international purposes. I concur – merely adding, however, that each benefit or cost may be analysed separately, without serious loss of accuracy, *if we are consistent in specifying the hypothetical alternative growth path or income level to which each effect is defined*. Specifically, the assumptions on which the estimates of the different effects are based must not be mutually contradictory. The same standard of comparison – that is, the same alternative measure of welfare – must be used for each different effect. So long as each effect is compared with the *same* hypothetical alternative, there is no reason why the separate estimates cannot be regarded as roughly consistent and therefore sufficient for our purposes.

The separate roles

Because international monetary theorists have until quite recently tended not to distinguish systematically among international money's six distinct roles, none of the published cost–benefit analyses has much to say on the question of the extent to which separate effects can be attributed to specific functions.[1] But the logic of attribution does in fact follow directly from the theory of the roles of currencies developed in the previous chapter, and from the enumeration of possible gains and losses developed in the present chapter. Considering in turn all of the benefits and costs listed in Table 2.1, we shall examine the extent to which each effect can be allocated – in terms of the taxonomy of roles in Table 1.1 – 'vertically' among monetary functions and 'horizontally' between levels of international transactions.

However, first it should be remarked that in this discussion we shall ignore, for now, any of the empirical problems implied by the question of attribution; formidable as these problems may be, they are best left until we reach the analytical chapters of Part Two. Here in Part One we are concerned exclusively with issues of theory – though, regrettably, theoretical discussions do have a tendency to create a spurious illusion of unattainable refinement. Distinctions which seem

[1] The Aliber, Karlik and Salant analyses are all concerned solely with the role of the dollar at the level of official international transactions. Although this is invariably described as the 'reserve-currency' role of the dollar, the analyses in fact encompass the dollar's functions as intervention currency and unit of account as well as reserve currency *per se*. However, none of the three attempts to attribute separate gains or losses to any of these three functions.

Grubel, and Kirman and Schmidt, are concerned with the roles of, respectively, the dollar and sterling at both levels of international transactions, private as well as official. Grubel speaks of America's position as 'world banker', Kirman and Schmidt of Britain's position as 'key-currency country'. But neither attempts to allocate separate gains or losses between the two levels of transactions – let alone among the three monetary functions of a currency at each of the two levels.

valid and precise in theory are often impossible to define in practice. Therefore, it is necessary to caution the reader here against what may appear to be a relatively high degree of precision in allocating the potential benefits and costs of an international currency. As we shall see in Part Two, precision in these matters is really very difficult in empirical terms, even if it seems appropriate in theoretical terms.

In theory, the first direct benefit of an international currency – the seigniorage benefit – may be allocated vertically partially to the medium-of-exchange function and partially to the store-of-value function. This is so even though the exchange function would appear, superficially, to have little or nothing to do with this particular gain. After all, the residents of a country can enjoy an expansionary income effect of greater balance-of-payments deficits only in so far as foreigners are prepared voluntarily to *accumulate* balances of their currency for asset and/or reserve purposes. Moreover, as we observed in the previous chapter, a currency may function as store of value *regardless* of whether it functions also as medium of exchange. Therefore, it would appear that if foreigners are in fact prepared to include the currency among their private assets and/or among their official reserves, it does not matter whether the currency serves additionally as international exchange intermediary. Take away the medium-of-exchange function but preserve the store-of-value function, and the seigniorage gain still accrues to the issuing country.

True, but as we also learned in the previous chapter, take away the medium-of-exchange function, and the store-of-value function may possibly be diminished; foreigners may not find it necessary, or be willing, to accumulate balances of the currency *to the same extent* as before. Accordingly, the *magnitude* of the gain accruing to the country may possibly be diminished. Or, to stand the point on its head, the additional role of exchange intermediary is likely to add marginally to the expansionary income effect by inducing foreigners to accumulate larger balances than they would otherwise if the currency were used just for asset and/or reserve purposes alone. In other words, the seigniorage benefit really consists of two effects – a *primary* effect and an *incremental* effect. The effect of the store-of-value function is primary: the currency *must* serve as a means of holding wealth if the gain is to accrue at all. But there is also an incremental effect, and this must be attributed to the medium-of-exchange function of the currency.[1]

---

[1] Note that the primary effect is primary only in a functional sense: of the two, the incremental effect may actually be the larger in quantitative terms.

FS C

In turn, the primary effect may be allocated horizontally between the levels of private and official international transactions in proportion to the extent that the currency is accumulated, respectively, in private asset balances and in official reserve balances. The incremental gain may be similarly allocated in proportion to the extent that use as either transactions currency or intervention currency adds to use, respectively, as either asset currency or reserve currency. In effect, therefore, four of the six possible roles of an international currency share in the seigniorage benefit. If a currency plays even just one of these roles, the issuing country has an opportunity of enjoying the expansionary income effect of greater balance-of-payments deficits. If the currency plays all four roles, the country's opportunity is very great indeed.

By the same token, in so far as the country does enjoy the benefit of seigniorage, it must also suffer the expense of interest payments to foreigners on their accumulated balances. This is the potential direct cost of an international currency. Its allocation parallels precisely the allocation of the expansionary effect of greater deficits.

The net income gain from increased foreign demand for national banking services, like the seigniorage benefit of an international currency, may be allocated vertically partially to the medium-of-exchange function and partially to the store-of-value function. However, without knowing the motivations of individual real-world transactions, it is impossible *a priori* to be very specific about this allocation. For instance, some of the gain is undoubtedly attributable to a money's use as a transactions or intervention currency: this probably includes the bulk of commissions earned on foreign-exchange transactions as well as much of the interest earned on foreign loans and investments. But some of this income is also likely to accrue on account of the store-of-value function. Conversely, some of the gain is undoubtedly attributable to a money's use as asset or reserve currency: this probably includes the bulk of the commissions earned on investment services. But some of this income is also likely to accrue on account of the medium-of-exchange function. Moreover, with respect to earnings based on the store-of-value function, allowance must be made too for an incremental gain attributable to the medium-of-exchange function, in so far as this latter role adds marginally to the total of these earnings. And finally, all these benefits must be allocated horizontally in proportion to the currency's use at the two levels of international transactions.

By contrast, the allocation of the net income gain from increased foreign demand for other national financial and commercial services is much more specific. All of this benefit is attributable exclusively to a money's use as a transactions currency. To the extent that foreigners find it convenient to make additional use of the services of local commodity and transport exchanges, brokerage houses and insurance companies, it is because they use the local currency as exchange intermediary; these services are all ancillaries of the kinds of activities that require a currency for private transactions purposes. It does not matter whether the currency is used as well as an intervention currency or for store-of-value purposes. Here it is only the private exchange function that matters.

The allocation of both the flexibility advantage and the constraint disadvantage parallels precisely the allocation of either the expansionary effect of greater deficits or the cost of interest payments on foreign balances – and precisely for the same reasons. Although each derives primarily from the store-of-value function, in each case allowance must also be made for an incremental effect attributable to the medium-of-exchange function; and both primary and incremental effects must also be allocated horizontally in proportion to the currency's use at the two levels of international transactions. Likewise, the income effect of supplying reserves must be attributed to both the medium-of-exchange and store-of-value functions, though clearly only at the level of official international transactions. The income effect of supplying a unit of account for the purpose of expressing par values is of course attributable exclusively to a money's use as unit of account.

The allocation of the separate benefits or costs to specific monetary functions is summarised in Table 2.2. Virtually all of the effects are shared among four of the six roles – the medium-of-exchange and store-of-value roles at both levels of transactions. The unit-of-account role at the level of official international transactions has but one benefit or cost – the income effect of supplying a standard for expressing par values. Interestingly, the unit-of-account role at the level of private international transactions has no benefit or cost at all. A country neither gains nor loses from the international use of its money strictly as a quotation currency.

This concludes Part One, the theoretical introduction to our study. Table 2.2 provides all the information we need for understanding the potential social gains or losses of each function of an international currency. It will be our fundamental analytical framework, the basis for the empirical cost–benefit analysis of the international roles of sterling in Part Two.

Table 2.2

Attribution of the Potential Benefits and Costs of an International Currency

Function	Medium-of-Exchange Transactions currencies:	Unit-of-Account Quotation currencies:	Store-of-Value Asset currencies:
PRIVATE TRANSACTIONS	*Benefits:* 1. Seigniorage based on private asset accumulation (incremental gain). 2. Net income gain from banking services provided for private transactions. 3. Flexibility advantage based on private asset accumulation (incremental gain). 4. Net income gain from other financial and commercial services. *Costs:* 1. Interest payments on foreign private deposits (incremental cost). 2. Constraint disadvantage based on private asset accumulation (incremental cost).		*Benefits:* 1. Seigniorage based on private asset accumulation (primary gain). 2. Net income gain from banking services provided for private investments. 3. Flexibility advantage based on private asset accumulation (primary gain). *Costs:* 1. Interest payments on foreign private deposits (primary cost). 2. Constraint disadvantage based on private asset accumulation (primary cost).

Table 2.2 (continued)

Attribution of the Potential Benefits and Costs of an International Currency.

	Intervention currencies:	Unit-of-account currencies:	Reserve currencies:
OFFICIAL TRANSACTIONS	*Benefits:* 1. Seigniorage based on official reserve accumulation (incremental gain). 2. Net income gain from banking services provided for official transactions. 3. Flexibility advantage based on official reserve accumulation (incremental gain). *Costs:* 1. Interest payments on foreign official deposits (incremental cost). 2. Constraint disadvantage based on official reserve accumulation (incremental cost). *Benefit or cost:* Income effect of supplying reserves (incremental effect).	*Benefit or cost:* Income effect of supplying a unit of account for par values.	*Benefits:* 1. Seigniorage based on official reserve accumulation (primary gain). 2. Net income gain from banking services provided for official investments. 3. Flexibility advantage based on official reserve accumulation (primary gain). *Costs:* 1. Interest payments on foreign official deposits (primary cost). 2. Constraint disadvantage based on official reserve accumulation (primary cost). *Benefit or cost:* Income effect of supplying reserves (primary effect).

PART TWO

The Benefits and Costs of Sterling

3 Introduction

STERLING, second only to the dollar, is the national money most widely used as an international currency. It is a fully developed international money, serving all six monetary functions. At the level of private international transactions, the pound is an important asset currency. Moreover, at least 20 per cent of all international trade is invoiced in sterling and settled through sterling bank accounts. Virtually every country in the world makes use of the currency at one time or another: at this level of transactions the pound performs its roles on a truly global scale. However, relative to the dollar it is only within the sterling area that the pound is used really often. Outside the sterling area the currency is just one of several international moneys; inside the sterling area, on the other hand, it predominates.

Consequently, inside the sterling area the pound also predominates at the level of official international transactions. In intervening to support local-currency values, member-governments of the bloc find it most efficient to buy and sell sterling. The principal transactions currency is also the principal intervention currency. In addition, the pound traditionally serves as the principal reserve medium and as a peg for currency values. But it is only within the sterling area, and not elsewhere, that the pound serves these three official functions. At this level of transactions, sterling is most definitely just a regional currency.

Regrettably, few systematic attempts have ever been made to measure the costs and benefits of the international use of sterling. That will be my objective here in Part Two of this study. Specifically, my objective will be to estimate, as accurately as is possible, the social gains or losses of *each specific function* of the pound.

The time perspective of the analysis will be current and prospective. What is the net benefit or cost for Britain of each of sterling's separate roles today, and what is the prospective benefit or cost of maintaining these roles in the future? I will not be concerned, except incidentally, with the retrospective question of whether *to date* Britain has on balance gained or lost from sterling's international functions. Without a doubt this is an interesting question; however, in a discussion of foreign economic policy it is also an academic one. For a policy–maker, the past is not a matter of much serious concern; even last year is already practically 'ancient history'. What really concerns him is the present and the future – how affairs stand today, and what the outlook is for tomorrow. Accordingly, only one chapter here will be devoted to the history of sterling. Chapter 4 will review the pound's development as an international currency, from earliest colonial days down to the Basle agreements of 1968. The purpose of Chapter 4 is to set the stage for the empirical investigation that follows in the remainder of Part Two. The chapter will comment only briefly and impressionistically on the question of past gains or losses for Britain.[1]

The empirical investigation will proceed by considering, in order, each of the potential benefits and costs enumerated in Table 2.1. Estimates of magnitudes will be derived and allocated among specific functions – but, of course, *only to the extent possible*. The reader is cautioned again not to expect a very high degree of precision. I do not want to give a spurious illusion of unattainable refinement. As I have already insisted, for the most part empirical precision in these matters is very difficult. My objective will be much more prudent – to give simply some rough idea of rank order of magnitude. That must necessarily be the limit of my ambition.

Within this limit, a single unique magnitude will be estimated for each of the specific, continuing effects of the international use o sterling. These include the benefits derived from seigniorage and from increased foreign demand for national banking, financial and commercial services; they also include the cost of interest payments on foreign balances. But they do not include any of the several indirect effects operating through public policy. These latter are neither specific nor continuing. They are contingent effects; no single unique magnitude can be associated with any of them. Rather, in each case there are several different magnitudes, each associated with one of several alternative contingencies. Estimates of these effects must therefore specify a *range* of magnitudes, rather than any single number.

Inevitably, the calculation of many estimates will require a choice among higher or lower figures. For the sake of consistency, I shall always try to err on the side of overstated benefits or understated costs,

---

[1] Of the five published cost–benefit analyses cited in Chapter 2, only one – John Karlik's – used the retrospective approach. All of the other four were concerned, as my own will be, with current and/or prospective gains and losses.

rather than the reverse. My preference is for a methodology that places the burden of proof on those who would alter the *status quo*, rather than on those who would preserve it.

In estimating all benefits and costs, an identical standard of comparison will be adopted. I shall assume that sterling is not used at all for any international purpose, the whole of the resources involved reverting to exclusively domestic employment. Benefits or costs will then be reckoned as the gain or loss of income relative to that hypothetical alternative.

The standard of comparison will be defined independently of any particular reform of sterling as an international currency. Over the years, as we know, many alternative reforms of sterling have been proposed. However, since any one of them would generate its own costs and benefits, specification of any single reform in the future would inevitably tend to bias the calculation of the pound's various costs and benefits as they are at present.[1] Accordingly, the hypothetical alternative adopted here will not specify any single reform. It will simply assume that somehow sterling's international roles suddenly disappear. In effect, it will compare Britain's position with what that position would be if, moving along a different time dimension, the pound had never begun to be used for international purposes at all. Admittedly, this is an unrealistic assumption. In actuality, the pound did begin to be used for international purposes. Moreover, any decline of sterling's status would normally be expected to occur gradually rather than suddenly, and some reform would almost necessarily be implied. Unrealism, however, is implied by the adoption of any hypothetical alternative. It is simply an analytical device. The test of the device is not whether it is especially realistic, but rather whether it is especially useful for analysis. For the purpose at hand, the hypothetical alternative I have specified will, we shall see, prove to be very useful indeed.

The analysis itself will be divided into four chapters. Chapter 5 will consider jointly the possible gain from seigniorage together with the interest cost of accumulated balances. The net gains from increased foreign demand for national banking, financial and commercial services will be treated in Chapter 6, and the flexibility advantage and the constraint disadvantage in Chapter 7. Chapter 8 will examine the last two potential effects, which may be either benefit or cost.

The analysis will be summarised in Chapter 9.

---

[1] Part Three will critically evaluate the potential costs and benefits of alternative reforms of sterling.

4 The History of Sterling as an International Currency

THE story of sterling has oft been told,[1] and this study does not require yet another detailed rehearsal. Therefore, our narrative will simply skim the surface of the tale, concentrating only on those details that are directly relevant to the analysis in the chapters which follow.

The story of sterling as an international currency is essentially quite simple. In its evolution the pound has passed through two distinct periods – first, a period of 'globalisation', as the effective British market area carried beyond the geographic confines of the United Kingdom itself; and second, a period of 'regionalisation', as the British economy has tended to shrink relative to the rest of the world. The first phase was highlighted by the establishment in London of more or less common financial facilities for all foreigners and for British residents alike; the second phase, by a kind of regional retreat, a regrouping of financial facilities along lines that have made transactions among sterling-associated countries – the sterling bloc or sterling area – easier than transactions with other countries. The globalisation of the pound began early in the 1800s and continued for more than a century, yielding only gradually to regionalisation in the period 1914–31. Since 1931 the trend toward the consolidation of sterling regionality has predominated, and persists even today.

I. GLOBALISATION

Up to the First World War

The years before 1914 were the halcyon days of sterling's globalisation. For a century or more, until convertibility was suspended with the

---

[1] Among the numerous 'histories' of sterling, perhaps the two best are A. C. L. Day, *The Future of Sterling* (London: Oxford University Press, 1954) chaps. 2–4;

outbreak of the First World War, the pound functioned as by far the most important international currency, and London as by far the most important financial centre. The largest proportion of world trade was financed, invoiced and settled in sterling; the largest proportion of internationally owned assets was denominated in sterling; and the largest proportion of official reserves, apart from gold, was held in sterling. The pound bestrode the financial world like a colossus.[1]

The reasons for sterling's emergence as the world's leading international currency during this period are familiar.[2] In the first place, the convertibility of the pound was unquestioned. This was the era of the gold standard, when gold was the ultimate reserve asset of the system. To be generally acceptable as an international means of payment, therefore, a currency first of all had to be convertible into gold – but not only that: the gold-convertibility pledge had to be credible. At this time, there was no currency more credibly gold-convertible than the pound. Britain was not only the world's principal creditor-nation; she was also the greatest exporter of new capital.[3] Moreover, while it is true that the ratio of British gold reserves to sterling liabilities generally tended to remain relatively low, it is also true that virtually any amount of money could be drawn into London, whenever it was necessary to maintain external liquidity, by raising interest rates. Nor

---

and Judd Polk, *Sterling: Its Meaning and in World Finance* (New York: Harper & Bros, for the Council on Foreign Relations, 1956) chaps. 2–4. For briefer and more-up-to-date treatment, see J. M. Livingstone, *Britain and the World Economy* (London: Penguin Books, 1966) chap. 2; and Fred Hirsch, *Money International*, rev. ed. (London: Penguin Books, 1969) pp. 480–9.

[1] It is important, of course, not to exaggerate too much the predominance of the pound in the nineteenth century. Sterling *was* the most important international currency of the period, but it was not *alone*. Other currencies were also used to a significant extent for international purposes, including especially the German mark and the French franc. See Peter H. Lindert, *Key Currencies and Gold, 1900–1913*, Studies in International Finance, No. 24 (Princeton: International Finance Section, 1969) pp. 16–21.

[2] These reasons have been frequently discussed. For a useful and concise treatment, see Day, op. cit., chap. 2.

[3] By 1913 Britain's net overseas assets are reckoned to have reached a total of nearly £4 billion. During the previous century there were just three years when the country imported capital, on balance, rather than exported it. See Albert H. Imlah, *Economic Elements in the Pax Britannica* (Cambridge, Mass.: Harvard University Press, 1958) pp. 70–5.

should it be forgotten that there were few countries that could match the stability of Britain's political and social institutions. For all these reasons, prospective foreign users of sterling could take the right of convertibility virtually for granted.

Given an assured right of convertibility, prospective sterling users tended to become actual sterling users because there was also no other currency in the nineteenth century that was nearly so attractive for transactions purposes. Britain, as the home of the industrial revolution, had grown to become the world's richest nation and its greatest trader (until the 1890s, at least). In addition, she was unrivalled in providing services ancillary to trade, such as shipping and insurance, and also most organised commodity markets were established in London. Consequently, British goods and services were in demand everywhere, and British imports of foodstuffs and raw materials were enormous.[1] Trade with the United Kingdom was a large part of the trade of practically every country in the world. To be sure, British trade was not always the largest part: there were countries that had trading relations with Britain's rivals which were more important than their trading relations with Britain. But the British were unique in having important trading relations with more countries than any others had. No country had such strong trade ties with so many countries in so many widespread parts of the globe as Britain had.

The predominant position of the British in world trade meant that foreigners were continually earning large incomes in Britain or else in countries making payments there, and also continually making payments to Britain or else to countries earning incomes there. Inevitably, the lines of clearance of commercial debt came to pass through London, and therefore it was logical that sterling should come to be used for denominating and settling contracts. Especially after 1860, the pound came to circulate almost universally as a transactions and quotation currency.[2]

As Alan Day has explained:

> In general the more connexions a country has and the stronger they are, the more connexions she is likely to attract. This meant that because Britain had

---

[1] In 1800 the British market was taking more than 40 per cent of the rest of the world's merchandise exports. In the 1860s the percentage was still over 30, and in the 1890s still over 20, though by 1913 it was down to just 17. See Imlah, op. cit., p. 191.

[2] See David Williams, 'The Evolution of the Sterling System', in C. R. Whittlesey and J. S. G. Wilson (eds), *Essays in Money and Banking* (Oxford: Oxford University Press, 1968) pp. 266–72.

very extensive trading . . . connexions, sterling would be all the more useful to a country which chose to use it; and as more people came to use it, sterling would be all the more attractive as a means of international payment to everyone. The very strength and importance of sterling attracted more strength and more importance.[1]

Sterling's strength derived initially from its differentially broader purchasing power, but it was enhanced by the availability of relatively cheap credit facilities in London. In the nineteenth-century, the City was predominant as a source of both short- and long-term capital. The importance of the bill of exchange drawn on London in the financing of trade during this period has often been remarked; so too has the importance of capital issues in London in the development of overseas economies.[2] This added to the eminent transactions attractiveness of the pound.

During this period sterling was eminently attractive also as a store of value. In part, of course, this was a natural corollary of the currency's usefulness for transactions purposes: it would clearly be convenient for foreign transactors to hold considerable working balances in London in order to meet sterling obligations. This was remarked decades ago by that shrewd observer, Walter Bagehot:

> London has become the sole great settling-house of exchange transactions in Europe, instead of being formerly one of two. And this pre-eminence London will probably maintain, for it is a natural pre-eminence. The number of mercantile bills drawn upon London incalculably surpasses those drawn on any other European city; London is the place which receives more than any other place, and pays more than any other place, and therefore, is the natural 'clearing-house'. . . .
>
> Now that London is the clearing-house to foreign countries, London has a new liability to foreign countries. At whatever place many people have to make payments, at that place those people must keep money. A large deposit of foreign money in London is now necessary for the business of the world. . . .[3]

However, additionally, London offered unrivalled facilities for the deposit and investment of funds in excess of what was required for working balances. The City's financial markets were the broadest, deepest and most resilient in the world. No other currency offered such a high degree of capital certainty as did sterling. And, of course, given

---

[1] Day, op. cit., pp. 15–16. See also Williams, op. cit., pp. 266–8.

[2] See, e.g., A. K. Cairncross, *Home and Foreign Investment 1870–1913* (Cambridge: Cambridge University Press, 1953).

[3] Walter Bagehot, *Lombard Street*, 12th ed. (London: Kegan Paul, Trench, Trubner & Co. Ltd, 1908) p. 34.

the wide use of sterling for transactions purposes, no other currency offered such a high degree of exchange convenience either. Therefore, pounds soon came to be held widely, purely for private asset purposes.

Pounds also came to be held for official reserve purposes – though not so widely as for private asset purposes. Few central banks or governments held large amounts of foreign exchange as a reserve under the gold standard, and those that did acquired it mainly after 1900. The ratio of world foreign-exchange reserves to world gold reserves remained relatively low even in 1913.[1] It is often claimed that the gold standard was in reality a sterling standard, but this is misleading in so far as most official reserves before 1913 were still held in gold, not sterling; and in so far as gold, not sterling, was still the preferred medium for intervention purposes. Furthermore, during this period most independent countries were explicitly concerned to maintain the gold value of their currencies, not the sterling value. Gold was the *de jure* unit of account for expressing par values in the nineteenth century. As a unit of account, sterling functioned only on a *de facto* basis, and not for all nations. (Mainly it was for those nations that after 1931 elected to maintain the relationship of their currencies vis-à-vis the pound rather than vis-à-vis gold.)

Yet the fact remains that in some sense the gold standard *was* in reality a sterling standard. Certainly at the level of private international transactions the pound was the most important international currency – more important even than gold. And this pre-eminence of sterling resulted in an asymmetry of the international adjustment mechanism that distinctly favoured Britain. No other country was able to use interest rates so effectively to manage the balance of payments. Not only were international capital flows highly sensitive to changes of London interest rates; so too were prices in international trade – and especially the prices of the primary-product exports of less developed countries, most of which were financed in sterling. When, for instance, a deterioration of the British balance of payments led the Bank of

[1] See Arthur I. Bloomfield, *Short-Term Capital Movements under the Pre-1914 Gold Standard*, Studies in International Finance, No. 11 (Princeton: International Finance Section, 1963) pp. 7–19; and Lindert, op. cit., pp. 9–16. Bloomfield's ('almost complete') figures of official foreign-exchange holdings show a total of $963 million at end-1913, up from $60–70 million in 1880 and $130–150 million in 1899. Lindert's figures ('at least 90 per cent of the world total') show a total of $1,132 million at end-1913. The resulting ratios of gold: foreign-exchange reserves of 5:1 (Bloomfield) or 4:1 (Lindert) compare with a ratio of roughly 2:1 today.

England to increase Bank Rate, importers of staple goods, finding financing more difficult, would be compelled to liquidate inventories, thus forcing down the prices of Britain's chief import goods. And this meant an improvement of Britain's terms of trade, since such declines could be expected to be far larger than those in the less sensitive prices of British industrial exports. Consequently, higher interest rates would improve the balance of payments not only on capital account (by inducing a net inflow of capital) but also on current account (by inducing lower prices on imports).[1]

In brief, Britain enjoyed a flexibility in dealing with payments imbalances during this period that was unique. This was a significant benefit of the international use of sterling. Britain also enjoyed an expansionary income effect of greater balance-of-payments deficits than would otherwise have been possible, as foreigners accumulated sterling balances in London; and the income gains from increased foreign demand for national banking, financial and commercial services were also probably quite large. On the other hand, the interest payments on foreign balances were apparently not so large[2] and the authorities seemed to experience no additional constraint on their domestic economic policies. There can be little doubt, therefore, that prior to 1913, on balance, Britain gained significantly from the globalisation of sterling.

1914–31

If the years before 1914 were the halcyon days of sterling's globalisation, the years from the Great War to the Great Crash were the twilight. During this period the pound lost its absolute dominance in the world of finance. The return to convertibility in 1925 restored the gold

[1] See Robert Triffin, 'National Central Banking and the International Economy', in *International Monetary Policies*, Postwar Economic Studies, No. 7 (Washington: Federal Reserve Board of Governors, 1947) pp. 52–3, and *The Evolution of the International Monetary System: Historical Reappraisal and Future Perspectives*, Studies in International Finance, No. 12 (Princeton: International Finance Section, 1964) pp. 5–6. But cf. P. M. Oppenheimer, 'Monetary Movements and the International Position of Sterling', in D. J. Robertson and L. C. Hunter, *The British Balance of Payments* (Edinburgh: Oliver & Boyd, 1966) pp. 95–7; and Lindert, op. cit., pp. 44–6.

[2] The balance on interest and dividends in the U.K. balance of payments was positive in every single year from 1815 to 1913. See Imlah, op. cit., pp. 70–5.

standard, but the system was no longer a sterling standard, nor was it any longer centred uniquely on London. The pound's global monopoly was broken.

What broke the pound's monopoly was the emergence of the dollar and, to a lesser extent, the French franc as serious competitors.[1] Even after 1925 sterling still accounted for the largest proportion of international trade, as well as the largest proportion of international assets. But this was in good measure the result of inertia in trade and financial relationships. America had already eclipsed Britain as the world's richest nation and as its greatest trader, and both New York and Paris had grown to challenge London as international financial centres. Both offered relatively cheap credit facilities for borrowers as well as profitable investment opportunities for lenders. By 1925 it was becoming clear that the pound did not have as much of an advantage over its rivals as it had once had, in terms of either transactions attractiveness or capital certainty.

In terms of the credibility of its gold-convertibility pledge, the pound did not have any advantage left at all; indeed, it was at a disadvantage. For when Britain returned to gold in 1925, she did so at the pre-war parity of $4.86 to the pound, which was, in view of the intervening changes in national price levels, a manifestly overvalued exchange rate. The dollar and franc, meanwhile, were both undervalued, the former slightly, the latter excessively. Thus to maintain parity after 1925, Britain had to tolerate high levels of unemployment; and so long as the City continued lending and investing abroad at long term, it had to borrow large amounts of foreign money at short term. Indeed, at each hint of crisis, foreigners were likely to withdraw balances from London. Capital flight was now a constant threat. Moreover, London was now less well placed to discourage a capital flight or to offset it by short-term inflows or by compensating improvements of the terms of trade. Now there were rival financial centres where funds could be lodged or where trade could be financed. Interest rates could no longer be so heavily relied upon to manage the balance of payments.

In brief, Britain no longer enjoyed an extra degree of flexibility in dealing with payments imbalances. Indeed, by the late 1920s there could be little doubt that it was now the constraint disadvantage that

---

[1] These developments have been discussed numerous times. The classic source is William A. Brown, Jr, *The International Gold Standard Reinterpreted, 1914–1934* (New York: National Bureau of Economic Research, 1940).

predominated, not the flexibility advantage. The high levels of domestic unemployment were sufficiently eloquent testimony, as were the exceptionally high rates of interest that were required to keep foreign money from leaving London. Although the City was still probably deriving a net income gain from providing its services to foreigners, it is likely that, on balance, the country as a whole was losing because of sterling's international functions. Certainly that was implied by the decision in September 1931 to suspend the convertibility of the pound. That decision brought into being a region of sterling-associated countries – the 'sterling bloc' or, as it is usually called today, the 'sterling area'. In effect, suspension of convertibility signalled the end of sterling's global status and the beginning of its regionalisation.

II. REGIONALISATION

Since 1931 the predominant trend has been toward the regionalisation of sterling's international status. The trend has not been a steady one; rather, it has been like the ebb and flow of an outgoing tide. But the tide has been inexorable. After a third of a century there can be no doubt that the global position of the pound is drastically shrunken. Not only has membership of the sterling world tended gradually to erode over time; likewise, so too have the monetary functions of sterling. Moreover, the relative importance of sterling as an international currency has tended to decline not just outside the sterling region but inside it as well. The pound today is but a shadow of its former self.

Shrinkage of sterling's world

In a sense, before 1931 all of the world was a sterling region. That was the meaning of globalisation. But with the suspension of convertibility, sterling's world began to shrink – and it is not at all certain that shrinkage has yet come to an end. Membership of the sterling region was still eroding even as late as the 1950s and 1960s.

Although the region did not emerge as a reasonably coherent body until 1931, its roots go much further back. From the very beginning of the pound's globalisation, different countries were attached to it with differing degrees of firmness: the currency was like the core of a series of concentric circles.[1] Thus the change after 1931 was more evolutionary than revolutionary. The sterling-regional system that developed in the twentieth century was already implicit in the gold-standard system of the nineteenth century.

Traditionally, the nearest circle to sterling comprised the British colonies and other dependent territories (protectorates, mandates, etc.). Before the extension of self-governing status to various 'dominions' (a designation now gone out of fashion), the Government in London was ultimately responsible for currency arrangements in all parts of the Empire. Each colony and territory was permitted an individual coinage and note issue, identifiable as its own. But from as early as 1704 the tendency was to use the pound throughout the Empire as unit of account for both private and official purposes, in order to regularise and simplify local conditions.[2] Behind this lay force of habit: it was natural that British settlers should cling to their old ways of thinking and calculating in terms of money.

In the same way, it was natural that as the foreign trade of the colonies developed, these same settlers should begin to use the pound not only as the standard, but also as the actual instrument, of settlement – and not just as that but as a store of value too. For not only was it true that most colonial trade flowed in the direction of the home country; it was also true that most trade finance was obtained there or from British 'overseas' banks established in the colonies themselves. From about 1850 a large number of banks were organised with head offices in London and operating branches overseas, especially in the colonies; at the same time, colonial banks were busily establishing branches in London.[3] The international banking network that resulted provided an institutional framework for the colonial sterling system. The pound became the logical medium for the financing of colonial trade. It also became the logical medium for the investment of private assets.

During the last third of the nineteenth century, instability of exchange rates in some of the colonies led to direct British Government regulation of local currency issues, further consolidating colonial links to sterling. The colonies were obliged to hold sterling assets to the full extent of local currency issues, to establish complete external con-

[1] Day, op. cit., pp. 24–6; and Hirsch, op. cit., pp. 481–2.
[2] Day, op. cit., p. 24; and W. F. Crick, *Origin and Development of the Sterling Area* (London: University of London and the Institute of Bankers, 1948) p. 10.
[3] Williams, op. cit., p. 270.

vertibility of the local currency with sterling at a fixed rate of exchange, and to maintain parity by buying and selling sterling in London on demand in exchange for the local currency. The pound became intervention currency, unit-of-account currency and reserve currency all rolled up into one. This was *par excellence* a sterling-exchange standard, holding together a group of dependent currencies ultimately under British Government control. The system was later formalised in the form of various currency boards.[1]

The next circle around sterling comprised the self-governing parts of the Empire – the Commonwealth dominions of Australia, New Zealand and South Africa.[2] Currency boards were never established in these three countries; moreover, their banking systems always stayed rather more independent of London than did those of the other colonies. Yet close ties with the pound developed, owing to the multitude of trade, financial and (not least) political connections with Britain. Sterling came to be used as backing to the home currency, the largest part of banking assets came to be invested in London, and most foreign trade came to be invoiced and transacted in pounds.

Similarly, close ties developed with a number of other countries which, though never formally part of the British Empire, were otherwise scarcely distinguishable from the dominions in so far as their external financial relations were concerned. These countries, too, maintained a multitude of trade and banking connections with Britain: they too backed their local currencies with sterling, and they too employed pounds for all international monetary functions. This group comprised the third circle around sterling. Because the membership of the group fluctuated over time, its constituents cannot be identified precisely, but at various dates it included Argentina and several other Latin American states, Japan, Thailand, Iran, and even a few peripheral European states (the Scandinavians, the Baltic nations, parts of the Balkans, and Ireland and Portugal).

These three circles constituted the pre-1931 sterling system. Of course, most other countries also employed sterling for various international monetary functions. But their trade and financial connections with Britain were not usually quite so close. They were the outer

---

[1] Williams, op. cit., pp. 272–4; and W. F. Crick, 'The Framework of Inter-Relations', in W. F. Crick (ed.), *Commonwealth Banking Systems* (Oxford: Oxford University Press, 1965) pp. 3–17.

[2] Canada, the remaining dominion, is excepted here: her main economic connections have always been with the United States.

circle, where other international moneys competed with the pound in both private and official transactions. In Europe and the United States, gold was used as backing to the home currency, not sterling; and frequently as well, local currencies were used in financing foreign trade instead of the pound, and most banking assets were invested at home instead of in London. In these areas sterling may have been still the leading international currency, but it was by no means the only international currency.

Before 1914, the discontinuity between the inner circles around sterling and the outer circle hardly mattered in practical terms. Sterling reigned supreme; it was a distinction without a difference. But in the 1920s it began to matter very much indeed, as sterling's supremacy was challenged. And in 1931 it led, finally, to a serious rupture of the international monetary system. When the convertibility of the pound was suspended, governments had to decide whether to maintain their currencies in terms of sterling or in terms of gold (or, in a few cases, in terms of some other currency such as the dollar). The outer circle, by and large, elected to stabilise exchange rates in terms of gold (or the dollar); the inner circles, by contrast, elected to stabilise in terms of sterling. These decisions formally defined the sterling region.

At the outset the region embraced, in addition to the Empire and Commonwealth (with the usual exception of Canada), two European states (Ireland and Portugal) and two Arab states (Egypt and Iraq, even though each had only recently broken close political ties with Britain). To this group were soon joined Thailand (1932), the Scandinavian countries and Estonia (1933), and Iran and Latvia (1936). These constituted the sterling bloc of the 1930s, a large and important grouping at the time. Members were effectively identified by two main characteristics. First, they maintained their currencies in a fixed relationship with sterling even after the suspension of convertibility (thus continuing to use the pound as unit of account for expressing par values); and second, they held their external reserves largely if not wholly in the form of sterling balances in London (thus continuing to use the pound also as principal intervention and reserve currency).[1] Overseas sterling-area countries could thus be defined as those where the pound generally retained all of its monetary functions at the level of official international transactions. In addition, sterling-area countries generally also tended to continue using the pound as their main international currency at the level of private transactions.

[1] League of Nations, *International Currency Experience* (1944) chap. 3.

For some years a number of other countries also continued to peg their exchange rates to the pound. These included Japan (after 1933), Argentina (after 1934), Greece, Turkey and Yugoslavia (after 1936), and France (after 1938). However, within this group, reserves were not generally held in the form of sterling; gold or the dollar was the preferred medium. Therefore, these countries were not usually regarded as members of the sterling bloc proper.[1] And of course, the rest of the world was even more definitely 'off' sterling: there the pound was no longer being used even as a unit of account. On the other hand, most non-sterling-area countries did continue to use the pound for private purposes, though not exclusively.

In 1939, after the outbreak of war, most of the non-British members of the bloc also went 'off' sterling. The group was thus constricted, to become practically coterminous with the borders of the Empire and Commonwealth. At the same time it was formalised, to become a clearly circumscribed and identifiable statutory entity for the first time. Before the Second World War there had been no written constitution or central organisation. But suddenly, from September 1939, membership became a matter of precise and legal status. In order to protect its monetary reserves in wartime, Britain decided to put into force a comprehensive system of exchange-control regulations; but from the beginning the Government chose to operate exchange-control around the whole group of sterling-associated countries rather than around the United Kingdom alone. Restrictions on payments for foreigners were not applied to countries which, in addition to (1) keeping their currencies pegged to the pound and (2) maintaining their reserves in London, also agreed (3) to enforce a system of exchange controls similar to Britain's. Only countries fulfilling all three conditions were henceforth regarded as members of the sterling area, as it now became known. In technical terms, the group became a monetary region defined by British exchange-control regulation.[2]

In more general terms, of course, the group remained what it had

---

[1] League of Nations, op. cit., ch. 3.

[2] The principal statutory authority for exchange control in the United Kingdom today is the Exchange Control Act of 1947, which superseded the emergency wartime regulations. Curiously, in the 1947 Act and subsequent amendments, despite common usage, the words 'sterling area' themselves never appear: member-countries are just referred to, drily, as the 'scheduled territories'. For a valuable survey of British exchange controls over the years, see 'The U.K. Exchange-Control; A Short History', *Bank of England Quarterly Bulletin*, VII 3 (Sep 1967) 245-60.

always been – a voluntary association with Britain of certain other countries using sterling as their principal or exclusive international currency. The principal of voluntarism is key: members have always been free to leave, others to join. During the 1930s this meant that membership tended to expand: ever since the 1930s, this has meant that membership has tended to shrink. Only two independent countries have joined the sterling area since 1939 – Iceland (after British wartime occupation and then independence from Denmark in 1944) and Libya (1952). On the other hand, a larger number have left or been excluded, including Israel (after partition of the British mandate of Palestine in 1948), Egypt (1947), Iraq (1959), Rhodesia (1965) and Burma (1966). In addition, other members have considered leaving from time to time.[1]

Shrinkage of sterling's functions

Before 1931 sterling was the world's leading international currency. It performed all monetary functions over vast parts of the globe. But since 1931 the currency's relative importance has declined. Outside the sterling area, except for special circumstances, the pound is no longer used at all for official purposes; and at the level of private transactions, its use has rapidly shrunk. Moreover, even inside the sterling area some of the pound's roles have declined, especially within the last decade.

It is not difficult to explain why sterling's functions have shrunk: the reasons are to be found in the shrinkage of the British economy itself relative to the rest of the world. Britain is no longer predominant, either in world trade or in international finance. As a trader, the country now ranks no higher than third;[2] and as a provider of services ancillary to trade, no higher than second.[3] Commercial ties around the

---

[1] A complete list of the sterling area's present membership is provided in an appendix to this chapter.

[2] In 1967, the United Kingdom accounted for roughly 7 per cent of world exports and 8 per cent of world imports, third behind the United States (16¼ and 13¼ per cent) and West Germany (10¼ and 8 per cent). See International Monetary Fund, *Direction of Trade.*

[3] In 1964, the United Kingdom accounted for roughly 15 per cent of total world invisible exports, second to the United States (26½ per cent). See Committee on Invisible Exports, *Britain's Invisible Earnings* (London: British National Export Council, 1967) chap. 3.

globe are not nearly so strong or so widespread as they used to be. Consequently, the lines of clearance of commercial debt no longer pass exclusively through London. The pound is not nearly so attractive for transactions purposes as it used to be.

Furthermore, Britain no longer ranks high as a source of either short-term or long-term capital. To be sure, the City of London is still a major international financial centre, perhaps still *the* international financial centre; certainly it still boasts some of the finest credit and investment facilities available anywhere in the world. But London itself no longer has the money to finance world trade or overseas development. Today it functions primarily as a processor rather than as a provider of funds – as a financial middleman or entrepôt for other people's money. The capital that comes out of London now is mainly Euro-dollar capital, not sterling. Inevitably, this too has diminished the transactions attractiveness of the pound.

Perhaps what has diminished the attractiveness of the pound most is the precarious state of the British balance of payments, particularly since the Second World War. Britain's pledge of convertibility at a fixed rate and on unqualified terms is, to say the least, no longer unquestioned. Twice, in 1949 and again in 1967, the pound has been devalued; and a quarter of a century after the war's end it is still the most extensively controlled of any major currency. Moreover, since 1945 there have been eight major sterling crises, as well as even more numerous minor frights. Naturally, this has tended to discourage the use of sterling as either medium of exchange or unit of account, let alone as a store of value.

At the level of private international transactions, the pound reached the peak of its importance between 1860 and 1914, when, it is estimated, at least 60 per cent of world trade was invoiced and settled in sterling.[1] The descent from that peak since has been long and painful. At first, it was a gentle decline: as late as the early post-Second World War years, the pound was still the world's most important transactions and quotation currency, accounting for perhaps half of all trade.[2] But after devaluation in 1949 the descent apparently tended to accelerate, despite sterling's gradually widening transferability and eventually its return to convertibility in 1958. By the early 1960s not even the most optimistic observer was willing to place the figure at more than one-

[1] Williams, op. cit., p. 268.

[2] Ibid.; and W. M. Clarke, *The City in the World Economy* (London: Institute of Economic Affairs, 1965) p. 211.

third.[1] In 1967, an official Government publication placed the proportion of trade invoiced and settled in sterling at 'about 30 per cent'.[2]

Recently, for the first time, systematic attempts were made to give these estimates greater precision. One effort was by *The Economist* in its 'British Banking Survey 1966',[3] another by the Committee on Invisible Exports in its report on *Britain's Invisible Earnings*.[4] Both arrived at even lower proportions of world trade, in the range of 25–29 per cent in the 1960s up to 1965 (see Table 4.1).

Table 4.1

Estimates of Proportion of World Trade Settled in Sterling, 1960–5
(in percentages)

Estimates by:	1960	1961	1962	1963	1964	1965
The Economist	27·1	26·5 ·	26·6	27·8	25·6	n.e.
Committee on Invisible Exports	n.e.	n.e.	n.e.	n.e.	26–29$\frac{1}{2}$	25$\frac{1}{2}$–29

n.e.: Not estimated.
Sources: See footnotes in text.

These two sources used roughly comparable techniques. Both assumed that virtually all of the trade within the sterling area is transacted in pounds (*The Economist* estimated 95 per cent, the Committee 90 per cent), as well as most of the trade between the sterling area and the rest of the world (both estimated about 70 per cent). On the other hand, the pound was assumed to account for very little of the trade between non-sterling-area countries. *The Economist* estimated a gradual increase from 5 per cent to 7$\frac{1}{2}$ per cent during the early 1960's, the Committee estimated a range of 5–10 per cent. With the wisdom of hindsight, we can now see that for the most part these assumptions

[1] Clarke, op. cit., p. 211; and 'Sterling as a "Key" Currency', *Midland Bank Review* (Aug 1963) p. 3. Estimates for the 1950s tend to vary widely, from one-third (Williams, op. cit., p. 268) to 40 per cent (Oppenheimer, op. cit., p. 125), to one-half (Polk, op. cit., p. 3; and John Wood, 'What Price the Sterling Area?', *The Listener*, LVIII 1496 (28 Nov 1957) 875). Paul Einzig insists that the decline in the use of sterling as a transactions and quotation currency did not begin until the middle 1960s. See Einzig, 'The Declining Use of Sterling as a Trading Currency', *Westminster Bank Review* (May 1968) p. 2.
[2] 'The Role of Sterling', *D.E.A. Progress Report*, no. 27 (Apr 1967) p. 1.
[3] *The Economist*, 18 June 1966, pp. x–xiii.
[4] Committee on Invisible Exports, op. cit., pp. 254–5.

were rather sanguine. In fact, well-informed sources in London indicate that by 1965 not more than 90 per cent of trade within the sterling area at most was actually being transacted in pounds, not more than 60 per cent of trade between the sterling area and the rest of the world, and not more than 5 per cent of trade between non-sterling-area countries. Using these lower proportions, I have calculated that in 1966 and 1967 sterling really accounted for only about 22½ per cent of world trade (see Table 4.2). And since 1967, probably even that

Table 4.2

Estimated Proportion of World Trade Settled in Sterling, 1966–67
(in £ million; final row in percentages)

	1966	1967
Sterling-area trade		
Total	3,940	4,020
of which: settled in sterling	3,550	3,620
Sterling-area trade with non-sterling		
Total[a]	15,400	16,720
of which: settled in sterling	9,240	10,030
Non-sterling-area trade		
Total[b]	48,350	51,780
of which: settled in sterling	2,420	2,590
Trade settled in sterling		
Total	15,210	16,240
Percentage of world trade	22·5	22·5

Note: The estimates of amounts settled in sterling assume that 90 per cent of sterling-area trade is settled in pounds, 60 per cent of sterling-area trade with the rest of the world, and 5 per cent of non-sterling-area trade.

[a] Includes both exports (f.o.b.) and imports (c.i.f., reduced by 10 per cent to bring them to an f.o.b. basis).

[b] Includes also Soviet-bloc trade, estimated at £2,900 million in 1966 and £2,960 million in 1967.

Sources: Board of Trade, *The Commonwealth and the Sterling Area*, selected issues; and International Monetary Fund, *Direction of Trade*, selected issues.

estimate has come to be on the high side. There are indications that increasingly, since devaluation, other currencies have been substituted for the pound in invoicing and settling trade – and not just in non-sterling-area trade, but even in sterling-area trade with non-sterling countries.[1] And a further blow was struck in October 1968 when exchange-control authority for sterling credits on third-country trade

[1] John Cooper, *A Suitable Case for Treatment: What to Do About the Balance of Payments* (London: Penguin Books, 1968) pp. 299–301.

was suddenly withdrawn.[1] Today it is unlikely that the pound accounts for much more than about 20 per cent or so of the overall total of world trade.

Taking the long view, therefore, there can be little doubt that the pound has indeed tended to decline in importance as a transactions and quotation currency, particularly outside the sterling area. True, the decline has been in *relative* rather than absolute terms. The actual *amount* of trade invoiced and settled in sterling is in fact greater than ever before, reflecting the growth of world trade in general. But once the pound stood alone as an international currency. Now pride of place goes to the dollar, which today is thought to account for at least one-third and possibly as much as one-half of all global commerce.[2]

Equally, there can be little doubt that the pound has declined in relative importance as an asset currency. In 1951, foreign private holdings amounted to £918 million. A decade and a half later, at end-1966, these holdings were still just some £1·95 billion – a rise of only a little more than a billion pounds – and, not surprisingly, almost all of the rise occurred within the sterling area rather than outside it.[3] During the same period, private dollar balances increased from $3·7 billion (£1·3 billion) to $14·2 billion (£5·1 billion) – a rise of some ten and a half billion dollars (£3·75 billion).

At the level of official international transactions, the pound did not reach its peak of importance until the 1940s. As previously indicated, sterling was still being used prominently as a unit of account for expressing par values even after the 1931 suspension of convertibility, and not only within the sterling area but outside it as well. However, that did not last long. After the 1949 devaluation, although sterling-area members continued to peg their currencies to the pound, others did not. True, many others did devalue in the wake of sterling. But these countries chose to revise their exchange rates principally because they wanted to maintain their trading positions and payments balances, not because they any longer regarded the pound as an international

[1] *Bank of England Quarterly Bulletin*, VIII 4 (Dec 1968) 347–8. The restriction was introduced because it was thought that overseas traders were using such finance as a means of speculating against the pound.

[2] *The Economist*, loc. cit., p. xiii.

[3] It should be noted that because of an important break in the statistical series in 1962, the published figures for 1951 and 1966 are not strictly comparable – though they are sufficiently consistent to be used for the illustrative purposes of this chapter. For sources, and for further discussion and analysis of the sterling balances, see Chapters 5 and 7.

accounting unit. By 1949, the sterling yardstick was being used only by the sterling countries. And by 1967 it was not even being used by all of them. When the pound was devalued again, this time only some of the smaller members together with Britain's dependencies went along. The majority of the membership made no move at all.[1]

Sterling's importance as a reserve and intervention currency, too, peaked in the 1940s. This was an importance that had only recently been attained. Before 1914 gold had been the only important reserve and intervention medium; the gold-exchange standard was not even initiated until the Genoa Conference of 1922.[2] And for a time even after the Genoa Conference gold tended to retain its traditional predominance. In 1928, world reserves totalled approximately $13 billion. Of this amount, three-quarters was held in the form of gold, only one-quarter ($3·25 billion) in the form of foreign exchange. In 1938, official reserves reached a level of nearly $28 billion. Foreign-exchange reserves, however, actually declined, to just $1·8 billion – only one-sixteenth of the total.[3] Most of these were of course sterling reserves held by sterling-area countries.

In 1918 United Kingdom net sterling liabilities to all foreigners (private as well as official) probably amounted to no more than £300 million.[4] In 1931 external liabilities were still only about £400 million, in 1937 (the peak of the inter-war period) only about £800 million, and in 1938 and 1939 they actually declined by £300 million. Thus, at the start of the Second World War Britain was again, as two decades earlier, very nearly in a balanced position. All that was changed, however, by the war itself. During the next six years sterling liabilities increased enormously as a result of British military expenditures overseas, particularly in Egypt, India and certain other sterling countries. In 1945 overseas sterling balances amounted to some £3·6 billion. Almost exactly two-thirds of the total (£2·35 billion) was held within the sterling area itself, and of this no less than £1·9 billion represented official reserve holdings.[5]

Since 1945, and especially since the 1949 devaluation, sterling's

---

[1] Only six non-sterling-area countries (all relatively minor financial powers) devalued their currencies following sterling in 1967: Brazil, Denmark, Israel, Macao, Nepal and Spain. For a complete list of the sterling-area members that devalued following sterling, see Chapter 8.

[2] League of Nations, op. cit., chap. 2.

[3] Robert Triffin, *Gold and the Dollar Crisis* (New Haven: Yale University Press, 1960) pp. 72–3.

[4] Williams, op. cit., p. 288.   [5] For sources, see Chapter 5.

importance as a reserve and intervention currency has declined. Liabilities to official holders outside the sterling area have never been large. At the end of the war they amounted to only some £840 million; by 1962 they were down to less than half that figure. And while it is true that since the early 1960s non-sterling-area official balances have tended to increase sharply again – indeed, in 1968 they actually went over the £2 billion level – for the most part these recent acquisitions have been held to oblige the British authorities rather than from choice. Mostly, they have arisen as the counterparts of foreign credits arranged during the periodic crises of the British balance of payments. They cannot be regarded as genuine reserve holdings.

Furthermore, even inside the sterling area the reserve and intervention roles of the pound have dwindled. In 1951, sterling accounted for more than 90 per cent of all the reserves of overseas sterling-area countries. Over the next decade, however, official sterling-area balances actually declined, albeit very slightly, while total sterling-area reserves were rising. Overseas members were beginning to diversify their reserves, and by 1961 the proportion accounted for by sterling had dropped to only 80 per cent.[1] After 1961 the process of diversification actually tended to accelerate.[2]

Before 1961 the process of diversification largely reflected the changing composition of reserve holdings within the overseas sterling area. Overall reserves of members whose trade links with Britain were strongest (e.g. India) happened to be declining, while the reserves of those whose trade links with Britain were weaker (e.g. Kuwait) happened to be rising. After 1961, on the other hand, the process reflected mainly deliberate policy decisions by certain overseas members from that date to treat the pound asymmetrically – to accumulate non-sterling assets when reserves were rising, but to sell off sterling assets when reserves were falling. Australia was a prominent example. Members recognised that their trade, financial and even political connections with Britain were weakening, while conversely their links with other areas (the United States, Europe, Japan) were growing.

[1] International Monetary Fund, *International Financial Statistics*. 1961 is the last year for which such data are officially available.

[2] According to the Chief Secretary of the Treasury (in a written answer to a parliamentary question): 'My best estimate from published sources is that the proportion of sterling held in the reserves of Overseas Sterling Area countries at the end of September 1967 was about two-thirds, compared with about three-quarters at the end of 1964.' *Hansard*, 30 Jan 1968. See also *The Basle Facility and the Sterling Area*, Cmnd 3787 (Oct 1968) pp. 2–4.

Britain was becoming less important as a trading partner (see Table 4.3), and as a source of longer-term capital and development assistance.[1] In addition, local banking systems were loosening their ties with London and building up relationships elsewhere.[2] Diversification of international reserves was regarded by overseas members as a natural corollary of the diversification of their international relations in general.

Until 1967, the process of diversification was restrained by a general desire of members to preserve the sterling area in some form. But the devaluation in November proved to be a severe shock. With many members feeling that their financial connections with Britain had been

Table 4.3

Britain–Overseas Sterling Area Trade, 1948 and 1967
(in percentages)

	1948	1967
Britain:		
Imports from O.S.A., as percentage of total imports	35·6	27·4
Exports to O.S.A., as percentage of total exports	46·8	29·9
Overseas Sterling Area:		
Imports from Britain, as percentage of total imports	34·4	22·7
Exports to Britain, as percentage of total exports	33·7	22·6

Source: Board of Trade, *The Commonwealth and the Sterling Area.*

loosened still further, diversification was increased; and in contrast to earlier periods, there was a significant fall in the total of official holdings, especially after the first quarter of 1968, as governments actively switched into other reserve media. Between March and

[1] The United Kingdom has gradually whittled away some of the privileges of the overseas sterling area affecting the flow of capital and outward investment. See 'The U.K. Exchange-Control: A Short History', loc. cit., pp. 257–60. As a source of official development assistance, Britain is now outranked in much of the sterling area by the United States and by international organisations. See Susan Strange, *The Sterling Problem and the Six*, European Series, No. 4. (London: Chatham House and P.E.P., 1967) p. 15.

[2] New restrictions have been placed on the operations of British overseas banks; local banks have been set up in competition; and other foreign banks have been welcomed in. See Crick (ed.), *Commonwealth Banking Systems, passim.*

September 1968 official sterling-area balances were decreased by £312 million – a net depletion of more than 15 per cent. Furthermore, it was clear that more depletions were in store unless some action was taken to prevent them. In the Government's words:

> . . . it became clear that there was a need for new and far-reaching arrangements to give greater stability to the sterling system. It no longer seemed likely that the United Kingdom, acting alone, would be able to contain the situation in traditional ways. The achievement of a balance-of-payments surplus by the United Kingdom was more necessary than ever, but it could no longer be assumed that, even with such a surplus, sterling area countries would wish to hold as much sterling in their reserves as in the past.
>
> At the same time, there was never any possibility that the reserve role of sterling could simply be abandoned. . . . It was therefore clear that new means had to be found to accommodate unavoidable reductions in the reserve balances; but at the same time to ensure that sterling would be willingly held in reserves at levels not significantly below the present.[1]

The new means that eventually were found constituted the most significant reform of sterling, as an international currency, to date – the so-called Basle facility and associated bilateral agreements between the United Kingdom and overseas sterling-area countries. The reform was announced in September 1968 and fully described in a White Paper a month later.[2] It consisted of three parts. First, the central banks of twelve major industrial countries[3] agreed to provide Britain with a $2 billion stand-by credit through the Bank for International Settlements to finance any further net withdrawal of sterling-area balances. Private as well as official balances were covered. The facility was to have a ten-year life, with drawings to be permitted during the first three years (1968–70). Repayments were to be made between the sixth and tenth years (1973–7).

Secondly, the United Kingdom guaranteed 'to maintain the dollar value of eligible official sterling reserves of sterling area countries'.[4] The guarantee applied to all of each member's reserve balances in London except for a portion equal to 10 per cent of its total reserves. (In other words, 10 per cent of each country's total reserves would henceforth be held in the form of unguaranteed sterling.) In the event of any future devaluation of the pound vis-à-vis the dollar, each country would receive a payment in sterling to restore the dollar value of the

---

[1] Cmnd 3787, p. 4.   [2] Ibid.

[3] Austria, Belgium, Canada, Denmark, Germany, Italy, Japan, the Netherlands, Norway, Sweden, Switzerland and the United States.

[4] Cmnd 3787, p. 6.

guaranteed portion of its reserves. The guarantee did not extend to private sterling-area holdings of pounds.

In return for the guarantee, there was only one counterpart concession on the part of sterling-area members: each country pledged to keep not less than an agreed percentage of its total reserves in sterling. This was the outer area's *quid pro quo*. 'The guarantee is conditional on each country maintaining at all times a Minimum Sterling Proportion in its reserves.'[1] The precise proportion in each case was arrived at through negotiation. Terms were set out in bilateral agreements between Britain and overseas members which were to remain in force for three years, with a provision for extension for a further two years by mutual agreement.

There is no need to discuss the Basle reform at length here; Part Three will analyse it in sufficient detail. I mention it now only to emphasise the extent of the shrinkage of sterling's reserve and intervention functions since the war. Not only was it necessary in 1968 for Britain to extend exchange guarantees in order to preserve what was left of these functions; it was also necessary to make the guarantees conditional on each member maintaining a minimum proportion of sterling in its reserves at all times. Holdings are no longer quite as voluntary as they used to be. Times have certainly changed.

Advantages and disadvantages of the sterling area

The advantages and disadvantages of the sterling area must be separated conceptually from the benefits and costs of the international use of sterling. The two sets of effects are actually quite distinct, even though, of course, in practice, they do tend to coincide to a considerable extent. The pound *does* tend to function as an international currency within the sterling area. But it does not tend to function *just* there; it is used elsewhere as well, at least at the level of private international transactions, and the gains or losses from these uses have nothing to do with the sterling area *per se*.

Conversely, there are gains or losses from the sterling area which have nothing to do with the international use of sterling *per se* – specifically, the benefits or costs of discriminatory exchange restrictions. The following chapters will be concerned in particular with the effects of the international use of sterling (including the effects of the sterling

[1] Cmnd 3787, p. 6.

area in so far as these coincide); the reader in a hurry can move on immediately. But before I conclude this chapter, it might be appropriate to comment briefly on the independent effects of the sterling area through the years.[1]

The outstanding feature of the sterling area through the years is that it has always been essentially a defensive mechanism. At no time has it represented a deliberate belief in the monetary virtues of a regional system: Britain did not set out with the specific intention of constructing a less-than-world-wide financial region. Quite the contrary, successive Governments have tried explicitly to resist the shrinkage of sterling's once-global scope. But in policy terms the result has always been the same. Defence of the pound has ordinarily taken the form of discrimination between sterling-associated countries and others. Inevitably, therefore, efforts to deter the disintegration of the pound's international position have succeeded only in so far as they have built up its regional status instead.

In the 1930s the sterling bloc was purely an arrangement *de convenance* – an informal grouping of countries with mutually close commercial and financial connections. For overseas members, Britain was an important trading partner (often the *most* important trading partner) as well as the repository of most external banking assets and official reserves, and the source of most foreign capital. The advantages of stabilising domestic moneys in terms of the pound rather than in terms of gold were therefore obvious. Members could simultaneously safeguard their competitive position in the British market, maintain the local-currency value of their external assets, and avail themselves of special treatment in the administration of U.K. controls on overseas lending.[2] At the same time there were obvious advantages for the British, who could thereby preserve their access both to commercial

---

[1] The advantages and disadvantages of the sterling area have been discussed innumerable times. The following is just a very partial list. Day, op. cit., chaps. 5–7; Polk, op. cit.; Philip W. Bell, *The Sterling Area in the Post-war World* (London: Oxford University Press, 1956); A. H. Conan, *The Rationale of the Sterling Area* (London: Macmillan, 1961); the symposium on the sterling area in *Bulletin of the Oxford University Institute of Statistics*, xxi 4 (Nov 1959); and Andrew Shonfield, *British Economic Policy since the War* (London: Penguin Books, 1958) chap. 6. For useful summaries of the arguments on both sides, see Oppenheimer, op. cit., pp. 131–5; Livingstone, op. cit., pp. 59–65; and Hirsch, op. cit., pp. 486–9.

[2] These controls began in 1934 and were formalised in 1936. See Thomas Balogh, *Studies in Financial Organisation* (Cambridge: Cambridge University Press, 1947) pp. 268–73.

markets and sources of supply overseas, and to profitable investment outlets for surplus domestic savings. In brief, for all its members, Britain as well as overseas, the sterling bloc minimised the effects of the outside pressure of adverse economic forces. In an era of unprecedented exchange instability and economic restrictions, the system of *ad hoc* sterling arrangements offered its adherents the continuing benefits of substantial exchange stability and reasonably free trade and capital movements.

With the coming of war, the nature of the system was altered dramatically by the first appearance of what was later to be known as 'the dollar shortage'. In 1939, the British Government realised that its external reserves of gold and dollars would not be equal to the demands that were likely to be made on them. Exchange controls were therefore regarded as imperative. However, as already indicated, it was also regarded as imperative that the pound's international monetary functions be preserved. Accordingly, from the beginning the Government chose to operate exchange control around the whole of the group of sterling-associated countries, rather than around the United Kingdom alone. With the co-operation of the overseas member-countries, a high fence of exchange restrictions was constructed around the entire sterling region. Inside the area, payments could still be made freely and flexibly. But with respect to payments outside the area – and, in particular, with respect to payments in the United States – the system became rigid and discriminatory. The sterling area became a formal, collective arrangement for discriminating against the scarce dollar.

A significant corollary of the revised arrangement was the new emphasis on reserve 'pooling' within the group. Of course, even before 1939, sterling countries were effectively pooling most of their reserves. That was inherent in the practice of maintaining reserves in London: countries earning gold and dollars generally tended to exchange them for pounds, thus making their non-sterling surpluses available to other countries including Britain that were in deficit on non-sterling account. But before the appearance of the dollar problem this was all quite informal and relaxed. The British Government could still manage the central reserve mainly in relation to its own payments position, like any other government, rather than in relation to the payments position of the bloc as a whole. The central reserve was its own, not the sterling area's. After the appearance of the dollar problem, on the other hand, a much greater awareness developed of the need for unity within the group. Collective discrimination against the scarce dollar would be difficult if members earning dollar surpluses declined to continue making them available to members in dollar-deficit. It was therefore felt that the practice of pooling holdings would have to become much more formal and deliberate. Henceforth, the central reserve was regarded as an integral part of the ongoing sterling system.

Since 1939, the essential nature of the sterling area has not changed significantly. Three decades later its two basic features still remain: (1) exchange discrimination as a group against non-members (although, since 1958, exchange discrimination has applied mainly to capital-account transactions only); and (2) the pooling of gold and dollar reserves. Historically, the two features tended to develop jointly. Conceptually, however, they are independent.[1] The reader is reminded that only the latter feature has anything to do with the international use of sterling *per se*. Any group of countries can elect to discriminate against transactions with non-members – whether or not they pool their reserves, whether or not they use one of their currencies for international purposes, indeed whether or not they otherwise co-operate financially at all. Conversely, any group can elect to economise on the need to hold external reserves by pooling holdings – whether or not members choose to discriminate against outsiders. No group need elect to do both (though as it happens the sterling area did). That is why I feel it is important to emphasise the distinction between the problem of the sterling area and the problem of the pound as an international currency. The two are not identical.

Although the essential nature of the sterling area has not changed significantly since 1939, the circumstances affecting it have altered substantially. As a result the economic rationale for the grouping has weakened to a considerable extent. Traditionally, the system had rested on a trio of mutually beneficial reciprocal links between Britain, at the centre, and the overseas members. In the first place, the temporal pattern of payments between centre and periphery had generally tended to be complementary. Britain was a major industrial country, exporting mostly manufactured goods, while the overseas members in the main were primary producers, exporting mostly foodstuffs and raw materials. Consequently, the payments positions of the two sides usually tended to move in opposite directions, that of the periphery improving when Britain's weakened, and vice versa. Surpluses and

[1] Richard N. Cooper, 'The Balance of Payments', in Richard E. Caves and Associates, *Britain's Economic Prospects* (Washington: The Brookings Institution, 1968) p. 181.

deficits tended to offset one another. This complementarity made the pooling of reserves mutually beneficial. Members automatically economised on the need to hold gold and dollars, since together they required fewer reserves than if each were operating independently. The deliberate emphasis on reserve pooling after 1939 merely formalised an arrangement that had already been long in existence.

The second reciprocal link between Britain and the overseas members concerned the geographic pattern of payments between centre and periphery. This had also tended to be complementary. Historically, Britain usually earned net trade surpluses in the overseas sterling area offset by net deficits elsewhere; the outer members, usually the reverse. Consequently, each side was structurally dependent on the other in maintaining the overall pattern of its foreign payments and receipts – Britain providing net imports for the outer sterling area, the latter in turn providing Britain with the wherewithal to finance net imports from non-members. Accordingly, in this respect too both sides stood to benefit from a system of reserve pooling.

Finally, Britain and the overseas members had been linked by the complementarity of their capital needs. Since the periphery did not begin to develop economically until well after Britain at the centre was approaching maturity as an industrial society, the British found themselves with a growing surplus of domestic savings and exchange resources at just the time when the outer sterling area was starting to experience increasing capital and exchange shortage. Consequently, both sides were able to benefit from the huge exports of funds by Britain that began as early as the late eighteenth century. These investments in the outer area were facilitated by the existence of the traditional sterling system of reserve pooling. In the opinion of some writers, this was the *principal* rationale for that system.[1]

The imposition of collective discrimination beginning in 1939 can be interpreted, in economic terms, as an effort by Britain together with the overseas members to preserve the historical benefits of the sterling area during an era of general dollar shortage. Certainly, the damage to international trade and welfare resulting from collective discrimination was far less than if each country had tried to move on its own to maintain its payment position. The arrangement was a favourable alternative to the rigid bilateralism of the day, affording real gains for all its members, including Britain, compared with what would have been likely in its absence. Members could still enjoy among themselves

[1] See, e.g., Williams, op. cit., pp. 280–4.

the wider benefits of exchange stability and reasonably free trade and capital movements. During the 1940s, therefore, and even into the early 1950s, the sterling system could still be rationalised on these grounds. However, by the later 1950s this was no longer possible. Once the liberalisation of commerce and payments got under way, especially after 1958, the rationale for the system weakened considerably. The advantages of collective discrimination against the dollar were now no longer quite so intuitively obvious. Indeed, now it was the disadvantages that were becoming obvious – especially the cost of wholesale evasion of exchange control by and through countries of the outer sterling area, where collective discrimination is enforced with much less rigour than it is in the United Kingdom itself.

Furthermore, by the late 1950s all three of the traditional links on which the system was based had begun to wither away – if not break altogether. In the first place, the temporal pattern of payments between centre and periphery seems to have become substantially less complementary than it once was, especially after about 1958. Before that date, the payments positions of the two sides still tended to move in opposite directions, but since then movements have become much more closely parallel.[1] Probably the most important reason for this change is the decline in relative importance of trade between Britain and the outer area. The higher the level of intra-area trade, the more complementary the payments positions of the two sides are likely to be. But since the war, as already indicated (see Table 4.3), each side has grown less dependent on trade with the other. Consequently, both sides show greater response than formerly to economic developments elsewhere, especially in the United States and Europe, and this results in sympathetic rather than complementary movements in net payments. Secondarily, there has in some instances been increasing direct competition between the exports of Britain and some of the overseas members, as the latter themselves have grown and matured as industrial nations.

In addition, the geographic pattern of payments between centre and periphery seems to have become substantially less complementary than it once was. Specifically, whereas Britain still tends to run a net trade deficit vis-à-vis non-sterling areas, the overseas members as a group no longer tend to earn a net trade surplus to cover it. Partly, this change seems to reflect the increase of long-term capital imports into the outer area from non-sterling sources such as the United States. However, the main reason seems to have been the dissatisfaction of

[1] Richard Cooper, 'The Balance of Payments', loc. cit., pp. 182–3.

certain newly independent members, beginning with India and Pakistan and continuing later with Ghana and others, over the traditional practice of reserve pooling. In some instances the members felt exploited, compelled to spend the bulk of their earnings in a market that was not necessarily the cheapest, and to hold the remainder of their earnings in a form that was not necessarily the safest. In other instances they simply wanted to increase their overall imports in line with domestic development programmes. In either event, they were determined to spend their money as much as they liked and where they liked, and (after 1961) even to diversify their reserves if they felt like it. The overseas sterling area as a result today tends towards a persistent current-account deficit with the outside world, despite the maintenance of discriminatory exchange restrictions on (mainly capital) transactions with non-members. In most years since the later 1950s, the sterling area's central reserve would have been seriously depleted by the outer members' trading deficit had it not been for the even larger sustained net inflow of long-term capital from non-sterling sources.[1]

Finally, the capital needs of centre and periphery seem to have become less complementary than they once were. True, the overseas members are still eager for capital imports from Britain – for direct investments, for long-term loans, for development assistance. Britain, however, no longer has the same surplus of exchange resources with which to finance such a movement of resources. Consequently, the outer area has become increasingly dependent on imports of capital from the United States and from international organisations, and decreasingly on capital imported from the United Kingdom.[2]

In summary, all of the advantages of the sterling area have declined considerably since the late 1950s, and not only for the overseas members but for Britain as well. For both sides, the economies to be derived from reserve pooling have diminished. For the outer area, in addition, the British cannot be relied upon as before as a source of capital imports; while for the British, the outer area cannot be relied upon as before to help maintain the structural pattern of foreign payments. At the same time, the disadvantages of the system have grown. For the outer area the system of reserve pooling can now be quite costly, as the 1967 devaluation experience demonstrated; and as the accelerated post-devaluation diversification of reserves demonstrated, much of the outer area now would apparently like to see the arrangement

[1] A. R. Conan, *The Problem of Sterling* (London: Macmillan, 1966) chap. 4.
[2] Ibid.

modified or loosened in some way – or perhaps even terminated. The British, on the other hand, apparently still feel obliged to keep the arrangement going. Consequently, for the British too the system now is costly. For example, the Government has had to provide exchange guarantees under the Basle reform of 1968; likewise, the Government has had to maintain, at least to a degree, the outer sterling area's privileged access to British capital exports.[1] In effect, these facilities may be regarded as a kind of ransom paid by Britain to keep the sterling system going.

Therefore, I would conclude that as far as the United Kingdom is concerned, the sterling area today is on balance considerably more costly than it used to be. The increased net cost derives from both the basic features of the system. However, only the feature of reserve pooling will be included in the cost – benefit analysis that follows in the remainder of Part Two. The independent effects of exchange discrimination will not be considered, since conceptually these are distinct from the effects of the pound's use as an international currency.

APPENDIX: STERLING–AREA MEMBERSHIP

The legal definition of the Scheduled Territories is given in the First Schedule to the Exchange Control Act, 1947, as amended. The latest version reads as follows:

> The United Kingdom (including the Isle of Man and the Channel Islands), all other countries within the British Commonwealth (except Canada and Rhodesia), the Irish Republic, British Trust Territories, British Protectorates and Protected States, Iceland, the Hashemite Kingdom of Jordan, Kuwait, Libya, South Africa and South West Africa, the People's Republic of Southern Yemen, and Western Samoa.

A list of countries and territories covered by this definition would include:

[1] In the opinion of some writers, this has become the basic feature of the sterling area today: it has become an arrangement for accommodating the long-term development needs of the overseas members, in return for their agreement to hold on to their sterling balances. In the words of Andrew Shonfield: 'The essential fact is that the sterling area has changed its character. It has ceased to be an old-fashioned bank: its members now regard it as an investment fund.' Shonfield, op. cit., p. 128. See also Williams, op. cit., pp. 294–7.

Antigua
Australia

Bahamas
Bahrain
Barbados
Bermuda
Botswana
British Honduras
British Indian Ocean Territory
British Solomon Islands
British Virgin Islands
Brunei

Cayman Islands
Ceylon
Cyprus

Dominica

Falkland Islands
Fiji

Gambia
Ghana
Gibraltar
Gilbert and Ellice Islands
Grenada
Guyana

Hong Kong

Iceland
India
Irish Republic

Jamaica
Jordan

Kenya
Kuwait

Lesotho
Libya

Malawi
Malaysia
Malta
Mauritius
Montserrat

Nauru
New Guinea
New Zealand
Nigeria

Pakistan
Papua
Pitcairn Islands

Qatar

St Helena (with Ascension Island
        and Tristan da Cunha)
St Kitts, Nevis, Anguilla
St Lucia
St Vincent
Seychelles
Sierra Leone
Singapore
South Africa
South West Africa
Southern Yemen
Swaziland

Tanzania
Tonga
Trinidad and Tobago
Trucial States (Ajman, Abu Dhabi,
        Dubai, Fujairah, Ras al Khaimah,
        Sharjah, Umm al Qaiwain)
Turks and Caicos Islands

Uganda
United Kingdom including Isle
        of Man and the Channel Islands

Western Samoa

Zambia

5 Seigniorage and Interest

Two of the most important presumed effects of the international use of a currency are, first, the potential benefit of being able to run a greater cumulative balance-of-payments deficit than would otherwise be possible, which is sometimes described as the gain from 'seigniorage'; and second, the direct offset to that benefit, which is the cost of interest paid to non-residents in their accumulated past balances. This chapter will consider the extent to which Great Britain today is subject to each of these effects as a result of the international use of the pound. Since both are reflected in the trend of accumulated foreign liabilities, we shall begin by looking carefully to discover what data are available on the sterling balances. We shall then consider separately the benefit and the cost.

I. THE STERLING BALANCES

The available data on the sterling balances go back almost three decades, as far as 1941. Unfortunately, though, the series does not run forward continuously from that date to the present day. There are two important breaks in the published statistics, in 1945 and again in 1962.

The data on sterling balances from 1941 to 1945 were summarised in a 1951 White Paper.[1] Additionally the White Paper also reported figures for U.K. external liabilities from 1931 to 1941, but these included *all* foreign balances, whether expressed in pounds or in other currencies, and not enough information was provided to permit separation of the sterling balances from the others. After 1941, on the other hand, liabilities in currencies of non-sterling-area countries were excluded. External liabilities from 1931 to 1941 are reproduced in Table 5.1. The early sterling data from 1941 to 1945 are reproduced in Table 5.2.

[1] *Reserves and Liabilities 1931 to 1945*, Cmd 8354 (Sep 1951).

Before 1945, liabilities were reported including all loans to the British Government expressed in pounds or sterling-area currencies. After 1945 such loans were excluded. That was the first important break in the sterling series. The second important break, in 1962, came when the old series was entirely revamped and replaced by a new set

Table 5.1

United Kingdom External Liabilities, 1931–41[a]
(in £ millions)

Date	Total	British Empire	Rest of World
1931: December	411	195	216
1932: June	457	238	219
December	468	246	222
1933: June	518	281	237
December	538	275	263
1934: June	591	337	254
December	580	316	264
1935: June	544	301	243
December	600	346	254
1936: June	645	357	288
December	721	358	363
1937: June	770	410	360
December	808	387	421
1938: June	778	380	398
December	598	339	259
1939: June	542	328	214
December	517	362	155
1940: June	543	434	109
December	680	544	136
1941: June	881	676	205
December	1170	924	246

[a] The figures show net liabilities, whether expressed in sterling or in foreign currencies. Loans to the British Government expressed in sterling or sterling-area currencies are included.

Source: *Reserves and Liabilities 1931 to 1945*, Cmd 8354 (Sep 1951).

of statistics. The contents of the two series and the differences between them were described in a special article in the June 1963 issue of the *Bank of England Quarterly Bulletin*.[1] The principal difference was that, in the old series, U.K. liabilities had been published *net* of U.K. claims,

[1] 'New Series of External Liabilities and Claims in Sterling', *Bank of England Quarterly Bulletin*, III 2 (June 1963) 98–105. See also 'Overseas Sterling Holdings', *Bank of England Quarterly Bulletin*, III 4 (Dec 1963) 264–78.

whereas in the new series liabilities were published on a *gross* basis, liabilities and claims being shown separately. In addition, there were substantial differences in the definition of certain items and in the classification of certain holders.

Changes due to redefinition of items resulted at the time in a large net difference between the two series in their overall total of liabilities

Table 5.2

United Kingdom Sterling Liabilities, 1941–5[a]
(in £ millions)

Date	Total	Sterling area	Non-sterling area
1941: December	1272	665	607
1942: June	1285	759	526
December	1642	987	655
1943: June	1967	1171	796
December	2350	1433	917
1944: June	2680	1655	1025
December	3015	1914	1101
1945: June	3354	2132	1222
December	3688	2454	1234

[a] The figures show net liabilities in sterling. Loans to the British Government expressed in sterling or sterling-area currencies are included.

Source: *Reserves and Liabilities 1931 to 1945*, Cmd 8354 (Sep 1951).

for the overlap year of 1962 – £387 million on the basis of statistical information then available. The discrepancy had three sources. First, the new series excluded net liabilities expressed in currencies of sterling-area countries, which had been included in the old series; in 1962 these were thought to amount to approximately £80 million. Secondly, the new series excluded all overseas holdings of British Government or Government-guaranteed stocks not held specifically for banking or central monetary purposes, retaining just the holdings of banks and central banks. The old series had contained the holdings of other official agencies as well (mainly the Crown Agents' special funds), estimated at some £197 million in 1962. And third, the new series excluded overseas residents' temporary loans to local authorities, which had been partially covered (to the extent of £110 million) in the old series. Subsequently, the new series (back to 1962) was redefined again, this time to *include* overseas residents' temporary loans to local authorities, and also deposits with hire-purchase finance companies.

This amendment, plus other revisions of the statistics as the information base was brought up to date, had the effect ultimately of reducing the overall discrepancy between the two series for 1962 to just £42 million (see Table 5.3).

There was only one important change of classification. The old series had divided holdings into 'central bank and other official' funds and 'other funds'; the new series distinguished between 'central monetary institutions' and 'other holders'. Mainly this meant that funds held by central monetary institutions with commercial banks in the United Kingdom, which previously had been included among privately owned balances, were now included among officially owned balances. The reclassification had no effect on the overall total of liabilities shown by the two series for the year 1962. However, it did result in a net shift of £84 million from private to official account.

In May 1968 the Bank of England republished the old series (1945 – 1962) on a gross basis, showing liabilities and claims separately in so far as was possible.[1] This was still not enough to make the two series strictly comparable: for one thing, the revised old series was still net to the extent that liabilities to and claims on overseas offices and branches of returning institutions were reported net at the time; and for another, all of the other substantial differences of definition and classification still remained. But it was enough to make comparisons between pre- and post-1962 significantly easier than before; with proper caution, the gross data from 1945 can now be analysed as if they were one continuous series. In any event, gross figures, not net, are most appropriate for our own analytical purposes. Therefore, it is these statistics that we shall use in this and subsequent chapters. They are reproduced in Table 5.3, showing U.K. sterling liabilities from 1945 to 1969. The reader will note that two sets of figures are presented for the year 1962, where the old and new series overlap.

II. SEIGNIORAGE

I noted in Chapter 2 that there are two parts to the seigniorage benefit of an international currency – a current portion and a capital portion. For the United Kingdom, the current portion of the gain from sterling

[1] *U.K. External Liabilities and Claims in Sterling: 1945–62 (Old Series)* (Bank of England, May 1968).

Table 5.3

United Kingdom Sterling Liabilities, 1945–69[a]

(in £ millions)

Date	Total	International organisations	Official holders[b]	Other holders	Overseas sterling countries Total	Official holders[b]	Other holders	Non-sterling countries Total	Official holders[b]	Other holders
1945	3602	–	2765	837	2348	1923	425	1254	842	412
46	3690	26	2746	918	2335	1889	446	1329	857	472
47	3970	388	2762	820	2239	1819	420	1343	943	400
48	3650	398	2463	789	2165	1734	431	1087	729	358
49	3835	576	2477	782	2176	1757	419	1083	720	363
1950	4242	577	2703	962	2598	2109	489	1067	594	473
51	4396	566	2912	918	2745	2252	493	1085	660	425
52	3974	567	2496	911	2569	2019	550	838	477	361
53	4196	511	2677	1008	2800	2203	597	885	474	411
54	4390	476	2720	1194	2920	2260	660	994	460	534
1955	4286	469	2705	1112	2874	2266	608	943	439	504
56	4345	669	2640	1036	2842	2240	602	834	400	434
57	4183	645	2510	1028	2727	2126	601	811	384	427
58	4235	623	2392	1220	2642	1993	649	970	399	571
59	4503	705	2491	1307	2852	2165	687	946	326	620
1960	4811	549	2528	1734	2685	2029	656	1577	499	1078
61	4890	958	2537	1395	2812	2097	715	1120	440	680
62	4535	605	2431	1499	2866	2056	810	1064	375	689

64	5409	991	2470	1948	3048	1947	1101	1370	523	847
1965	6016	1481	2540	1995	3061	1911	1150	1474	629	845
66	6401	1655	2793	1953	3084	1855	1229	1662	938	724
67	6689	1540	3247	1902	2982	1736	1246	2167	1511	565
68 I	7127	1543	3700	1884	3120	1815	1305	2464	1885	579
II	7212	2136	3251	1825	2796	1531	1265	2280	1720	560
III	7383	2109	3397	1877	2788	1506	1282	2486	1891	595
IV	7671	2082	3821	1768	2881	1650	1231	2708	2171	537
69 I	7611	1967	3931	1713	3070	1847	1223	2574	2084	490
II	7517	2101	3695	1721	3120	1921	1199	2296	1774	522
III	7432	2102	3756	1574	3071	1977	1094	2259	1779	480
IV	7356	2123	3554	1679	3170	2037	1133	2063	1517	546

a The figures show gross liabilities in sterling, both before 1962 (old series) and after 1962 (new series); for residual differences of definition between the two series, see the text.

b In the old series, classified as 'central bank and other official'; in the new series, as 'central monetary institutions'.

c Includes estimated breakdown of funds with local authorities and hire-purchase finance companies between official and other holders.

Sources: *Bank of England Quarterly Bulletin*; and *U.K. External Liabilities and Claims in Sterling: 1945–62 (Old Series)* (Bank of England, May 1968).

accrued mainly during the Second World War. Before the war, sterling balances over the long term were relatively constant in total; likewise, since the war there has been comparatively little secular change, apart from increases of liabilities associated with international support operations for the pound. Only during the war were the British actually able to absorb significant additional imports of goods and services because of the willingness of foreigners to accumulate sterling as an international currency. Since then, this portion of the benefit has become not much more than a faint memory. Britain today has ceased to obtain any *current* seigniorage gain from the international use of the pound. But on the other hand, Britain does continue to obtain a *capital* seigniorage gain from the international use of the pound. This portion is still very much alive. We shall look at each of these two portions of the seigniorage benefit in turn.

The current portion

Table 5.1 shows how relatively stable British external liabilities were over the long term before the war. Between 1931 and 1939 the greatest year-to-year change was only some £236 million (June 1938 to June 1939) – and that was a *decrease*. The greatest year-to-year *increase* was just £125 million (June 1936 to June 1937). Over the period as a whole balances rose by only £106 million. That is not what one would describe as a significant current 'credit' from foreigners.[1]

By contrast, once the war started, balances began to rise at a tremendous rate. Between 1941 and 1945 net sterling liabilities increased by almost £2.5 billion (Table 5.2); in addition, in 1940 and 1941 they must have increased by at least £0·5 billion more (Table 5.1). This may certainly be described as a significant 'credit' from foreigners. From a very nearly balanced portion, Britain became a foreign short-term debtor on a truly grand scale. This was practicable only because of the international status of the pound, which allowed the country to run a much greater cumulative deficit than it could otherwise have done.

[1] Neither did Britain, apparently, enjoy much of a 'credit' from foreigners before 1931. Net sterling liabilities in 1918 have been estimated at about £300 million. This indicates that there was very little net rise over the next thirteen years, since as Table 5.1 indicates, liabilities in 1931 were still only £411 million, including liabilities in foreign currencies. See David Williams, 'The Evolution of the Sterling System', in C. R. Whittlesey and J. S. G. Wilson (eds), *Essays in Money and Banking* (Oxford: Oxford University Press, 1968) p. 288.

The deficit was associated with war expenditures, of course, particularly in the Middle and Far East; it did not necessarily expand incomes in Britain. But it did enable the country to avoid even greater income reductions than those which were in fact required by the war effort overseas. Current foreign expenditures of this magnitude simply would not have been possible had sterling not been a major international currency. This was an important benefit of the use of the pound; indeed, in the opinion of some, the *most* important benefit: 'The major economic support obtained in that conflict is probably the biggest gain Britain has derived from the sterling system.'[1]

Whether this is the biggest gain of the sterling system or not, it is clearly not a gain that has persisted in the post-war period. The fundamental point of the seigniorage benefit is that accumulations are more or less voluntary: they reflect foreign confidence in a money's usefulness as an international store of value. During the Second World War the foreign beneficiaries of British war expenditures did show the necessary confidence: they were willing – or were successfully persuaded – to hold pounds rather than to demand dollars or gold. However, since the war there has been regrettably rather less such foreign confidence in sterling. True, there have been increases of sterling balances – indeed, enormous increases. Over the twenty-four years from 1945 to 1969, U.K. liabilities rose by more than £3·75 billion (most of this increase occurring only after 1963). But comparatively few of these new balances represented genuinely voluntary acquisitions of an international currency. Most in fact had nothing at all to do with the traditional roles of the pound. Rather, they were accumulated largely as counterparts of foreign support operations for sterling, and are still held largely to oblige the British authorities rather than from choice.

For example, between 1945 and 1962 sterling liabilities rose by a little over £900 million (Table 5.3). But of this amount, almost two-thirds was accounted for by Britain's subscriptions to and drawings from the International Monetary Fund. At most, therefore, only about one-third (£328 million) represented genuinely voluntary acquisitions of the traditional type. Once again, this is not what one would describe as a significant current 'credit' from foreigners. Similarly, from 1964 to 1969 – the years of Britain's most serious and

[1] P. M. Oppenheimer, 'Monetary Movements and the International Position of Sterling', in D. J. Robertson and L. C. Hunter (eds), *The British Balance of Payments* (Edinburgh: Oliver & Boyd, 1966) p. 132.

prolonged post-war payments crisis – sterling liabilities rose by some £2½ billion. However, all of the rise and then some was accounted for by international support operations. Almost £1·7 billion represented subscriptions to and drawings from the Fund,[1] and another £1·1 billion represented credits acquired in consequence of Britain's various swap arrangements with other major financial powers.[2] Conventional holdings of sterling actually declined by £300 million. Certainly this is strong evidence for the conclusion that the United Kingdom has ceased to obtain any current seigniorage gain from the international use of the pound (except in the negative sense that increases of world price levels in the post-war period have meant a reduced burden of debt in real-value terms).

Some observers object to this conclusion. It is true, they say, that the U.K. no longer obtains a current seigniorage gain *in the traditional sense*; on a net basis today there are few genuinely voluntary acquisitions of sterling. But, they insist, there may nevertheless be a sense in which the country does still manage to enjoy a current seigniorage gain. Attention is focused on the various international swap arrangements and other central-bank credit facilities arranged on Britain's behalf since 1964. These have given the U.K. access to vast amounts of credit – far more than has been made available to any other country (with the exception of the United States). Presumably this is because of the sterling balances: no other currency (except the dollar) has such a large 'overhang' of liabilities, consequently no other currency (except the dollar) requires so much support at times of crisis. In other words, Britain gets so much credit only because the pound is an international currency. *Ipso facto*, it is supposed to follow that these credits are a seigniorage gain from sterling.[3]

[1] In March 1966, as part of an overall expansion of I.M.F. resources, Britain increased its subscription by £175 million – raising its total quota to $U.S. 2440 million (approximately £1 billion at the post-devaluation rate). The remainder of the increase of liabilities to the Fund represents the unpaid balance on drawings of £1000 million in December 1964 (repaid in 1967), £1400 million in May 1965, $1400 million in June 1968, and a further $1000 million in several instalments from June 1969 (excluding a final instalment of $150 million in March 1970). See Chapter 10.

[2] Between 1964 and 1969 sterling liabilities increased net by £287 million to Western European central banks, and by £820 million to the central banks of Canada and the United States. *Bank of England Quarterly Bulletin*, recent issues.

[3] It is difficult to find this argument formalised in print. As presented here, it has been pieced together from conversations in London with various interested individuals.

Now, no one would deny that the support Britain has received since 1964 has been substantial. The country has been given access to truly vast amounts of credit.[1] In September 1964 seven central banks (Belgium, Canada, France, Germany, Italy, the Netherlands and Switzerland) arranged short-term facilities totalling $500 million in Britain's favour; this was in addition to the $500 million swap arrangement already in existence with the United States Federal Reserve System. In November 1964, when the great balance-of-payments crisis first broke, the facilities available were raised to $3 billion, including a $250 million increase in the Federal Reserve swap line and a $250 million stand-by facility with the U.S. Export-Import Bank. The European portion of these arrangements expired the following summer, but was replaced in September 1965 by a new credit facility with nine central banks (the seven above, less France, but including Austria, Japan and Sweden) and the Bank for International Settlements, plus a separate, renewable three months' facility with the Bank of France, together totalling $1 billion. This was renewed in 1966 and again in 1967, and in November 1967, at the time of devaluation, it was increased to an amount officially reported to be 'in excess of' $1·5 billion. Meanwhile, the Federal Reserve swap line had also been raised in several steps to $2 billion. Thus, by 1969 the British had at their disposal short-term facilities amounting to a minimum of $3·5 billion – certainly a lot of credit,[2] and certainly more than has been made available to any other country apart from the United States.[3]

[1] The information in this paragraph is all public. It was gleaned from the 'Commentary' section of various issues of the *Bank of England Quarterly Bulletin*, vols IV–IX (1964–9).

[2] In fact, short-term facilities appear to have been considerably larger than this publicly revealed minimum. In its *Annual Report* for 1969 (p. 65), the I.M.F. disclosed that at end-1968 U.K. *drawings* on such facilities were already up to £2 billion ($4·8 billion). In addition, since 1964 the U.K. has received loans of $80 million and $40 million from the Swiss Government (December 1964 and May 1965, respectively, each in conjunction with a simultaneous British drawing from the I.M.F.); of $103 million from a consortium of three Swiss commercial banks (October 1967); of $250 million from 'a number of central banks' (November 1967, used to repay the balance of Britain's 1964 I.M.F. drawing); and of $50 million and $125 million from the Deutsche Bundesbank (April 1968 and August 1969, respectively, to offset British military expenditures in Germany).

[3] As of March 1970 the Federal Reserve System's swap network totalled $10,980 million, more than twice as much as the $3·5 billion minimum at Britain's disposal. On the other hand, Britain's $3·5 billion minimum is considerably greater than the next largest credit packages ever provided – to Italy in

Furthermore, no one would deny that the British get so much credit only because the pound is an international currency. Quite the opposite, in fact: much money is provided for precisely this reason. In June 1966, for instance, the European central banks made available to the U.K. a separate facility of $1 billion 'specifically designed to counter the stresses to which sterling is subject as a reserve and international trading currency'.[1] This facility was replaced in September 1968 by the $2 billion credit line through the B.I.S., which of course was also intended to relieve stresses arising from the international use of sterling – specifically, 'to offset fluctuations in the sterling balances of the sterling area countries'.[2] In fact, the new facility was projected as an indispensable condition of the so-called Basle reform of the sterling system (see Chapter 4).

However, even granting that the credits are substantial and that they are connected to sterling, it does not follow that they are a current seigniorage gain. The essence of the seigniorage benefit from an international currency is that it is a kind of *free* command over real resources: it is characterised by both unconditionality and indefinite maturity. That is what is implied by the voluntary nature of acquisitions (see Chapter 2). But the credits that the British have obtained since 1964 have been of an entirely different kind. They have been both conditional and of fixed (usually very short) maturity; in other words they have been exactly like any other series of loans between governments. In this sense, there is nothing special about them at all – certainly nothing distinguishing them specifically as seigniorage gain. In truth, because of their short term and firm 'strings', they should be more properly regarded as evidence of the increasing constraint on British policy resulting from the international use of sterling. We shall return to this point in Chapter 7.

An alternative objection to the conclusion that, for Britain, the current benefit of seigniorage is a thing of the past, has been raised by John Knapp. He argues that the U.K. still derives a special kind of seigniorage gain from the sterling area itself, specifically from the

---

March 1964 ($1 billion) and to France in June and November 1968 ($1·3 billion in June plus $2 billion more in November).

[1] *Bank of England Quarterly Bulletin*, vi 3 (Sep 1966) 209.

[2] *The Basle Facility and the Sterling Area*, Cmnd 3787 (Oct 1968) p. 2. From 1966 to 1968 the facility had covered both sterling-area and non-sterling-area balances. By contrast, since 1968 the facility relates only to balances held by residents of sterling-area countries. Ibid., p. 5.

convention of reserve pooling.[1] His argument goes like this. Britain supposedly enjoys access to a greater flow of gold and foreign exchange, to finance imports from non-sterling-area sources, than would otherwise be possible, and this (according to Knapp) is because it is unlikely that anything like equally profitable outlets for U.K. exports would be available outside the sterling area as are available within it. Britain runs a large and persistent current-account surplus vis-à-vis the other sterling-area countries. 'This, together with the fact that the United Kingdom is in large and persistent current account deficit with the non-sterling areas means . . . that the reserve currency arrangements which secure the large inter-area transfers the United Kingdom can use for settling her non-sterling deficits may well be of very great benefit to her.'[2]

Now, this is a most confused argument. It may actually be true, of course, that Britain does find it easier to sell within the sterling area than outside it. Suppose it is true. It does not therefore follow that the benefit depends directly on the system of reserve pooling. What it does depend on are Commonwealth Preference and the exchange-discrimination features of the sterling area, and neither of these has anything at all to do with the international use of sterling *per se* (see Chapter 4). In other words, even if there is such a special kind of current seigniorage gain, it does not require an international currency. But I would go even further than that: I would contend that there is *no* such special gain. Knapp overlooks the empirical fact that whereas the U.K. still tends to run a net trade deficit in relation to non-sterling areas, the overseas members as a group no longer tend to earn a net trade surplus to cover it (again, see Chapter 4). Consequently, Britain's large and persistent current-account surplus with the outer sterling area no longer earns as much in the way of gold and foreign exchange as it once did. In truth, the main source of replenishment of the central reserve today is the sustained net inflow of long-term capital from sources such as the United States. Surely no one would consider *that* a seigniorage gain from the international use of sterling.

The capital portion

Although for Britain the current benefit of seigniorage is now a thing of the past, nevertheless some seigniorage gain remains from the

[1] John Knapp, 'Would Britain Profit from the E.E.C.?', *The Round Table*, no. 226 (Apr 1967) 172–4. [2] Ibid., p. 174.

international use of the pound. For while it is true that conventional holdings of sterling are not being increased significantly at the present time, so it is also true (at least since Basle) that they are not being reduced very much either. Consequently, the United Kingdom is under no compulsion to sell off foreign assets; whereas if sterling balances were actually being repatriated from London, a portion of these overseas investments would have to be liquidated. In other words, the British are in the fortunate position of being able to continue enjoying whatever rate of return is yielded by their own capital held abroad. This is the capital portion of the seigniorage benefit of sterling. How large may we reckon this gain to be? To make such a calculation, we must estimate, first, the *size* of sterling-related investments abroad; and second, their average rate of *profitability* to the British economy. We must then try to allocate the total capital gain among the separate roles of the pound.

The size of sterling-related investments abroad is indicated by the corresponding total of foreign balances in London that would have to be repatriated if the pound were to become a purely domestic currency. This total, of course, excludes the balances of international organisations and non-sterling-area official holders. As I have already stressed, very few of these have anything to do with the traditional roles of the pound. True, some small part of them are in fact held by certain non-sterling governments (e.g. in Scandinavia, Spain, Portugal and Greece) because sterling is still an international currency. However, the published statistics are not detailed enough to let us identify which these balances are; and in any event the amounts involved are not apt to be significant enough to make an uninformed breakdown worth while. Private holdings, on the other hand, should not be excluded; nor should the official holdings of overseas sterling-area countries. These, it must be presumed, would all have to be repatriated if the pound were to become a purely domestic currency. These are the *conventional* holdings of sterling. They are all clearly related to the currency's traditional international functions.

Table 5.4 provides a breakdown of these conventional holdings of sterling for the years 1965-9. (This period was chosen because it is both long enough to even out short-term fluctuations in the total and composition of foreign balances, and yet recent enough to be relevant.) At the end of 1969 private holdings of sterling in London, plus the official holdings of overseas sterling-area countries, amounted to some £3716 million, down only some £200 million net from 1965, despite rather substantial intervening fluctuations. Over the five-year period as a whole conventional holdings averaged approximately £3700 million. In the following discussion, the size of sterling-related British investments overseas will be assumed equal to that sum. The figure accounts for less than one-third of the total of British private long-term investments abroad outstanding during the same half-decade, and for not much more than one-quarter of the total of all British private foreign assets outstanding (short-term as well as long-term).[1]

Our next step is to estimate the average rate of profitability of this amount of sterling-related investments. This is not an easy problem to solve. Relevant data are especially difficult to come by. In fact, to date there has been only one systematic attempt to analyse the real rate of return of a major portion of Britain's foreign assets. That was the effort by Professor W. B. Reddaway included in his well-known recent study of the various effects of U.K. direct investment overseas.[2] Most of Reddaway's work was concerned specifically with balance-of-payments effects. However, in his *Final Report* (chapters 23–26) he did comment as well on real-income effects for Britain. These comments of his should suffice us as input here for our own analytical purposes.[3]

Reddaway's research indicated that the most important income effects of U.K. overseas investment are those which accrue through the level of profits (net of tax paid to foreign governments) and through the gain from 'knowledge-sharing' (knowledge of new techniques, new products, new methods of marketing and so on). Together, after appropriate adjustment of depreciation rates and also after allowing for capital appreciation, these produce an operating return of 6 per cent on the total of capital invested – a reasonable figure, though not a

---

[1] See Central Statistical Office, *United Kingdom Balance of Payments 1969*, pp. 44–6.

[2] W. B. Reddaway in collaboration with J. O. N. Perkins, S. J. Potter and C. T. Taylor, *Effects of U.K. Direct Investment Overseas: An Interim Report* (Cambridge: Cambridge University Press, 1967); and W. B. Reddaway in collaboration with S. J. Potter and C. T. Taylor, *Effects of U.K. Direct Investment Overseas: Final Report* (Cambridge: Cambridge University Press, 1968).

[3] To be sure, Reddaway's comments applied only to British *direct* investments overseas; he never considered the effects of either long-term portfolio or short-term investments. But that should not trouble us here: apart from the fact that direct investments account for well over half of all British private foreign investments, it seems reasonable to assume, given the fungibility of capital, that at the margin there would not be much divergence among the rates of return to various classes of overseas investment.

Table 5.4

United Kingdom Sterling Liabilities Related to the International Functions of Sterling, 1965–9
(in £ millions)

	Current and deposit accounts	Treasury bills	Other bills	British Government stocks	Local authority temporary loans	Finance-house deposits	Total
Total liabilities, all holders							
1965	1783	538	80	1209	170	126	3906
1966	1831	441	90	1190	119	137	3808
1967	1746	399	97	1175	119	102	3638
1968	1670	373	123	1129	71	51	3418
1969	1747	312	194	1312	97	57	3716
Of which:							
1. Official holders (overseas sterling countries only)							
1965	217	520	–	1043	131	–	1911
1966	310	427	–	1006	105	7	1855
1967	291	370	–	953	104	19	1736
1968	270	368	–	938	59	14	1650
1969	421	307	–	1198	87	25	2037
2. Other holders (total)							
1965	1566	18	80	166	39	126	1995
1966	1521	14	90	184	14	130	1953
1967	1455	29	97	222	15	83	1902
1968	1400	5	123	191	12	37	1768
1969	1326	5	194	114	10	32	1679

(a) Overseas sterling countries

1965	866	11	28	144	26	75	1150
1966	922	12	39	165	10	81	1229
1967	908	12	45	204	11	65	1246
1968	937	3	75	178	9	32	1231
1969	862	2	139	98	9	28	1133

(b) Non-sterling countries

1965	700	7	52	22	13	51	845
1966	599	2	51	19	4	49	724
1967	547	17	52	18	4	18	656
1968	464	2	48	14	3	5	537
1969	464	2	61	15	1	4	546

Note: Detail may not add to total because of rounding.
Source: *Bank of England Quarterly Bulletin.*

very high one.[1] But this is not the figure we need for our purposes. This is a measure of *private* gain only. What we need is a measure of *social* gain – the true benefit to the economy of the United Kingdom as a whole. As indicated in Chapter 2, to measure this social gain we must compare the operating return of British assets overseas with what the same capital would earn if it were invested at home rather than abroad. Reddaway suggests that the most appropriate figure for the domestic 'opportunity' cost is of the order of 3 per cent (gross of tax paid to domestic government). In turn, this suggests that the *net* gain to Britain is really quite low – not more, in fact, than about 3 per cent of the total amount of capital invested.[2] We may take this figure as roughly indicative of the average rate of profitability of all British investments overseas, including those assets that may be considered sterling-related.

We can now estimate the magnitude of the capital seigniorage gain to Britain. Sterling-related investments were previously reckoned to average approximately £3700 million over the half-decade 1965–9. Their average rate of profitability is now reckoned to amount to approximately 3 per cent of the capital invested. These two figures together yield a total capital gain of the order of £110 million a year. This, we may conclude, is all the seigniorage benefit that remains from sterling's continued use as an international currency.

Our last step is to allocate this capital seigniorage benefit among the separate roles of the pound. The gain may be attributed to both the medium-of-exchange and store-of-value functions of the pound at both the private and official levels of international transactions. The question is: in what proportions? The answer is: in proportion to the ratio of working balances to investment balances at each level. Working balances are associated directly with the transactions and intervention roles of sterling. They represent the incremental effect mentioned in Chapter 2 – the holdings that are in excess of the amount that foreigners would otherwise accumulate if the currency were used for store-of-value purposes only. All other holdings represent foreign investments in the United Kingdom; they are associated directly with the asset and

[1] Cf. W. A. P. Manser, 'Professor Reddaway's Last Word?', *National West-minster Bank Quarterly Review* (Feb 1969) pp. 44–9.
[2] This low figure is corroborated by some alternative data on the profitability of British overseas investment collected by Richard N. Cooper. See his chapter on 'The Balance of Payments' in Richard E. Caves and Associates, *Britain's Economic Prospects* (Washington: Brookings Institution, 1968) pp. 175–6.

reserve roles of the pound. Our problem now is to determine the approximate ratio of working balances to investment balances at each level of transactions.

A clue to the solution of this problem was first provided by the Committee on Invisible Exports in its 1967 report on *Britain's Invisible Earnings*.[1] In discussing current and deposit accounts held by foreigners in British banks, the Committee estimated that probably only about 25 per cent of the total represent genuine working balances. These were defined as 'the level of balances which overseas traders and banks need to maintain in London in order to conduct their day-to-day business'.[2] The remaining 75 per cent of bank deposits were regarded as a form of investment in the United Kingdom.

Now, from an operational point of view this does not seem an unreasonable figure. Most foreign deposit holdings in London are not in fact used to conduct day-to-day business in sterling. Most are held, rather, as cash reserves or compensating balances, etc. – in other words, as convenient and highly liquid stores of value. Unfortunately, in the present context an operational approach is unduly restrictive. For our purposes here, the issue is not what percentage of sterling deposits is actually *used* to conduct the day-to-day business of international trade or currency intervention. The issue is rather what percentage is actually *held* because the pound is used for such purposes – a very different question indeed. In brief, what percentage depends on the fact that sterling functions *not only* as store-of-value *but also* as medium of exchange?

My guess is that virtually all bank deposits depend on this fact. In view of the lack of confidence in sterling in recent years, it would indeed be surprising if we were to find that as much as three-quarters of the total were still being held *solely* for investment purposes. By and large, deposit accounts are not usually held for investment purposes at all. True, cash balances and compensating balances are not used from day to day; but true also, they can hardly be said to be motivated essentially by asset or reserve considerations. The truth of the matter is that they are motivated basically by just one consideration – the role of the pound as an exchange intermediary. Transfer that role to another currency, and the balances would not be likely to

---

[1] Committee on Invisible Exports, *Britain's Invisible Earnings* (London: British National Export Council, for the Financial Advisory Panel on Exports, 1967). See also Chapter 6.

[2] Ibid., p. 190.

remain long in sterling. I conclude, therefore, that for our present analytical purposes all bank deposits should be treated as working balances, and none as investment balances.

But of course bank deposits are not the only form of sterling liabilities to foreigners. The published data reproduced in Table 5.4 classify the sterling balances into a total of six major categories, including, in addition to (1) bank deposits: (2) Treasury bills; (3) other bills (including both prime bank bills and other trade bills); (4) British Government stocks; (5) temporary loans to local authorities; and (6) deposits with hire-purchase finance companies. Few of these liabilities are held solely for medium-of-exchange purposes. Quite the opposite, in fact. Government stocks and other securities are not nearly so liquid as current or deposit accounts; they must usually be converted to bank money first before they can be employed for transactions or intervention purposes. Besides, their interest yields tend generally to be higher. Consequently, more are likely to represent investment balances than working balances. But not all: even among these, we must admit, there is some percentage that is held directly in connection with the medium-of-exchange function of sterling. What percentage? Here I shall apply the ratio suggested by the Committee on Invisible Exports: I shall assume that 25 per cent of these other holdings are working balances, and that 75 per cent represent foreign investments in the United Kingdom.

Given these assumptions, we may now proceed to allocate the seigniorage benefit of sterling's international functions. Consider Table 5.4. It is interesting to observe the striking contrast in the composition of private and official balances of sterling. Of the latter, nearly four-fifths during the years 1965-9 were held in the form of British Government stocks and Treasury bills; at the same time, a virtually identical fraction of private balances was held in the form of current and deposit accounts with U.K. banks. This suggests that relatively different emphases are placed on the separate roles of sterling at the two levels of international transactions. At the level of official transactions, it is the store-of-value function that predominates. The comparatively large holdings of Government securities indicate that central banks use the pound more as an international reserve medium (or as backing for their local currencies) than for active intervention purposes. At the level of private transactions, by contrast, it is the medium-of-exchange function that predominates. The comparatively large holdings of bank deposits indicate that international traders and investors, and the banks who service international traders and investors, hold the pound more for working-balance purposes than as an asset currency.

The significance of these contrasting emphases may be plainly seen in Table 5.5 which gives the estimated breakdown, of total liabilities between working balances and investment balances at each of the two levels of transactions. As we would expect, at the level of official international transactions investment balances exceed working balances by a considerable margin – by a ratio of close to 2:1 on average. At the level of private international transactions, by contrast, it is working balances which predominate – by a ratio of more than 5:1 on average. Overall, the transactions-currency role of sterling accounts for about 42 per cent of the total of sterling liabilities; the asset-currency role, for about 8 per cent; the intervention-currency role, for about 19 per cent; and the reserve-currency role, for about 31 per cent. These are the proportions we need to allocate the seigniorage gain of sterling's international functions. Rounding to the nearest quinquevalent, we derive the following attribution:

Official transactions	
Intervention currency	£20 million
Reserve currency	35 million
Private transactions	
Transactions currency	45 million
Asset currency	10 million
Total	£110 million

III. INTEREST

While Britain today does continue to enjoy some seigniorage gain from sterling, that benefit is not without its price. The British must pay for their privileged position of being able to continue to enjoy the return on capital invested abroad. Just as any single investor, managing his portfolio, must pay interest for any borrowed capital which is then re-lent, so the U.K. must pay interest abroad on the accumulated sterling balances. This is the direct cost of the international use of the pound. Our problem now is to determine just how large these interest charges are, and then just how they are allocated among the separate functions of sterling.

Table 5.5

Estimated Breakdown of Working Balances and Investment Balances, 1965–9ᵃ
(in £ millions)

	Total sterling liabilities		Working balances		Estimate of Investment balances	
	Amount	Percentage of total	Amount	Percentage of total	Amount	Percentage of total
Total liabilities, all holders						
1965	3906	100·0	2314	59·2	1592	40·8
1966	3808	100·0	2325	61·1	1483	38·9
1967	3638	100·0	2219	61·0	1419	39·0
1968	3418	100·0	2107	61·6	1311	38·4
1969	3716	100·0	2240	60·3	1479	39·8
Of which:						
1. Official holders (overseas sterling countries only)						
1965	1911	48·9	641	16·4	1270	32·5
1966	1855	48·7	696	18·3	1159	30·4
1967	1736	47·7	652	17·9	1084	29·8
1968	1650	48·3	615	18·0	1035	30·3
1969	2037	54·8	826	22·2	1212	32·6
2. Other holders (total)						
1965	1995	51·1	1673	42·8	322	8·2
1966	1953	51·3	1629	42·8	324	8·5
1967	1902	52·3	1567	43·1	335	9·2
1968	1768	51·7	1492	43·7	276	8·1
1969	1679	45·2	1414	38·1	267	7·2

Note: Detail may not add to total because of rounding.
ᵃ Working balances are estimated to constitute 100 per cent of current and deposit accounts, plus 25 per cent of all other sterling liabilities; the remainder are estimated to constitute investment balances.
Source: Table 5.4.

Estimates of the interest cost of the sterling balances have occasionally been suggested elsewhere, but these have usually been not nearly so precise as one might prefer.[1] Here we shall attempt to be quite precise about the question. Since comprehensive interest-rate series are published regularly for all of the six reported categories of sterling liabilities,[2] it should be a relatively simple matter to proceed to an accurate estimate of the overall total of interest charges.

For this purpose, I shall again concentrate on the years 1965 to 1969. This will ensure consistency with the discussion in the previous section. Likewise, I shall again concentrate on just those sterling liabilities that are clearly related to the traditional roles of the pound – all private holdings, plus the official holdings of overseas sterling-area countries.

The published interest-rate series corresponding to the sterling liabilities in Table 5.4 are shown in Table 5.6. These are average annual rates, calculated from rates effective at the last working day of each month. One adjustment of these data is necessary in order to make them useful for our purposes. Just as the rate of return on British capital invested abroad had to be adjusted for the discrepancy between the private and social gain from foreign investment, so these data on interest rates must be adjusted for the discrepancy between the private and social *cost* of sterling. The raw series in Table 5.6 are a measure of *private* cost only – the price Britain must currently pay to hold on to its imported capital. But that is not the true cost to the economy of the United Kingdom as a whole, for even if this capital had been raised at home rather than abroad there would have been a price to pay. This price, we may assume, is equal to the domestic 'opportunity' cost suggested by Professor Reddaway – namely, 3 per cent of the capital borrowed, Accordingly, the *social* cost of the sterling balances may be assumed to be, for each category of liability, 3 per cent lower than as shown in Table 5.6. This adjustment is provided in Table 5.7.

There is of course no series in either Table 5.6 or Table 5.7 for current accounts (demand deposits, in American parlance): these liabilities do not pay interest. But on the other hand, the sterling-balance statistics do include current accounts jointly with deposit

[1] For example, in a speech before the Press Club on 13 June 1969, the Financial Secretary to the Treasury suggested a figure of 'over £200 million' for the total of sterling balances. This is typical of the ambiguity of official estimates. And private estimates are even less satisfactory. See, e.g., John Cooper, *A Suitable Case for Treatment: What to do About the Balance of Payments* (London: Penguin Books, 1968) p. 274; and Richard N. Cooper, op. cit., p. 187.

[2] *Bank of England Quarterly Bulletin*, statistical annex, Tables 23–25.

accounts (time deposits, in American parlance); therefore, some further adjustment of the data is necessary to take account of this additional fact. We must remove the current accounts from the first

Table 5.6

Selected United Kingdom Interest Rates, 1965–9[a]
(in per cent per annum)

	Deposit accounts	Treasury bills	Other bills[b]	British Government stocks[c]	Local authority temporary loans	Finance – house deposits
1965	4·42	5·82	6·88	6·60	6·78	6·96
1966	4·50	6·07	7·09	6·86	6·84	7·21
1967	4·54	5·79	6·70	6·75	6·22	6·40
1968	5·42	6·95	8·03	7·60	7·85	8·08
1969	6·00	7·69	8·96	8·91	8·83	9·74

[a] All rates are calculated as annual averages of rates effective at the last working day of each month.

[b] Mean of spread between the rate on prime bank bills (three months) and a representative rate at which trade bills (three months) of good average quality are discounted.

[c] Mean of spread of short-term (five years), medium-term (ten years) and long-term (twenty years) British Government stocks; calculated as average redemption yields.

Source: *Bank of England Quarterly Bulletin.*

Table 5.7

Adjusted United Kingdom Interest Rates, 1965–9[a]
(in per cent per annum)

	Deposit accounts	Treasury bills	Other bills	British Government stocks	Local authority temporary loans	Finance- house deposits
1965	1·42	2·82	3·88	3·60	3·78	3·96
1966	1·50	3·07	4·09	3·86	3·84	4·21
1967	1·54	2·79	3·78	3·75	3·22	3·40
1968	2·42	3·95	5·03	4·60	4·85	5·08
1969	3·00	4·69	5·96	5·91	5·83	6·74

[a] For notes, see Table 5.6.
Source: Table 5.6.

column of Table 5.4, for if we do not we would run the risk of greatly exaggerating the interest cost of the pound. We would be attributing interest charges to accounts which are not in fact interest-bearing.

Unfortunately, the published data do not provide enough information for this purpose. On the other hand, a quite useful estimate has been provided by the Committee on Invisible Exports.[1] I have already mentioned the Committee's estimate that only about one-quarter of foreign-owned bank deposits in London represents genuine working balances; I have also suggested that from an operational point of view this does not seem an unreasonable figure. Since the remaining three-quarters of bank deposits are thus regarded as a form of investment in the United Kingdom, they may all be assumed to be interest-bearing deposit accounts. The Committee further reckoned that half of working balances as well consist of deposit accounts. The conclusion follows that just one-eighth of the total of deposit holdings are in fact current accounts. I see no reason for questioning the Committee's view on this matter, which is after all purely operational: most of its members were bankers, who ought to know the breakdown of their own deposit liabilities. Therefore, I shall use the Committee's estimate in the present context. One-eighth (12·5 per cent) of bank deposits will be assumed to consist of current accounts, and seven-eighths (87·5 per cent) to consist of deposit accounts. The calculation is summarised in Table 5.8.

Given the information in Tables 5.4, 5.7 and 5.8, we can quickly estimate the total social interest cost of sterling for the years 1965-9. This is shown in Table 5.9. The implied cost of each category of liability is computed by applying the relevant (adjusted) rate of interest from Table 5.7. The costs of all six categories are then summed. We find that the overall cost to Britain rose steeply over the five-year period, paralleling the extraordinary rise of world interest rates in general. On average, a net amount of some £110 million was paid out annually to foreigners on their accumulated balances. Of this amount, approximately £70 million a year was paid to official holders and £40 million a year to private holders. In the following discussion these average figures, evening out shorter-term fluctuations, will be treated as approximately representative of the actual interest cost for Britain today resulting from the continued international use of the pound.

Significantly, this cost is identical to the amount of seigniorage *benefit* estimated in the previous section to be still remaining from the international use of the pound. Both are of the order of £110 million a year. This means that, on balance, the United Kingdom today no

[1] Committee on Invisible Exports, op. cit., p. 191.

FS E

longer gains anything at all from the management of that part of its international investment portfolio which is directly related to sterling's position as an international currency. The total social benefit yielded by sterling-related investments overseas is now just matched by the total social cost of retaining the sterling balances in London. Competition from the dollar and other international currencies, apparently, has become sufficiently keen to eliminate completely any vestige of mono-

Table 5.8

Estimated Breakdown of Current and Deposit Accounts, 1965-9
(in £millions)

	Current and deposit accounts (from Table 5.4)	Estimate of	
		Current accounts	Deposit accounts
Total accounts, all holders			
1965	1783	223	1560
1966	1831	229	1602
1967	1746	218	1528
1968	1670	209	1461
1969	1747	218	1529
Of which:			
1. Official holders (overseas sterling countries only)			
1965	217	27	190
1966	310	39	271
1967	291	36	255
1968	270	34	236
1969	421	53	369
2. Other holders (total)			
1965	1566	196	1370
1966	1521	190	1331
1967	1455	182	1273
1968	1400	175	1225
1969	1326	166	1160

Note: Detail may not add to total because of rounding.

ᵃ Current accounts are estimated to constitute 12·5 per cent ($\frac{1}{8}$) of the total of bank accounts, and deposit accounts to constitute 87·5 per cent ($\frac{7}{8}$) of the total.

Source: Table 5.4.

polistic advantage that Britain might once have enjoyed as a source of international money (see Chapter 2).

Like the capital seigniorage gain, the interest cost of sterling may be attributed to both the currency's medium-of-exchange and store-of-value functions at both the private and official levels of transactions, in proportion to the ratio of working balances to investment balances at

Table 5.9

Interest Cost of the International Functions of Sterling, 1965–9
(in £ millions)

	Deposit accounts	Treasury bills	Other bills	British Government stocks	Local authority temporary loans	Finance-house deposits	Total interest cost
Total liabilities, all holders							
1965	22·2	15·2	3·1	43·5	6·4	5·0	95·4
1966	24·0	13·5	3·7	45·9	4·6	5·8	97·5
1967	23·5	11·1	3·7	44·1	3·8	3·5	89·7
1968	35·4	14·7	6·2	51·9	3·4	2·6	114·2
1969	45·9	14·6	11·6	77·5	5·7	3·8	159·1
Of which:							
1. Official holders (overseas sterling countries only)							
1965	2·7	14·7	–	37·5	5·0	–	59·9
1966	4·1	13·1	–	38·8	4·0	0·3	60·3
1967	3·9	10·3	–	35·7	3·3	0·6	53·8
1968	5·7	14·5	–	43·1	2·9	0·7	66·9
1969	11·1	14·4	–	70·8	5·1	1·7	103·1
2. Other holders (total)							
1965	19·5	0·5	3·1	6·0	1·5	5·0	35·6
1966	20·0	0·4	3·7	7·1	0·5	5·5	37·2
1967	19·6	0·8	3·7	8·3	0·5	2·8	35·7
1968	29·6	0·2	6·2	8·8	0·6	1·9	47·3
1969	34·8	0·2	11·6	6·7	0·6	1·9	55·8

Note: Detail may not add to total because of rounding.
Sources: Tables 5.4, 5.7 and 5.8.

each level. The implied cost of each function at each level, computed by applying the relevant (adjusted) rates of interest from Table 5.7 to the breakdown of liabilities in Table 5.5, is shown in Table 5.10. As we would expect, at the level of official international transactions we find that it was the pound's store-of-value function that was relatively more expensive over the four-year period 1965-9. Reserve-currency holdings of sterling cost Britain approximately £47 million a year in

Table 5.10

Allocation of the Interest Cost of Sterling, 1965–7
(in £ millions)

	Total	Functions: Medium of exchange	Store of value
Total			
1965	95·4	40·5	54·9
1966	97·5	42·4	55·1
1967	89·7	40·1	49·6
1968	114·2	55·1	59·1
1969	159·1	74·1	85·0
Level of official transactions			
1965	59·9	17·0	42·9
1966	60·3	18·2	42·1
1967	53·8	16·4	37·4
1968	66·9	21·0	45·9
1969	103·1	34·1	69·0
Level of private transactions			
1965	35·6	23·5	12·1
1966	37·2	24·3	12·9
1967	35·7	23·6	12·1
1968	47·3	34·2	13·1
1969	55·8	40·0	15·8

Note: Detail may not add to total because of rounding.
Sources: Tables 5.5, 5.7, 5.8 and 5.9.

interest payments; holdings related to the currency's use for intervention purposes, by contrast, cost only about £21 million annually. Also as we would expect, at the level of private international transactions, it was the pound's medium-of-exchange function that was the relatively more expensive. Asset-currency holdings of sterling cost only some £13 million a year. Annual interest charges on transactions-currency balances, however, amounted to more than £29 million. Rounding to the nearest quinquevalent, we derive the following attribution:

Official transactions
Intervention currency	£20 million
Reserve currency	45 million

Private transactions
Transactions currency	30 million
Asset currency	15 million
Total	£110 million

This attribution of the interest cost of sterling contrasts significantly with the attribution of the capital gain from seigniorage estimated earlier in the chapter. In only one case, that of the reserve-currency role of the pound, do benefit and cost appear to be roughly offsetting. Two roles, the store-of-value roles of reserve currency and asset currency, appear to be somewhat costly on balance. And conversely, one role, that of transactions currency, appears actually to yield a capital gain larger than its corresponding interest loss – half again as large, in fact. This function, as private exchange intermediary, seems to be the only one of sterling's several functions which is clearly beneficial to the U.K. on a net basis. The significance of this fact will become even more evident as we proceed in Chapter 6.

6 The City's Invisible Earnings

THE net income gains from increased foreign demand for national banking, financial and commercial services constitute a *social* benefit of the international use of a currency – even though the gains actually accrue to just a single *sector* of the issuing country's economy. In the case of the British economy this sector is commonly referred to as 'the City of London'. The income gains are commonly referred to as the City's 'invisible earnings'.

The invisible earnings of the City are generally regarded as the major benefit still accruing to Britain from the international use of sterling. Indeed, until just a few years ago this benefit was, in the view of many experts, thought to be sufficiently large to make worth while preserving *all* of the pound's international monetary functions *whatever* the offsetting costs. The City was bringing in a vast amount of income, income which would have been lost had the City not been supported by a great international currency; therefore, sterling's roles had to be maintained. Thus the argument went.[1] However, in more recent years this line of argument has been subjected increasingly to challenge and question. Are the earnings of the City really so vast? Are they really so dependent on the support of an international currency? And is it possible that they may depend more on some roles of sterling than on others? These are the questions we shall examine in the present chapter.

I. GROSS EARNINGS

Defining the City

How large are the City's invisible earnings in fact? This is not such an easy question to answer. In the first place, it is difficult in this context even to *define* the City in terms that are precise or statistically meaningful. Clearly the City cannot be interpreted, as it is often by the layman,

[1] See 'The Debate on Sterling', *Planning*, XXIV 421 (Apr 1958) 79–80.

as a purely geographic location – the 'square mile' bounded roughly by the Thames, the Tower, Aldersgate and the Temple.[1] This would lead to a meaningless division of many activities, such as banking and insurance, into business transacted within the geographic limits of the City, and business transacted elsewhere. It would also lead to the exclusion of some institutions (e.g. some insurance companies) which, although located physically outside the square mile, ought properly to be included in the analysis; and to the inclusion of some institutions (e.g. some accounting and actuarial firms) which, although located physically within the square mile, ought properly to be excluded.

For our purposes it is more appropriate to interpret the City selectively in functional terms – as a group of banking and certain financial and commercial institutions whose activities are historically associated with the City of London, whether or not they actually happen to be located there. Essentially this is an industrial classification; it is the definition usually employed in such discussions.[2] Four main industries are traditionally included:

1. *Banking*, comprising the domestic clearing banks, the merchant banks, the British overseas banks and the branches of Commonwealth and foreign banks.
2. *Insurance*, comprising the British insurance companies, Lloyd's underwriters and the insurance brokers.
3. *Merchanting*, comprising the organised commodity markets and the commodities section of the Baltic Exchange.
4. *Brokerage*, comprising the Baltic Exchange (other than its commodities section), the Stock Exchange and a number of smaller activities.[3]

An array of estimates

Until very recently, there were no reliable estimates at all of the invisible earnings of this quartet of industries. Primarily this was

[1] To be precise, the City of London occupies an area of 677 acres (1·06 square miles).

[2] See, e.g., Committee on Invisible Exports, *Britain's Invisible Earnings* (London: British National Export Council, for the Financial Advisory Panel on Exports, 1967) p. 187; and 'The Overseas Earnings of U.K. Financial Institutions', *Bank of England Quarterly Bulletin*, VIII 4 (Dec 1968) 402.

[3] These include mainly the gold and silver bullion markets and the services of Lloyd's Register of Shipping.

because of the substantial conceptual problems involved in making any such computations. Balance-of-payments accounts generally classify invisibles – imports and exports of services – by the nature of the transaction rather than by the nature of the industry or by the type of institution carrying out the transaction. Consequently, it has always been difficult to identify precisely the contribution made by individual industries to Britain's traditional surplus on invisibles. All early estimates were in fact no more than educated guesses – and were usually admitted as such. The first really detailed measurements appeared beginning only a little more than a decade ago. They are summarised in Table 6.1.[1]

There is an interesting history behind this series of measurements. Their genealogy apparently traces back to an exchange of lectures on the B.B.C. Third Programme in the autumn of 1957. At about this time the pound's future as an international currency was being hotly debated. The country had just gone through a serious exchange crisis: despite a substantial payments surplus, currency speculators, exploiting the mechanisms for exporting capital available in the City, had gambled on another sterling devaluation – and had almost succeeded. Many people began to ask if maintaining the international status of the pound was really worth all the trouble. With convertibility just beyond the horizon, the question at issue was whether Britain ought to retain and reinforce the sterling system, or renounce and dismantle it.[2] One expert who was most decidedly in favour of the latter alternative was Professor Alan Day, and in a Third Programme talk he dismissed the presumed major benefit of retaining the sterling system – namely, the City's overseas earnings. These, he insisted, were easy to exaggerate. 'I imagine it is unlikely that the net earnings arising from the international banking services provided by London amount to no more than £20,000,000 or at most £30,000,000 a year: and in these guesses I include various earnings which accrue indirectly.'[3] But these 'guesses' were roundly criticised in a rejoinder by Mr John Wood, a second expert and one most decidedly opposed to dismantling the

[1] For earlier estimates and guesses, see William M. Clarke, *The City's Invisible Earnings* (London: Institute of Economic Affairs, 1958) chap. 11, and *The City in the World Economy* (London: Institute of Economic Affairs, 1965) pp. 138–9.

[2] For a useful summary of the chief arguments at the time, see 'The Debate on Sterling', loc. cit. Also, see the later symposium on the sterling area in *Bulletin of the Oxford University Institute of Statistics*, xxi 4 (Nov 1959).

[3] A. C. L. Day, 'What Price the Sterling Area?', *The Listener*, lviii 1495 (21 Nov 1957) 824.

sterling system. Day's estimates, according to Wood, were 'ridiculously low'. In fact, the City's earnings were at least £110 million a year, and perhaps as high as £150 million. Wood admitted, however, that he too was frankly conjecturing.[1]

Table 6.1
Recent Estimates of the City's Invisible Earnings
(in £ millions)

Source	Year of estimate	Banking	Insurance	Merchanting	Brokerage	Total
1. Treasury (*Hansard*, 19 Dec 1957)	1956	25	40	30	30	125
2. William M. Clarke, *The City's In-Invisible Earnings* (1958)	1956	25–30	70	25–30	15–20[a]	135–50
3. William M. Clarke, *The City in the World Economy* (1965)	1963	45–50[b]	85	20–25	20–25[a]	170–85
4. Committee on Invisible Exports, *Britain's Invisible Earnings* (1967)	1965	82½	56[c] (81)	40 (85[d])	35	213½ (283½)
5. Central Statistical Office, *United Kingdom Balance of Payments 1969*	1965–8 (annual averages)	25	130	30–35	30	215–20

[a] Shipping brokers only; excludes other forms of brokerage (underwriting, etc.).
[b] Includes, for the first time, £15 million estimate for overseas earnings of bank branches abroad.
[c] Excludes income from portfolio investments.
[d] Includes U.K. import and export trade.
Sources: see text.

The considerable gap between these two estimates, which received wide publicity, illustrated just how little actually was known at the time about the City's overseas income. Yet it was agreed by all that this was a crucial datum in the debate on sterling's future. The effect therefore was catalytic. Both the Government and the City were

[1] John Wood, 'What Price the Sterling Area?', *The Listener*, LVIII 1496 (28 Nov 1957) 875–6, 886.

persuaded to try their own hands at measurement. An official estimate was produced within just a matter of weeks, in a written answer to a parliamentary question, given by the Economic Secretary to the Treasury.[1] And just a short while later a private estimate was produced as well, by William Clarke, in a study of the City's earnings commissioned by the Institute of Economic Affairs.[2] Both the Government's and Clarke's calculations were for the year 1956, and both built up their estimates by reckoning separately the earnings of the four main industries of the City. As the table shows (rows 1 and 2), the two sources showed a high degree of agreement – certainly a higher degree than Day and Wood had shown. The Government placed total earnings at about £125 million, Clarke at between £135 million and £150 million. The main difference between the two sources seems to have been in the extent of coverage of two of the City's industries, insurance and brokerage. Otherwise, they are entirely consistent.

The extent of consistency apparently satisfied the Government: no further attempts were made officially to examine the question in detail, although Government spokesmen were still prepared from time to time to guess at the City's earnings overall.[3] The Institute of Economic Affairs, on the other hand, was not prepared to rely indefinitely on these two sources alone. It was recognised that the coming of convertibility was bound to alter the environment in which the City functioned; within a relatively short time the 1956 estimates of earnings were bound to become obsolete. A few years later, therefore, Clarke was commissioned again to do a more comprehensive follow-up study of the same subject. This was published in 1965 under the title *The City in the World Economy*,[4] providing new figures for the year 1963 – figures based on data which were, broadly speaking, consistent with Clarke's earlier data for 1956 (see Table 6.1, row 3). In total, the earnings of the City were estimated to have risen to £170–£185

---

[1] *Hansard*, 19 Dec 1957.

[2] Clarke, *The City's Invisible Earnings*. I have been told on good authority that John Wood was instrumental in persuading Clarke to accept the Institute's commission.

[3] In 1963 the Central Statistical Office placed the City's overseas earnings at £150 million in 1961; this was published in the *Report of the Committee of Inquiry on Decimal Currency*, Cmnd 2145 (Sep 1963). In 1966 the Governor of the Bank of England reckoned £200 million for the year 1965. See 'Extracts from the Governor's Speech to the Confederation of British Industry, 18 May 1966', *Bank of England Quarterly Bulletin*, VI 2 (June 1966) 160.

[4] Clarke, op. cit.

million, an increase of £20 million in seven years (plus an increment of £15 million owing to the inclusion for the first time of the overseas earnings of bank branches abroad). Virtually all of the increase was recorded in the banking and insurance industries.

In 1966, yet another study was commissioned. Almost from the moment that the Labour Party had taken office in 1964, bankers and others in the City began to express misgivings about Government policy. The City was discriminated against, they said; its contributions to the balance of payments and national income were not sufficiently recognised. Clarke's 1963 estimates ought to have been adequate evidence of the City's continuing importance, but unfortunately a private analysis failed to carry enough weight to sway official policy. Therefore, what was needed was a formal inquiry backed by the City as a whole. This was how the Committee on Invisible Exports came to be formed, as an offshoot of the Financial Advisory Panel on Exports (which was the City's representative to the Government-sponsored British National Export Council). The Committee's *Report*, published in 1967, contains the most detailed examination to date of the City's invisible earnings, based on an exhaustive questionnaire survey.[1] The Committee's conclusions, which cover the year 1965, are summarised in row 4 of the table. Two alternative sets of estimates were provided, differing in the extent of coverage of the insurance and merchanting industries. The City's earnings were reckoned on one basis as between £205 million and £225 million, and on the other as between £275 million and £295 million. On either basis, the estimates were higher than any previous calculations.

In its *Report*, the Committee recommended that henceforth corresponding estimates of the City's earnings be made and published annually by an appropriate agency of the Government. This recommendation was eventually acted upon – though not without some modification of the Committee's initial conception. Concerned about the statistical difficulties involved in defining the City with any precision, the Government chose instead to estimate the overseas earnings of, simply, 'U.K. financial institutions'. These were not quite the same as the Committee's City of London. On the one hand, the Government's group of institutions did not include the branches of Commonwealth and foreign banks, even though these had been part of the Committee's definition of the banking industry; while on the other hand the Govern-

[1] Committee on Invisible Exports, op. cit., especially chap. 13. William Clarke was appointed the Committee's administrative director.

ment also included investment and unit trusts and pension funds, which the Committee and all other estimates of the City's earnings had traditionally excluded. The extent of coverage, therefore, differed considerably. The Government's first estimates, covering the years 1965-7, were published in the *Bank of England Quarterly Bulletin* for December 1968; later figures extending the estimates through 1968 were published in the balance-of-payments 'Pink Book' for 1969.[1] These figures were derived from the regular balance-of-payments data collected by the Government. The Government estimated that in the years 1965-7 the earnings of all U.K. financial institutions averaged some £255–£260 million a year (table 6.1, row 5). Excluding investment and unit trusts and pension funds, earnings averaged some £215–£220 million a year. Similar estimates are expected to appear regularly in the future.

Narrowing the range of estimates

This array of estimates gives us some broad idea of the range of magnitudes involved in the invisible earnings of the City – but it is still just that, just some idea of a range. We would prefer to identify the City's earnings more precisely. To do that, we shall have to examine some of the available estimates more closely. Specifically, we shall concentrate on the estimates by the Committee on Invisible Exports and by the Government (Table 6.1, rows 4 and 5). These two sets are the most detailed calculations available of the relevant data; they are also the most recent. By comparing them industry by industry, we ought to be able to construct a set of reliable and relatively more precise working estimates for the City of London as a whole.

1. *Banking.* The Committee and Government estimates of the overseas earnings of the banking industry are widely divergent: the former reckons £82$\frac{1}{2}$ million in 1965; the latter, only £32 million in 1965, even less in 1966 and 1967, and still only £40 million in 1968. Moreover, as Table 6.2 reveals, the Committee and Government are in relatively close agreement on only one item within the banking category – receipts for various services performed in London for foreigners (including, in particular, foreign-exchange dealing). They disagree markedly with respect to the other two items of revenue – earnings on interest account, and the profits of overseas branches and subsidiaries.

[1] 'The Overseas Earnings of U.K. Financial Institutions', loc. cit.; and Central Statistical Office, *United Kingdom Balance of Payments 1969*, pp. 59–61.

And they also disagree regarding the single item of cost listed – the interest paid on deposits taken from abroad. Unfortunately, it is not easy to reconcile these several disagreements.

There are two problems in particular. The first relates to the fact that the Government's estimate of interest income does not separate the interest earned on overseas loans and discounts expressed in foreign currencies from the interest earned on overseas loans and discounts in sterling, as the Committee's estimate does. And similarly, the Government's estimate of interest payments does not separate the interest paid on foreign-currency deposits from the interest paid on sterling deposits, as the Committee's does. Furthermore, to make matters worse, the Government merges its joint estimate of interest earnings together with the profits of branches and subsidiaries abroad; and analogously, merges its joint estimate of interest payments together with the profits of branches and subsidiaries of Commonwealth and foreign banks earned in the U.K. and remitted abroad. These latter profits are not deducted in the Committee's calculations.

The second problem relates to the fact that the Government includes in its estimate of interest payments *all* the interest paid to foreigners on their deposits, whereas the Committee does not. The latter's estimate of interest on sterling deposits includes only an amount paid on what the Committee regards as 'working balances', defined as 'the level of balances which overseas traders and banks need to maintain in London in order to conduct their day-to-day business'.[1] In practice (as we saw in the previous chapter), these are assumed to comprise 25 per cent of the total; the remainder of the sterling deposits are considered to be a form of investment in the United Kingdom. Likewise, the Committee's estimate of interest on foreign-currency deposits includes only an amount paid on funds which are thought ultimately to be re-lent abroad, excluding funds thought to be invested in Britain. In practice, the amount paid on the latter category of funds is assumed to be equal to the difference between the amount paid on the former and the total amount of interest earned on foreign-currency loans and discounts. In other words, interest income on foreign-currency credits and interest payments on foreign-currency deposits are assumed to cancel out.[2]

How shall we resolve these problems? Which source should we accept? As indicated in Chapter 3, as a general rule I shall always try to err on the side of overstated benefits or understated costs, rather than

[1] Committee on Invisible Exports, op. cit., p. 190.
[2] Ibid., p. 191.

the reverse. Accordingly, in this particular situation I shall rely upon the basic estimates of the Committee on Invisible Exports for all three revenue items, since in each instance the Committee's figure, for 1965, is larger than the corresponding estimate by the Bank of England for the same year. However, I shall also have to modify each of the Committee's figures in the light of subsequent developments as revealed by the Government's estimates for the later years 1966–8.

Table 6.2

The Invisible Earnings of the Banking Industry
(in £ millions)

	Committee on Invisible Exports 1965	Bank of England				
		1965	1966	1967	1968	Average
Services	19·5 ⎫	16	18	20	25	20
Interest on sterling loans and discounts	36·0 ⎪					
Interest on foreign-currency loans and discounts	73·5 ⎬	98	97	96	127	105
Overseas branches and subsidiaries	37·5 ⎭					
Less: Interest payments on sterling deposits	−10·5[a] ⎫					
Interest payments on foreign-currency deposits	−73·5[b] ⎬	−82[c]	−99[c]	−97[c]	112[c]	98[c]
Total	82·5	32	16	19	40	25[d]

[a] Includes only estimated interest paid on 'working balances'.
[b] Excludes estimated interest paid on deposits invested in the U.K.
[c] Includes the profits of foreign-bank branches and subsidiaries in the U.K.
[d] Detail does not add to total because of rounding.
Sources: Committee on Invisible Exports, *Britain's Invisible Earnings*, chap. 13; and Central Statistical Office, *United Kingdom Balance of Payments 1969*, p. 60.

There is little difficulty about the figure for services. Extrapolating the Committee's 1965 estimate forward to 1968 on the basis of the rising trend in the Government's figures, and rounding to the nearest quinquevalent, we obtain an average of about £25 million a year over the four-year period. Likewise, there is little difficulty about the figure for overseas branches and subsidiaries. Extrapolating the Committee's 1965 estimate forward to 1968 on the basis of the movement suggested by the Government's figures, and rounding, we obtain an annual average of roughly £40 million. But there is considerable difficulty about the figures for the interest account. Following the procedure just applied to overseas profits, we may reckon that earnings on sterling credits also averaged annually some £40 million in 1965–8, and that earnings on foreign-currency credits averaged some £80 million. The question is: what deductions should we make for interest payments?

Clearly, we do not wish to deduct the interest paid on deposits expressed in pounds. This has already been included in the analysis of the interest cost of sterling in the previous chapter. On the other hand, we most certainly do wish to deduct the interest paid on deposits expressed in foreign currencies, for otherwise the invisible earnings of the banking industry would be greatly exaggerated. Yet deducting the one and not the other might seem to be an inconsistent procedure. In fact, it is not inconsistent. If we assume, as the Committee on Invisible Exports does, that interest income on foreign-currency credits and interest payments on foreign-currency deposits are roughly matching, then the procedure cannot affect our estimate of total bank interest income: nor, since we may assume that the foreign-currency activities of the banks have nothing to do with sterling *per se*, can the procedure affect our estimates (to come) of the proportion of interest income which is dependent on the international use of the pound. In effect, what the procedure does is to limit the estimate of bank interest income to the gross amount of interest earned on sterling credits only; and since the gross amount of interest paid on sterling deposits has already been included elsewhere (Chapter 5), neither can this affect the overall analysis in Part Two of the pound's benefits and costs. Therefore, this is the procedure I shall follow. I assume that earnings on interest account averaged some £40 million a year in 1965–8.

What about the profits of branches and subsidiaries of Commonwealth and foreign banks? According to the data compiled by the Committee on Invisible Exports, these amounted to approximately £8 million in 1965.[1] Since they are all remitted abroad, logically it might appear most appropriate to deduct all of them from our estimate of the income which actually accrues to the City of London. Indeed, that is precisely the reasoning behind the procedure chosen by the Government in its own calculations. However, in our calculations most of the £8 million has already been deducted, since by far the largest part of the total derives not from sterling-based activities but rather from

[1] Ibid., p. 80.

foreign-currency activities – and these, following the Committee's example, have already been netted out. Consequently, there seems no need to make any further adjustment for this figure now.

In conclusion, therefore, total banking earnings in the period under review appear to have been of the order of some £105 million a year: services, £25 million; interest, £40 million; and overseas branches and subsidiaries, £40 million. Of course, these are just *direct* earnings. The figures ignore certain possibly substantial *indirect* social benefits accruing from banking activity. In particular, they ignore the 'considerable aid to exports arising from the City connection: whether as the result of accumulated goodwill or mere lethargy and habit, the financial services of the City undoubtedly help the British exporter to keep his market'.[1] Likewise, the financial services of the City undoubtedly help the British importer as well, and perhaps also the British shipper. However, regrettable though it may be, there really is just no way of knowing just how large these second-order effects of banking might be. Consequently, we have no choice but to follow the standard procedure of omitting them from our discussion here. Our estimate of banking earnings will have to remain limited to direct earnings only.

2. *Insurance.* In contrast to their divergent estimates of the banking industry, the Committee and Government estimates of the overseas earnings of the insurance industry are highly consistent. Both sources figure that in 1965 the British insurance companies and brokers and Lloyd's underwriters together earned a total of roughly £80 million on their overseas transactions. This comprised the premium income (less the cost of claims) on policies written in Britain on behalf of foreigners; net earnings on reinsurance business; the profits of branches and subsidiary or associate companies abroad; and income from overseas portfolio investment. Apparently 1965 was a bad year for the insurance industry: the incidence of Hurricane 'Betsy' in the United States in September led to heavy payments claims overseas.[2] But the following years were better, with earnings rising to as much as £177 million in 1968. I see no reason for not accepting as accurate the Government's claim that the gross overseas earnings of the insurance

---

[1] 'No Backsliding on Sterling', *The Banker*, cvii 383 (Dec 1957) 766. See also 'The Overseas Earnings of U.K. Financial Institutions', loc. cit., pp. 404–5; and Paul Bareau, 'The Importance of Invisibles', *The Banker*, cxvii 501 (Nov 1967) 927–32.

[2] Committee on Invisible Exports, op. cit., pp. 150, 192.

industry averaged annually £130 million over the four-year period.[1]

3. *Merchanting*. There is some difference between the Committee and Government estimates of the overseas earnings of the merchanting industry. The Committee reckons that in 1965 these added up to between £35–£45 million, including both the foreign income of the various organised commodity markets and the commodities section of the Baltic Exchange, and the profits earned by merchants on re-exports from the United Kingdom. The Government, by contrast, places the former at £25–£28 million in recent years, and the latter at only £5–£10 million – yielding a total just at the lower end of the Committee's range. However, we are adopting the methodology of erring on the side of overstated benefits; besides we want to allow for secular growth of merchanting earnings. Therefore, we shall assume that the invisible income of this industry averaged annually £45 million over the years 1965–8.

4. *Brokerage*. The Committee and Government estimates of the overseas earnings of the brokerage industry are highly consistent. The Committee places the 1965 total at between £30 million and £35 million – including perhaps £25 million earned by members of the Baltic Exchange, £3–£4 million earned by the stockbrokers and jobbers of the Stock Exchange, and £5 million earned by other related activities (mainly the gold and silver bullion markets and Lloyd's Register of Shipping). This coincides neatly with the Government's estimated total of roughly £30 million for the years 1965–8. This is the figure we shall rely on in our subsequent discussion.

5. *The City as a whole*. In summary, this gives us a set of working estimates of the invisible earnings of the City as a whole that are reliable and relatively precise. These estimates are as follows (annual averages for the years 1965–8):

Banking	£105 million
Insurance	130 million
Merchanting	45 million
Brokerage	30 million
The City	£310 million

[1] The Committee on Invisible Exports raises the question of whether the insurance industry's income from overseas portfolio investment ought properly to be included as an invisible earning of the City, on the grounds that if this income is included, then it would be difficult to exclude similar income earned by investment trusts, pension funds and other financial institutions. I disagree; the analogy is weak. The latter's overseas portfolio reflects their ordinary investment

II. NET EARNINGS

The sum of £310 million a year is not small: the invisible earnings of the City really are quite vast. And the City would not have us forget that fact, either.[1] But it is important to keep figures like this one in perspective. Three hundred and ten million pounds accounted for less than one-tenth of all invisible credits earned by Britain annually (on average) during the period 1965–8. It represented less than 6 per cent of annual average visible exports during the period, and less than 1 per cent of national income. The City's earnings may be large, but they do not appear quite so large when compared with some other economic magnitudes.

And yet for all that, the fact remains that £310 million a year is a lot of money. But a question also remains: how much of this amount actually represents a real gain to Britain from the international roles of sterling? The reader is reminded that these are the *gross* earnings of the City. They do not all add up to a social benefit of the pound's use as an international currency. That benefit is really much smaller. In the first place, not all of the City's gross earnings are directly dependent on the international status of sterling; only a fraction of them would actually be lost if the pound were to become a purely domestic currency. Moreover, not even all of this fraction of income would be lost to Britain irretrievably. Only a portion would be so lost, a portion equal to the *net* earnings of the City – equal, that is, to the difference between

---

activity. The insurance industry's overseas portfolio, by contrast, relates directly to its overseas business: its investments abroad reflect its need to match the diversity of the potential foreign-currency claims of its overseas customers.

[1] The original Committee on Invisible Exports recommended that 'some permanent organisation should be responsible for keeping a continuing watch on the whole field of invisibles' (op. cit., p. 259). This recommendation was soon acted upon. Early in 1968 a new, permanent Committee on Invisible Exports was formed 'to suggest, and where possible implement, measures for the encouragement of "invisible exports"'. (Once again, William Clarke was appointed the Committee's administrative director.) According to a press handout (Dec 1968), the new Committee intends, as one of its principal tasks, 'various efforts to publicise the size and widespread nature of Britain's invisible exports and their major contribution to the balance of payments'. For an example of one such effort, see 'Invisible Exports', *The Times*, 21 Mar 1969, supplement, pp. i–viii. Early in 1970, the private members of the Committee (that is, excluding government representatives) submitted a report to the Chancellor of the Exchequer, recommending important new tax incentives to further stimulate invisible exports. See *The Economist*, 10 Jan 1970, p. 56.

the gross income of services which are dependent on international sterling, and what the income of these services would be in their next-best alternative domestic use (see Chapter 2).

Our problem, therefore, is to reduce the gross figure of £310 million to the net income of the City – which is the real gain to Britain from the pound's international functions. We shall do this in two stages. First, we shall estimate the fraction of the gross total actually dependent on the international status of sterling, and then we shall estimate the net difference between this figure and what the income on these services would be in their next-best alternative domestic use. Finally, we shall have to allocate the real gain to Britain among the several functions of the pound.

Dependence on sterling

Our first stage is to ask what fraction of the City's gross earnings are directly dependent on the international status of sterling. In other words, how much of the overall total of £310 million would actually be lost if the pound were to become a purely domestic currency?[1] I shall attempt to answer this question by again examining separately each of the City's four main industries.

1. *Banking.* Superficially, of all the City's industries, banking might be thought to be the *most* directly dependent on the international use of the pound: sterling is its natural tool; the history of foreign activity of the clearing banks, merchant banks and overseas banks is intimately connected with sterling's earlier globalisation and later regionalisation.[2] Yet on closer inspection, only a comparatively small fraction of the industry's invisible income appears really to require the support of an international currency. Even if the pound were to cease altogether being used for international purposes, I submit that not much more than one-third of all banking earnings would be affected.

The banking industry's invisible income (some £105 million a year)

[1] Once again, the reader is reminded that this is simply an analytical device (see Chapter 3). In actuality, it is of course quite unrealistic to assume that the pound might suddenly, in a very short time, shed its international functions and become a purely domestic currency. In fact, any decline of sterling's international status would normally be expected to occur gradually over a rather long period measured in years – if not in decades.

[2] See above, Chapter 4; and also Clarke, *The City in the World Economy*, chap. 2; and David Williams, 'The Evolution of the Sterling System', in C. R.

is derived from three sources: (a) services performed in London for foreigners; (b) interest account; and (c) the profits of overseas branches and subsidiaries (see Table 6.2). Of these only the second is very closely related to the roles of the pound as an international currency – specifically, to its role as a transactions currency. The banks earn roughly £40 million a year from the provision of sterling credits to non-residents. Most of these credits are provided by way of short-term loans, advances and discounts. Almost all are for the financing of overseas trade, either between the United Kingdom and other sterling-area countries, within the sterling area, or between the United Kingdom or sterling-area countries and the rest of the world.[1] The earnings from this source are therefore directly dependent on the use of sterling as an international exchange intermediary.

What would happen to these earnings if sterling were to cease being used as an international exchange intermediary? By definition there would no longer be a significant foreign demand for sterling trade credits; the volume of loans, advances and discounts in pounds would certainly decline. But this does not mean that the banks' interest earnings would necessarily disappear. In this connection it is important to distinguish between the short run and the long run. In the short run, income on interest account might very well be maintained. For there would still be a significant foreign demand for trade credits of some kind: commerce would still have to be financed (and invoiced and transacted) in some currency. Most probably this currency would be the Euro-dollar, in which case London's banks would be especially favourably placed, since the City is generally acknowledged to be the functional centre of the Euro-dollar market.[2] Moreover, London's banks have expanded into the Euro-dollar market to a considerable

---

Whittlesey and J. S. G. Wilson (eds), *Essays in Money and Banking* (Oxford: Oxford University Press, 1968) pp. 266–97.

[1] The exchange-control authority for the use of sterling credits between non-sterling-area countries was withdrawn in October 1968 (see Chapter 4).

[2] It is estimated that about 80 per cent of all Euro-dollar transactions go through London. 'The Euro-Dollar Market: What it Means for London', *The Banker*, CXIX 522 (Aug 1969) 774. See also W. F. Crick, 'The City and the Pound: Yesterday, Today and Tomorrow', *The Banker*, CXVII 498 (Aug 1967) 700–7; George Bolton, 'Euro-dollar Efficiency Pays Off', *The Times*, 21 Nov 1968, supplement, p. iv; and Ira O. Scott, Jr, 'That Controversial Euro-Dollar Market', *National Westminster Bank Quarterly Review* (Aug 1969) pp. 4, 16. The Euro-dollar market apparently began in 1957 when, as a consequence of extreme pressure on sterling at the time, British banks were prohibited from

extent.[1] Consequently, there seems no reason why the banks should not be able to continue, for a time at least, to accommodate the trade-financing demands of their traditional customers.

Inevitably, however, over the longer term the change away from the pound would gradually tend to loosen financial ties to the City of London. Dollar working balances would replace sterling working balances. These could remain in London, but they might just as easily be shifted elsewhere – and if they are, then in time the loosening of ties would probably lead to a shifting of banking connections also. In the longer run, therefore, some trade-financing business would probably be transferred elsewhere. And indeed, even if most of the business remains in London, a good part of it would probably be transferred from British to non-British banks – in particular, to the American banks in the City. American banks have been crowding into London at an accelerating pace; near the end of 1969 some twenty-nine U.S. banking enterprises were represented directly in the City with branches or offices, and at least twenty more were represented indirectly through joint operations.[2] Not unexpectedly, the American banks tend to pre-dominate in the business of the Euro-dollar market, since effectively they have access to virtually unlimited resources in dollars. They can always rely on their head offices as lenders of last resort:

> That the American banks should have the lion's share of the Euro-dollar business is surely not surprising, because they are dollar banks. Furthermore,

---

financing trade between third countries in pounds. In order to preserve a lucrative business, the banks offered the same financing facilities in dollars instead, attracting the dollars by offering interest on short-term deposits. See 'The Euro-Dollar Market: What it Means for London', loc. cit., pp. 778–9; and Richard N. Cooper, *The Economics of Interdependence: Economic Policy in the Atlantic Community* (New York: McGraw-Hill, for the Council on Foreign Relations, 1968) p. 118.

[1] See, e.g., M. S. Mendelsohn, 'British Overseas Banks: No Place Like Home', *The Banker*, CXVIII 512 (Oct 1968) 880–4; and George K. Young, *Merchant Banking: Practice and Prospects* (London: Weidenfeld & Nicolson, 1966) chap. 3.

[2] 'Foreign Banks in London – Annual Review', *The Banker* CXIX 524 (Oct 1969) 1063. For discussions of the American banking invasion of London, see Richard S. Vokey, 'Impact of the U.S. Banks on British Banking', *The Banker*, CXIX 524 (Oct 1969) 1053–63; L. S. Thornton, 'Why the American Banks Come to London', *The Banker*, CXVIII 512 (Oct 1968) 895–903; Robin Pringle, 'Why American Banks Go Overseas', *The Banker*, CXVI 489 (Nov 1966) 770–85; and Philip Saunders, Jr. 'American Banks in London's Euro-dollar Market', *National Banking Review*, IV 1 (Sep 1966) 21–8.

the banks concerned are all large, if not very large, institutions. This combination of size and the fact that they are dealing in their own native currency makes it easier for them in comparison with big U.K. clearing banks and other major banks . . . who are not dealing in their own currency.[1]

The British banks in London have done their utmost to overcome this handicap of limited dollar resources. Some have formed partnerships with U.S. banks, or have sold them minority shares of their equity.[2] Others have established stand-by dollar credit facilities with American bank branches in London, or with their head offices in the United States. However, it is manifest that there are limits to devices such as these. There is potentially a real cost of partnership or minority shareholding, namely the possible dilution of management control. Likewise, there is in fact a real cost of stand-by credit facilities, namely the necessary commitment fee, which sometimes may be quite substantial. Inevitably, therefore, the British banks have remained at a competitive disadvantage in the London Euro-dollar market. The American banks are estimated to account for roughly one-half of all the Euro-dollar business done in the City today; and other foreign banks are thought to account for perhaps one-quarter more. That leaves only about 25 per cent of the total to be shared among the clearing banks, merchant banks and overseas banks.[3]

Of course, a very large part of the Euro-dollar activity of American banks in London is limited to repatriations to head offices back home. These transactions have nothing at all to do with the real business of the market – namely, trade financing. Accordingly, with respect to this business alone, British banks are much more prominent in Euro-dollar lending than their 25 per cent share of the overall total would suggest.[4] However, this remains so only because, prior to devaluation in 1967, the American banks largely refrained from competing directly

[1] Cyprian J. Bridge, 'U.S. Banks in London: Then and Now', *The Banker*, cxviii 512 (Oct 1968) 911. The profits of American (and other foreign) bank branches and subsidiaries in the United Kingdom which accrue to head offices or parent banks abroad are of course not included in this chapter's estimate of the invisible earnings of the City.

[2] 'Foreign Banks in London – Annual Review', *The Banker*, cxviii 512 (Oct 1968) 915; and *The Economist*, 4 Jan 1969, p. 44.

[3] 'The Euro-Currency Business of Banks in London', *Bank of England Quarterly Bulletin*, x 1 (Mar 1970) 30.

[4] One recent estimate suggests that British banks share about equally with the American banks in the business of Euro-dollar company lending. See 'Foreign Banks in London – Annual Review' (Oct 1969), loc. cit., p. 1077.

for the traditional clientele of the U.K. industry. Since 1967, American self-restraint has been crumbling – and as it has, British banks, given the handicap of their limited dollar resources, have found it increasingly difficult to prevent the U.S. banks from attracting away a considerable proportion of their overseas customers.

Suppose, then, that sterling were to cease altogether being used for international purposes. We may assume that most trade financing which presently is done in pounds would move over to a Euro-dollar basis; and we may assume that the British banks would do their utmost to retain their traditional clientele. But judging from current experience we should not expect that in the longer run they would be able to hold on to more than one-quarter – or, at most, one-third – of their foreign loan business. As much as £25 million a year of overseas interest earnings could eventually be lost to the industry.

However, this is the *only* source of bank earnings that is so closely dependent on the support of sterling. The other two sources of income are much less closely related to the international functions of the pound. Roughly £25 million a year is earned from the various services performed in London on behalf of foreign customers. These include all the usual ancillary international banking activities, such as dealing in foreign exchange; providing information and advice to facilitate overseas trade; making foreign remittances; registering and new issue business; and handling overseas securities. Significantly, none of these activities by its nature requires the propinquity of a strong international currency. What each does require is competitiveness, efficiency and widespread international connections. British banks, owing to their long history of foreign involvement, happen to be favourably endowed in all these respects, and that is the usual reason why so many non-residents tend to rely on them for international banking services – because they are expert and experienced, not necessarily because sterling is their regular working currency.

To be sure, at the margin there must be some customers who employ British banks for these services for just one reason – because the banks are also the source of their trade or other financing. Shift the source of their credits and they will shift their incidental business too. But the essential point is that the margin in fact probably is quite a bit narrower than one might think. After all, even if the pound were to become a purely domestic currency, there would still be the same foreign demand for international banking services – the same need to deal in foreign exchange (though now there would be more dealing in dollars and less in sterling), the same need for information and advice to facilitate overseas trade, the same need to make foreign remittances, and so on. And while British banks may be competitively handicapped by a lack of dollar resources in making credits, they are not at all handicapped by a lack of expertise or experience or connections in providing services. Indeed, in the latter respects they are probably at a competitive advantage vis-à-vis their American rivals in London, most of whom have only very recently entered the field of international banking. My guess, therefore, is that at most perhaps only 20 per cent of the British industry's total earnings from this source (that is, £5 million a year) is directly attributable to the use of the pound as an international currency.

Finally, the industry earns roughly £40 million a year from the profits of its overseas branches and subsidiaries.[1] This income is not closely related to the pound's international functions either. True, historically there was a close relationship: when they first began to be established abroad, foreign branches and subsidiaries generally were concerned exclusively with the financing and servicing of international trade (which was predominately with Britain) and with the transmission of British investment funds. Essentially they were British bank offices that happened to be situated outside of Britain: there was a genuine dependence on the globalisation of sterling. However, times have changed, and as they have changed so too has the nature of the industry overseas been altered.[2] From a narrow preoccupation with trade and investment, the foreign branches and subsidiaries of British

---

[1] Most overseas branches and subsidiaries are owned by the five principal British overseas banks (which are banks registered in the United Kingdom, where the central management is located and the capital largely held, but which do their main business overseas): Barclays Bank D.C.O.; Bank of London and South America; Chartered Bank; National and Grindlays Bank; and Standard Bank. (In May 1969 Chartered and Standard announced their intention to merge). To this group are often added Australia and New Zealand Bank; English, Scottish and Australian Bank; and Hong Kong and Shanghai Banking Corporation. Together these eight institutions have more than 5200 branches abroad. The clearing banks and merchant banks in general have only a few branches or subsidiary offices abroad. Their overseas transactions are normally handled through reciprocal arrangements with a world-wide system of correspondent banks. See Committee on Invisible Exports, op. cit., pp. 68–74; and H. D. Cayley, 'British Overseas Banks Find New Pastures', *Euromoney* (Sep 1969) p. 13.

[2] See, e.g., Lord Aldington, 'Growing Nations are Nourished', *The Times*, 21 Nov 1968, supplement, p. v; and Lord Carrington, 'City Remains Chief Centre for Expansion', ibid., p. viii.

banks gradually have broadened their scope to encompass the entire range of regular banking activities; in fact, even in so far as they are still involved in trade financing, they now use other currencies, including especially the Euro-dollar, as much as they use the pound, as a vehicle for commercial credits. Today they are essentially full-service local banks that just happen to be British-owned. Their profits are mainly dependent on developments in the local economics within which they are situated, not on the shrinking status of sterling. Perhaps only 20 per cent of earnings are still directly related to the financing and servicing of trade, and probably not much more than half of that still requires the support of the pound – say, some £5 million a year.

2. *Insurance.* The British insurance industry, which is made up of some 400 British companies plus Lloyd's underwriters and brokers, collectively comprises the largest international insurance market in the world.[1] However, as a market the industry is largely independent of the position of the pound. Of all the City's industries, this one is undoubtedly the least dependent on the continuing support of international sterling. Currency does not matter in this context. What does matter is established position, reputation, efficiency and contacts. There is no evidence, for instance, that the Swiss insurance industry is handicapped in any way in world markets by the fact that the Swiss franc is seldom used in international transactions; nor is there any evidence that the American industry is specially advantaged in any way because the dollar tends to be used so widely. But there is considerable evidence that the British industry is both efficient and reliable – in many ways its services are unique – and until now this has meant, as we have seen, a high and growing level of overseas income (£130 million a year in 1965–8). Hardly any of this amount is earned from the insuring of current trade or other transactions dependent on the international functions of sterling. Accordingly, there seems no reason why this income should not remain high and growing in the future, even if the pound ceases to be used for international functions. My presumption is that the industry would be unaffected by such a development.[2]

[1] Clarke, *The City in the World Economy*, chap. 5; and Committee on Invisible Exports, op. cit., chap. 9.

[2] The Committee on Invisible Exports concluded that 'it is clear that British insurance business overseas is now dependent on the efficiency of the insurance companies and Lloyd's, and the way they conduct their business, both in London

3. *Merchanting*. By contrast, the merchanting industry probably *would* be affected by such a development – and affected significantly. To be capable of functioning effectively, organised commodity markets require a completely stable unit of account and acceptable exchange intermediary. In other words, they require a strong international currency. We know that the pound used to be a strong international currency; indeed, its globalisation in the nineteenth century was a prime cause of London's emergence then as a merchanting centre. But we also know that the pound is no longer as strong as it once was, and this has already weakened somewhat the international position of the merchanting industry. It is difficult to see how that position could not but be further weakened if sterling were to become a purely domestic currency.

To be sure, historically the development of London's merchanting industry reflected more than just the globalisation of sterling – much more, in fact.[1] At least as important was the leading position of Britain itself as a trader of primary products. The country was the world's largest consumer of imported foodstuffs and raw materials; in addition, London was well placed to function as an entrepôt, being located directly on the main shipping routes from the commodity-producing areas of America, Asia and Africa to the main consuming areas of Europe. Not surprisingly, therefore, most organised international commodity markets came to be established in the City during the course of the nineteenth century. These included three types of markets: sales rooms, auction rooms and commodity exchanges proper.[2] Until 1939, London was unrivalled as a merchanting centre.

The Second World War and its aftermath threatened materially to damage London's leading position as a merchanting centre. Most markets were closed 'for the duration', and by the time they were able to reopen in the late 1940s and early 1950s numerous competing markets were already established elsewhere. Furthermore, Britain itself was reduced in importance as a consumer of primary products, as well

---

and in overseas markets, and not on the fact that sterling is an international currency' (op. cit., p. 252). See also 'The Debate on Sterling', loc. cit., p. 80; and Andrew Shonfield, *British Economic Policy since the War* (London: Penguin Books, 1958) pp. 157–8.

[1] For a valuable discussion of the important elements in the evolution of London's merchanting industry, see Graham Rees and Jack Wiseman, 'London's Commodity Markets', *Lloyds Bank Review*, no. 91 (Jan 1969) pp. 22–45.

[2] Committee on Invisible Exports, op. cit., pp. 104–6.

as an entrepôt for trade between producers and other consumers. Yet London's markets have managed to preserve their global pre-eminence. Most other markets are concerned mainly with domestic demand or domestic supply. The City's markets, by contrast, are still overwhelmingly international, and in the variety of commodities with which they deal they are still collectively the most important in the world. 'London has continued to throw off foreign competition, even through periods of severe stress.'[1]

In good part, London's ability to throw off foreign competition in the post-war period has been the result of special Government efforts to preserve the usefulness of sterling to the industry, in spite of the trials and tribulations of the pound. As soon as the war ended, the authorities turned to the task of reopening the commodities markets. There was a problem, however – the pound's inconvertibility. Convertibility for overseas customers was essential if London's markets were ever to regain their position as truly global exchanges: facilities had to be provided to foreign dealers for making and receiving payments freely in settlement of contracts. But convertibility was also potentially dangerous, in view of Britain's precarious foreign-exchange position. The problem was finally resolved by the introduction of special exchange-control arrangements known as Commodity Market Schemes, especially from 1951 onwards. By these means, years before formal convertibility in 1958, London's commodity markets were able to provide what amounted to virtually the same thing for their overseas customers. The pound remained useful as a medium of exchange.[2]

Official efforts were also responsible for the pound remaining useful as a unit of account. Owing to the frequent crises of the British balance of payments, sterling was very often under the threat of devaluation or depreciation. At such times stability in trading was difficult; the pound could not function as the invariant standard of value that commodity markets require. Nor could the authorities provide an invariant standard of value. But they could provide the next-best alternative to it, which is a smoothly functioning forward-exchange market, permitting dealings in the markets to take place with a kind of informal exchange guarantee attached. From early in the 1950s the Government encouraged the redevelopment of forward-exchange facilities in

---

[1] Clarke, *The City in the World Economy*, p. 83.

[2] Ibid., pp. 80–2; and 'U.K. Commodity Markets', *Bank of England Quarterly Bulletin*, IV 3 (Sep 1964) 194–5.

London.[1] From early in the 1960s, in addition, for a variety of reasons, the authorities even began to intervene regularly to cheapen artificially the cost of forward cover in sterling – thus offering a kind of officially subsidised exchange insurance benefiting, among others, dealers in the commodity markets.

So long as sterling remained useful as exchange intermediary and accounting unit, London was able to continue to maintain its position as a merchanting centre. But this position was rudely jolted by the devaluation of 1967. Traders in many of the markets were seriously affected, particularly those traders who had contracted to buy produce in sterling-area countries in currencies that were not devalued along with the pound;[2] and since devaluation, dealings in sterling have been much more expensive now that the Government is no longer so willing to subsidise the cost of forward sterling cover. In many of the City's markets there is increasing pressure to shift dealings from pounds to a dollar basis. One market, the diamond market, already has shifted. Others are thinking of it, and may follow before long.[3]

Suppose that all of the markets did in fact shift to a dollar basis, so that sterling were no longer used at all in this connection. What would be the result? Inevitably, as in the banking industry, the change away from the pound would gradually tend to loosen financial ties to the City of London, and in time this would probably lead to the shifting of some markets as well. The United States, after all, is a more logical location for many international commodity markets: America, not Britain, is now the world's leading trader of primary products. Of course, not all of the commodity markets would be likely to leave London. Many (such as cocoa, diamonds, rubber and tea) involve com-

---

[1] 'The U.K. Exchange Control: A Short History', *Bank of England Quarterly Bulletin*, VII 3 (Sep 1967) 256. Aiding the commodity markets, of course, was only *one* of the Government's motives in encouraging the redevelopment of the forward-exchange market. In fact, in so far as strictly intra-sterling-area trade was concerned, the Government *refused* to permit traders to cover their transactions forward in dollars.

[2] Rees and Wiseman, loc. cit., p. 43; and John Woodland, 'Commodity Markets Second to None', *The Times*, 21 March 1969, supplement, p. vii.

[3] Even the foreign-exchange market has come under pressure to shift dealings to a dollar basis, at least for quotation purposes. After the 1967 devaluation there was a growing demand for foreign-exchange brokers to quote currency cross-rates – that is, to quote various currencies against each other instead of simply against sterling. Effectively, this would mean quoting most currencies against the dollar. The brokers were reported to have accepted this demand in principle in the autumn of 1969. See *The Times*, 17 Oct 1969, p. 30.

modities whose production is concentrated almost entirely within sterling-area countries and in the hands of sterling-area companies. Britain is in any event likely to maintain strong trading connections along these lines. Besides, many of London's markets are highly efficient and might well survive and persist solely on the basis of their superior competitiveness. Merchanting activity often depends more on personal goodwill than on any other single factor. A good part of the industry might therefore remain right where it is and continue to earn invisible income for the City. But this income would almost certainly be reduced from what it is now.[1] My guess is that it would eventually amount to no more than two-thirds of the present £45 million a year – that is, to no more than £30 million.

4. *Brokerage*. Most parts of the brokerage industry also are significantly dependent on the support of international sterling. Certainly this is true of the largest part of the industry, the Baltic Exchange, which is the world's leading market for the chartering of ships and aircraft (and also for the purchase and sale of ships).[2] Essentially the Baltic functions just like any other type of commodity market, except that its major commodity is a service rather than a good. Thus, like any other market, the Baltic requires a completely stable unit of account and acceptable international exchange intermediary in order to be able to function effectively. Were sterling to cease being used for international purposes, the Baltic would probably continue to make money. But once again, the loosening of financial ties to the City of London would inevitably lead to the shifting of some business elsewhere. This danger has been remarked by the Committee on Invisible Exports:

One example is the foreign shipowner who fixes his vessels for cross trades with freights payable in sterling in London to the account of the shipowner's London brokers. This means the keeping of accounts for the foreign shipowner in the office of the London broker, which over the years, inevitably leads to a strengthening of ties between the shipowner and his London broker, and the likelihood of further business coming via London. If sterling became purely a

[1] Others have reached the same conclusion. See, e.g., Committee on Invisible Exports, op. cit., pp. 252–3; 'The Debate on Sterling', loc. cit., p. 80; and Shonfield, op. cit., p. 158.

[2] The Baltic Exchange was opened in its present form in 1903. Its full name is the Baltic Mercantile and Shipping Exchange Ltd. It also has a commodities section for the trading of grain, and also oil and oil seeds; however, this section is treated as part of the merchanting industry. See Clarke, *The City in the World Economy*, chap. 7; and Committee on Invisible Exports, op. cit., pp. 134–6.

national currency leaving the U.S. dollar as the sole world currency these same fixtures might well be fixed with freights payable in New York in U.S. dollars to the account of the shipowner's New York agents, inevitably leading to a loosening of the ties between the shipowner and his London broker, and giving an encouragement to the New York agent in his competitive efforts.[1]

By the same token, the loosening of financial ties to the City would inevitably lead to some shifting of most other types of brokerage business too. The overseas business of the Stock Exchange, for instance, would undoubtedly suffer some decline if sterling were no longer held widely as an asset currency (though it should be noted that the extent of the decline would be limited by a unique rule which permits London brokers, on behalf of their clients, to deal in any stock quoted in any currency on any other stock exchange in the world). In this category only the income of Lloyd's Register of Shipping is largely independent of the international use of the pound.[2] I would suppose, therefore, that as in the merchanting industry, so too in the brokerage industry, at least one-third of current invisible income eventually would be lost if sterling were to become a purely domestic currency.[3]

5. *The City as a whole.* In summary, the income of the City as a whole which is directly dependent on the international status of sterling appears to be considerably smaller than its overall gross income. Invisible earnings in the square mile are much less closely related to the pound's use as an international currency than is often supposed.[4] Only about one-third of the invisible income of the banking, merchanting and brokerage industries would be likely to be affected if present monetary arrangements were altered, and probably none of insurance income. That gives us a total figure of approximately £60 million a year, less than one-fifth of the City's gross earnings:

[1] Committee on Invisible Exoprts, op. cit., p. 251.

[2] Lloyd's Register of Shipping is an independent, non-commercial society whose aim is the establishment of standards of construction and maintenance, and the provision of a technical service to enable owners to maintain such standards. It surveys ships and also many kinds of industrial structures. Ibid., p. 137.

[3] See also 'The Debate on Sterling', loc. cit., p. 80. But cf. Shonfield, op. cit., p. 157.

[4] One source has suggested that as much as two-thirds of the City's invisible earnings may be attributable to the use of sterling as an international currency. See 'The Debate on Sterling', loc. cit., p. 80. Other sources, however, have been more cautious. See, e.g., Shonfield, op. cit., pp. 158–9; and John Cooper, *A Suitable Case for Treatment: What to do About the Balance of Payments* (London: Penguin Books, 1968) pp. 117–19, 274–5.

Banking (services, £5 million; interest, £25 million; branches and subsidiaries, £5 million)	£35 million
Insurance	nil
Merchanting	15 million
Brokerage	10 million
The City	£60 million

From gross to net

To measure the *net* earnings of the City, we need to compare two economic magnitudes: first, the current income of services which are directly dependent on international sterling; and second, an estimate of what the income of these services would be in their next-best alternative domestic use. The difference between these two magnitudes is the actual gain to Britain from sterling's several international functions.

We already know what the income is of services directly dependent on international sterling. It is £60 million a year, and we are probably safe in assuming that the figure will remain at least that high in the foreseeable future. What we do not yet know is what the income of these services would be if the pound were to become a purely domestic currency. What would these services earn in their next-best alternative domestic use?

To begin with, we can be quite certain that they would earn *something*. Otherwise, we would have to assume that there is no useful alternative domestic employment at all for the resources allocated to providing such services to foreigners, a condition of zero marginal cost – which is unlikely. True, there is much specificity about the resources of the City. Many of its workers have invested considerable time and effort in acquiring their present specialised skills; moreover, much of its physical plant and equipment has been designed with very precise commercial purposes in mind. Undoubtedly there would be serious problems involved in adapting to new modes of activity. But it is improbable indeed that adaptation would prove impossible. Zero marginal cost as a condition is actually quite rare in the real world.

Besides, there is considerable evidence that the City currently operates at something less than a full Pareto-optimum of efficiency. An inefficient allocation of resources is usually assumed to result from the presence of various kinds of restrictive practices which limit the degree of competition in the market. The fact is that the City has more than its share of restrictive practices – fixed underwriting commissions, demarcation agreements between jobbers and brokers in dealing, common interest rates paid on deposits, and so on. This implies that at least some of the institutions of the City could perform their jobs more economically than they do at present. Indeed, such institutions may be in the majority. In the opinion of one expert, 'there [are] more sleepers than thrusters in the Square Mile'.[1]

Does this mean that the services of the City might actually earn *more* in some alternative domestic use? Possibly, but I doubt it. Inefficient though they may sometimes be, market mechanisms do generally tend to direct resources to their most profitable employments. The £60 million that the City's services currently earn because the pound is an international currency is probably more than what they would earn otherwise. However, my guess is that the figure is not more than two to three times as great as what they would earn otherwise. To be certain of erring on the side of overstated benefits, let us assume that it is three times as great – a very generous assumption. In that case, the income of the City's services in their next-best alternative domestic use would be of the order of £20 million a year. The difference is £40 million, representing the actual gain to Britain from the international status of sterling:

Banking	£25 million
Insurance	nil
Merchanting	10 million
Brokerage	5 million
The City	£40 million

Allocating the gain

Virtually all of the social benefit of the City's invisible earnings may be attributed to just one of the international functions of the pound – its role as a transactions currency. Certainly this is true of the estimated £15 million a year contributed by brokerage and merchanting: as I argued in Chapter 2, the additional demand for services of industries

[1] George Cyriax, 'The City's Earnings', *Moorgate and Wall Street* (autumn 1965) p. 79.

such as these derives directly from a currency's use as a private exchange intermediary. And as it happens, this also seems to be true of most of the estimated £25 million a year contributed by banking. The substantial amount earned on interest account consists almost entirely of income on commercial credits; and the profits from overseas branches and subsidiaries are also directly related to the financing of trade. Likewise, a considerable proportion of the income earned from services reflects sterling's transactions role. True, some part of this last figure also depends on sterling's other roles. Some part of the earnings from foreign-exchange dealing, for instance, is probably attributable to the use of the pound as an intervention currency; similarly, some part of the earnings from underwriting and portfolio management is probably attributable to its use as an asset or reserve currency. But altogether these amounts are unlikely to add up to more than a couple of million pounds a year – a negligible fraction of the total of the City's net invisible income. For our purposes they can safely be ignored. We shall assume that, in practice, all of the City's net income depends exclusively on the private medium-of-exchange function of sterling.

7 Beyond Flexibility to Constraint

THE advantage of 'flexibility' in dealing with payments imbalances, and the disadvantage of 'constraint' in managing domestic income and employment, are both contingent effects of the international use of a currency. They manifest themselves in the gain or loss of degrees of freedom experienced by the authorities in the administration of public policy. As emphasised in Chapter 2, the gain and loss tend to apply sequentially rather than simultaneously.

In the case of the United Kingdom, it is evident that the sequence has already proceeded well beyond flexibility and well into constraint. True, even as late as the Second World War the British still seemed to be deriving some extra benefit, in terms of the timing and scope of adjustment policies, from the confidence of other countries – particularly sterling-area countries – in the pound's usefulness as an international store of value.[1] However, almost as soon as the war ended, confidence in sterling tended to decline, as we know, and as a result the comparatively wide latitude formerly afforded British policy was gradually constricted. By the middle and late 1950s, with the start of 'stop–go', it was clearly no longer the flexibility advantage that predominated in Britain; now it was the disadvantage of constraint. U.K. policy options were now limited by the threat of a reduction or withdrawal of the 'overhang' of sterling liabilities.

Before 1964, the external constraint on British policy tended to be more *de facto* than *de jure*. Since 1964, on the other hand, the tendency has been rather more to formalise it. To begin with, increasingly firm conditions were attached to the massive central-bank and I.M.F.

[1] Actually, the flexibility advantage enjoyed by the British during the 1930s and the Second World War represented the start of a *second* cycle of the flexibility–constraint sequence. There had already been an earlier cycle, beginning in the latter nineteenth century, during the period of sterling's globalisation, with Britain enjoying a flexibility in dealing with payments imbalances that was unique, and ending in the 1920s with the emergence of rival international financial centres (see Chapter 4). The second cycle began with sterling's regionalisation in 1931.

credits that Britain needed to help support the pound during the years of the great balance-of-payments crisis (see Chapter 5). As John Cooper has remarked, the 'arrangements . . . placed British policy firmly under the influence of foreign central bankers and supra-national officials'.[1] For example, following devaluation in 1967 (on 18 November), Britain requested a stand-by credit of $1·4 billion from the International Monetary Fund. The Fund, however, first required prior assurance from the British Government that tough internal measures to curb public expenditures and improve the balance of payments would be forthcoming. Such assurances were provided in a 'letter of intent' from the Chancellor of the Exchequer to the Fund's Managing Director, dated 23 November.[2] The stand-by was then approved. Even tougher 'strings' were tied to the $1 billion stand-by negotiated in June 1969.[3]

Likewise, firm conditions have been required to ensure that overseas sterling-area countries will continue in the future, as in the past, to help finance short-term deficits in the U.K. balance of payments. Particularly after devaluation, members began deliberately to switch *out* of pounds, and the drain could not be entirely blocked until the British Government, as part of the so-called Basle reform of the sterling area, pledged to guarantee the exchange value of the bulk of the bloc's official reserve balances (see Chapter 4 and below). Only then would members agree in future to hold on to most newly acquired sterling liabilities.

In short, for Britain, the constraint disadvantage would seem to have become quite serious. The question is: *how* serious? The answer depends on two essential factors: first, on the seriousness of the threat of reduction or withdrawal of sterling balances; and second, on the seriousness of the policy alternatives (the 'trade-offs') required to forestall the threat of overhang. These are the factors we shall be concerned with in the present chapter. Our procedure here, though, must necessarily be slightly different from what it was before. For unlike the effects considered in the previous two chapters, the effect to be considered in the present chapter – the constraint disadvantage – is neither specific nor continuing. It is a contingent effect. Therefore, in contrast to the

---

[1] John Cooper, *A Suitable Case for Treatment: What to Do about the Balance of Payments* (London: Penguin Books, 1968) p. 90.

[2] The full text of the letter was reprinted in the *Financial Times*, 1 Dec 1967, p. 13.

[3] See, e.g., *The Economist*, 28 June 1969, pp. 61–2.

previous effects, there is no single, unique magnitude that can be associated with it. In fact, there are several different magnitudes, each associated with one of the alternative contingencies (trade-offs) implied by it (see Chapter 3). Our problem, accordingly, will be to quantify not a single cost, but rather the whole *range* of alternative costs that is implied by the constraint disadvantage.

I. THE THREAT OF THE OVERHANG

How serious is the threat to the overhang of sterling balances? This is not an easy question to answer. Opinions on the matter differ sharply. At one extreme, Andrew Shonfield has written:

> There is no doubt that the Government has allowed its domestic policy since 1955 to be determined largely by the movement of international confidence in the pound sterling. . . . At the moment we have manœuvred ourselves into a position where our liberty of choice as sovereign nation in the field of social and economic policy is constricted by the views of a marginal holder of sterling in Zürich or some other foreign capital.[1]

At the opposite extreme, Peter Oppenheimer has written:

> . . . the international position of sterling has made little intrinsic difference to the U.K. balance-of-payments problem.[2]

And between them *The Banker* has suggested:

> The fact that sterling is so widely held, and can be freely converted into dollars at a very modest discount below the official rate, does make it especially vulnerable to disturbances. A banker always tends to be more vulnerable than a trader. But the extent of the dangers inherent in sterling's present status has been greatly exaggerated . . .[3]

Clearly, in fact no one *really* knows how serious the threat of the overhang might possibly be. Like any other country, Britain is subject to an independent balance-of-payments constraint on its domestic

---

[1] Andrew Shonfield, *British Economic Policy since the War* (London: Penguin Books, 1958) pp. 218, 269. See also John Cooper, op. cit., chap. 2.

[2] Peter M. Oppenheimer, 'Monetary Movements and the International Position of Sterling', in D. J. Robertson and L. C. Hunter (eds), *The British Balance of Payments* (London: Oliver & Boyd, 1966) p. 135.

[3] 'No Backsliding on Sterling', *The Banker*, cvii 383 (Dec 1957) 763–4.

economic and social policies. However, no one knows for certain what additional constraint, if any, ensues from the existence of the sterling balances. Is the payments constraint intensified by the overhang of liabilities, or is it not – and if it is, then to what extent?

There are three possible ways in which the overhang of liabilities might intensify the constraint of the balance of payments for Britain. In the first place, there might be a tendency toward persistent deficits in the balance of payments of the overseas sterling area vis-à-vis non-sterling areas: because of the tradition of gold and dollar pooling within the bloc, this would mean intensified pressure on Britain's reserve position over the long term. Alternatively, some or all of the sterling liabilities might be volatile in the short term, sensitive to shifts in confidence or to changes in the payments situation, and hence prone to move speculatively at a moment's notice. Or, third, even if the liabilities themselves are not prone to move speculatively, their very existence might induce or aggravate speculative movements of other funds, since the presence of large liabilities outstanding might be thought to make Britain's international liquidity position more precarious than it would be otherwise. We shall explore each of these three possibilities in turn.

Drawings on the reserve pool

The practice of reserve pooling in London has always been – and still is – one of the main pillars of the formal sterling area (see Chapter 4). Members in overall deficit with non-sterling areas draw on the pool of gold and dollars, running down their sterling balances; members in overall surplus, meanwhile, contribute at least part of their earnings to the pool, thereby building up their sterling balances. True, in the years after about 1961 the arrangement tended, in some instances, to become rather asymmetrical, owing to the accelerated process of reserve diversification in the outer area; certain countries began to accumulate non-sterling assets when their reserves were rising, though continuing to sell off sterling assets when their reserves were falling. For the most part, though, this process of diversification was effectively halted by the 1968 Basle reform, which stipulated that Britain's pledge of an exchange guarantee on reserve balances was to be matched by pledges from members to maintain not less than an agreed proportion of their total reserves in sterling. As a result, the pooling mechanism today is still working roughly as it originally did: when outer members as a group are in surplus vis-à-vis non-sterling areas, the central reserve benefits; when on the other hand members collectively are in deficit, drawings increase, the reserve declines, and the external constraint on Britain is intensified. The only new element in the picture is that now the U.K. is enabled to postpone the pressure of overseas sterling-area drawings on the central reserve, by drawing in turn on its own $2 billion stand-by facility with the Bank for International Settlements.

Table 7.1 shows the overall balance of payments of the overseas sterling area vis-à-vis non-sterling areas for the period 1958–68, together with the principal financing items: changes in I.M.F. accounts; changes in gold and dollar reserves; miscellaneous monetary movements; and 'inter-area transfers'. The last item is intended to measure that part of the payments balance with non-sterling areas which members finance by movements of sterling liabilities in London.[1] A negative figure under this heading means an increase of member balances; a positive figure, a decline.

The table indicates that despite a tendency toward persistent and often quite large current-account deficits, the outer-sterling countries managed to stay in overall surplus vis-à-vis non-sterling areas in every year but two (1965 and 1966), owing to an even larger sustained net inflow of long-term capital. The table also indicates that despite the tendency toward reserve diversification, especially after 1961, there were only a relatively few years (1964–6 and, of course, 1968) in which member balances were actually reduced – and, even then they were not reduced by very much (except in 1968). The data thus suggest that drawings on the sterling-area reserve pool have not in fact added to pressures on Britain's external position over the long term. To be sure, the situation could change in the future: for instance, the inflow of capital could dry up. However, at present there are no signs of any such change developing; moreover, even if it did develop, then undoubtedly some part of the outer area's current deficit would tend to dry up as well. And of course since the Basle reform of 1968 overseas reserve diversification is no longer a danger either. We may be permitted to assume, therefore, that any risks deriving from the reserve pool can be omitted from the following discussion: the mechanism does not at present seem to intensify significantly the balance-of-payments constraint for Britain.[2]

[1] Thomas M. Klein, 'The United Kingdom Balance-of-Payments Accounts', *Economic Journal*, LXXIV 296 (Dec 1964) 951–2.
[2] Cf. John Cooper, op. cit., pp. 240–2.

Table 7.1

Overseas–Sterling–Area Balance of Payments with Non–Sterling Areas, 1958–68
(in £ millions)

	Current balance	Balance of long-term capital	Balance of current and long-term capital	Changes in accounts with I.M.F.	Changes in holdings of gold and non-sterling currencies	Miscellaneous monetary movements	Inter-area transfers
1958	−321	+396	+75	+13	−15	−17	−56
59	+59	+380	+439	−55	−65	−1	−318
1960	−401	+406	+5	−31	+20	+16	−10
61	−194	+355	+161	+104	−112	−3	−150
62	−200	+440	+240	−65	−131	−	−44
63	−289	+530	+241	−27	−88	+16	−142
64	−633	+604	−29	−17	−73	+61	+58
1965	−1005	+883	−122	+64	−54	+94	+18
66	−469	+623	+154	+35	−335	+123	+23
67	−734	+1056	+322	+63	−266	+40	−159
68	−686	+1237	+551	−93	−735	+69	+208

Assets: increase − ; decrease + . Liabilities: increase + ; decrease − .

Source: Central Statistical Office, *Economic Trends*.

Volatility of the sterling balances

In exploring the possible short-term volatility of the sterling balances, we may immediately exclude certain categories of liabilities from consideration – specifically, the balances of international organisations and non-sterling-area official holders. Few, if any, of these liabilities are prone to move speculatively at a moment's notice. International organisations, of which the most important in this connection is the I.M.F., hold sterling in consequence of formal treaty obligations; similarly, non-sterling-area official holders, of which the most important in this connection are the central banks of Western Europe and the United States, hold sterling in consequence of their various swap arrangements with the Bank of England. By their very nature, these liabilities are unlikely to be liquidated at a time of weakening confidence in the pound – quite the reverse, as a matter of fact. And in any event these holders are all effectively guaranteed against loss in the event of a sterling devaluation. We may therefore be permitted to ignore them here.

This leaves us with just three categories of liabilities to consider – the balances of sterling-area official holders, sterling-area non-official holders, and non-sterling-area non-official holders. In other words, this leaves us with just those sterling liabilities that are directly related to the traditional roles of the pound, the same liabilities that concerned us in Chapter 5. A breakdown of these liabilities for the years 1965–9 is provided in Table 7.2 (reproducing Table 5.4); a further breakdown by quarters is provided in Table 7.3. In addition, in order to facilitate analysis of potential volatility, quarterly changes for each of the three types of holder in 1965–8 are plotted in Fig. 7.1 (see p. 187). The scale used is logarithmic, so as to highlight the *relative* volatility of each series in this recent period.

Consider Fig. 7.1. Of the three series shown, clearly the least volatile liabilities – until 1968, at least – were those of sterling-area official holders. From quarter to quarter over the first three years of the period barely any changes at all can be perceived. Nor should this be surprising. Many of these balances – perhaps as many as half[1] – represent backing for local currencies based on the pound. These are not the sort of liabilities that can be easily liquidated by their owners in the short term. And as for the remainder, these consist essentially of international

---

[1] J. M. Livingstone, *Britain and the World Economy* (London: Penguin Books, 1966) p. 42.

reserves held as a contingency against deficits in the nation's balance of payments. The central banks of overseas sterling-area members are not generally in the business of speculating against the pound at times of weakening confidence.

True, in 1968 the situation did alter somewhat. Chapter 4 has already described how, shaken by the windfall losses suffered on account of the 1967 devaluation of sterling, many overseas central banks began to switch into other reserve media. Fig. 7.1 shows that the decline of area reserve balances was severe: in the second quarter of 1968 alone, holdings dropped by nearly £300 million – a net depletion of roughly 15 per cent (Table 7.3B). And there can be little doubt that the decline would have persisted had the British not begun the negotiations which eventually led to the exchange guarantee on reserve balances announced in September 1968.

However, in fact, once the guarantee was announced, the decline of holdings was reversed, and the situation returned more or less to the *status quo ante*. The outer members no longer had an incentive to diversify out of sterling; quite the opposite, they now had an incentive to remain in sterling (at least up to their respective Minimum Sterling Proportions) in order to retain their eligibility for the guarantee pledged them. Thus, in effect, the balances of sterling-area official holders were transformed into something very much like the balances of international organisations and other official holders: like the latter, area reserve balances could now be assumed to pose no significant threat of sensitivity to short-term changes of sentiment. But such stability was not purchased without a price. For Britain, the Basle exchange guarantee represents an additional contingent cost of the international use of sterling. This cost is discussed separately in the last section of the present chapter.

Of course, even despite the guarantee, there is always the risk that some area reserve balances may be used for the purpose of political blackmail. It is not unknown for overseas members to threaten withdrawal of their holdings in order to exert pressure on the foreign and diplomatic policy of the British Government. There were, for instance, the well-publicised withdrawals of sterling by Arab countries during the Middle East crisis of 1967.[1] Similarly, Malaysia talked of 'diversifying' its reserve holdings during the period of 'confrontation' with Indonesia; and Zambia and other African countries have threatened from time to time to withdraw assets from London in the absence of a

[1] John Cooper, op. cit., pp. 57–8. Cooper calls these movements 'spite money'.

Table 7.2

United Kingdom Sterling Liabilities Related to the International Functions of Sterling, 1965–9 (in £ millions)

	Current and deposit accounts	Treasury bills	Other bills	British Government stocks	Local authority temporary loans	Finance-house deposits	Total
Total liabilities, all holders							
1965	1783	538	80	1209	170	126	3906
1966	1831	441	90	1190	119	137	3808
1967	1746	399	97	1175	119	102	3638
1968	1670	373	123	1129	71	51	3418
1969	1747	312	194	1312	97	57	3716
Of which:							
1. Official holders (overseas sterling countries only)							
1965	217	520	–	1043	131	–	1911
1966	310	427	–	1006	105	7	1855
1967	291	370	–	953	104	19	1736
1968	270	368	–	938	59	14	1650

2. Other holders (Total)

1965	1566	18	80	166	39	126	1995
1966	1521	14	90	184	14	130	1953
1967	1455	29	97	222	15	83	1902
1968	1400	5	123	191	12	37	1768
1969	1326	5	194	114	10	32	1679

(a) Overseas sterling countries

1965	866	11	28	144	26	75	1150
1966	922	12	39	165	10	81	1229
1967	908	12	45	204	11	65	1246
1968	937	3	75	178	9	32	1231
1969	862	2	134	98	9	28	1133

(b) Non-sterling countries

1965	700	7	52	22	13	51	845
1966	599	2	51	19	4	49	724
1967	547	12	52	18	4	18	656
1968	464	2	48	14	3	5	537
1969	464	2	61	15	1	4	546

Note: Detail may not add to total because of rounding.

Source: *Bank of England Quarterly Bulletin.*

Table 7.3A

Total Sterling Liabilities, Quarterly, 1965–9
(in £ millions)

		Current and deposit accounts	Treasury bills	Other bills	British Government stocks	Local authority temporary loans	Finance-house deposits	Total
1965	I	1659	602	73	1240	n.a.	n.a.	n.a.
	II	1637	554	66	1219	n.a.	n.a.	n.a.
	III	1699	500	75	1161	n.a.	n.a.	n.a.
	IV	1783	538	80	1209	170	126	3906
1966	I	1870	613	72	1114	n.a.	n.a.	n.a.
	II	1903	621	78	1189	n.a.	n.a.	n.a.
	III	1718	482	79	1195	n.a.	n.a.	n.a.
	IV	1831	441	90	1190	119	137	3808
1967	I	1967	484	86	1202	n.a.	n.a.	n.a.
	II	2008	426	88	1180	n.a.	n.a.	n.a.
	III	1836	468	89	1173	n.a.	n.a.	n.a.
	IV	1746	399	97	1175	119	102	3638
1968	I	1724	471	101	1171	119	111	3699
	II	1630	394	106	1074	77	76	3356
	III	1681	349	109	1116	67	61	3383
	IV	1670	373	123	1129	71	51	3418
1969	I	1690	412	155	1167	70	57	3560
	II	1769	339	177	1227	82	48	3642
	III	1665	322	180	1235	104	44	3551
	IV	1747	312	194	1312	97	57	3716

n.a. Not available.
Source: *Bank of England Quarterly Bulletin.*

Table 7.3B

Sterling Liabilities to Sterling-Area Official Holders, Quarterly, 1965–9
(in £ millions)

		Current and deposit accounts	Treasury bills	Other bills	British Government stocks	Local authority temporary loans	Finance-house deposits	Total
1965	I	172	570	–	1105	n.a.	n.a.	n.a.
	II	176	539	–	1093	n.a.	n.a.	n.a.
	III	224	484	–	1031	n.a.	n.a.	n.a.
	IV	217	520	–	1043	131	–	1911
1966	I	260	587	–	978	n.a.	n.a.	n.a.
	II	245	599	–	1037	n.a.	n.a.	n.a.
	III	284	462	–	1044	n.a.	n.a.	n.a.
	IV	310	427	–	1006	105	7	1855
1967	I	303	471	–	1013	n.a.	n.a.	n.a.
	II	344	400	–	1000	n.a.	n.a.	n.a.
	III	288	431	–	986	n.a.	n.a.	n.a.
	IV	291	370	–	953	104	19	1736
1968	I	283	447	–	963	95	27	1815
	II	220	386	–	860	51	13	1531
	III	201	342	–	901	48	14	1506
	IV	270	368	–	938	59	14	1650
1969	I	370	406	–	983	67	20	1847
	II	456	334	–	1049	70	11	1921
	III	440	318	–	1111	93	16	1977
	IV	421	307	–	1198	87	25	2037

n.a. Not available.
Source: *Bank of England Quarterly Bulletin.*

Table 7.3c

Sterling Liabilities to Sterling-Area Non-Official Holders, Quarterly, 1965–9
(in £ millions)

		Current and deposit accounts	Treasury bills	Other bills	British Government stocks	Local authority temporary loans	Finance-house deposits	Total
1965	I	847	26	23	111	n.a.	n.a.	n.a.
	II	814	11	21	103	n.a.	n.a.	n.a.
	III	820	11	21	107	n.a.	n.a.	n.a.
	IV	866	11	28	144	26	75	1150
1966	I	892	21	24	115	n.a.	n.a.	n.a.
	II	992	19	28	152	n.a.	n.a.	n.a.
	III	891	16	31	151	n.a.	n.a.	n.a.
	IV	922	12	39	165	10	81	1229
1967	I	922	10	33	171	n.a.	n.a.	n.a.
	II	890	10	32	165	n.a.	n.a.	n.a.
	III	883	10	33	173	n.a.	n.a.	n.a.
	IV	908	12	45	204	11	65	1246
1968	I	971	6	50	194	21	62	1305
	II	928	5	56	200	22	55	1265
	III	960	4	62	202	16	39	1282
	IV	937	3	75	178	9	32	1231
1969	I	902	3	105	171	10	33	1223
	II	871	2	121	165	9	32	1199
	III	821	2	125	110	10	25	1094
	IV	862	2	137	98	9	28	1133

n.a. Not available.
Source: Bank of England Quarterly Bulletin.

Table 7.3D

Sterling Liabilities to Non-Sterling–Area Non-Official Holders, Quarterly, 1965–9
(in £ millions)

		Current and deposit accounts	Treasury bills	Other bills	British Government stocks	Local authority temporary loans	Finance-house deposits	Total
1965	I	640	6	50	24	n.a.	n.a.	n.a.
	II	647	4	45	23	n.a.	n.a.	n.a.
	III	653	5	54	23	n.a.	n.a.	n.a.
	IV	700	7	52	22	13	51	845
1966	I	718	5	48	21	n.a.	n.a.	n.a.
	II	666	3	50	22	n.a.	n.a.	n.a.
	III	543	4	48	20	n.a.	n.a.	n.a.
	IV	599	2	51	19	14	49	724
1967	I	742	3	53	18	n.a.	n.a.	n.a.
	II	774	16	56	15	n.a.	n.a.	n.a.
	III	665	27	56	14	n.a.	n.a.	n.a.
	IV	547	17	52	18	4	18	656
1968	I	470	18	51	13	5	22	579
	II	482	2	50	14	4	8	560
	III	520	3	47	14	3	8	595
	IV	464	2	48	14	3	5	537
1969	I	418	3	50	13	3	4	490
	II	442	3	56	13	3	5	522
	III	404	2	55	14	1	3	480
	IV	464	2	61	15	1	4	546

n.a. Not available.
Source: *Bank of England Quarterly Bulletin*.

firm stand against Rhodesia.[1] Britain is thus to some extent a hostage of its short-term creditors. But it would be a mistake to exaggerate the problem. The British are not without political weapons of their own; and besides, they always have it within their power to block (indeed, *in extremis* even to confiscate) a member's sterling balances if they so desire. In any event, these considerations take us quite a bit beyond the limits of strictly economic analysis. Considering just the economics of the matter, it still seems reasonable to assume that sterling-area reserve balances are likely to remain relatively stable in the short term.

For related reasons, it seems reasonable to assume that sterling-area private balances are relatively stable in the short term also. These liabilities too traditionally show little sensitivity to temporary changes of sentiment. Consisting for the most part of working and trading balances, in the long run they tend to grow slowly in line with sterling-area trade in general, and in the short run to fluctuate only within comparatively narrow limits. To be sure, since the devaluation experience of 1967 there may well have been some increase in the sensitivity of these balances; this would not be surprising, in view of the windfall losses suffered by many sterling-area private holders because of the failure of local currencies to be devalued *pari passu* with sterling. But even if there has been such an increase in sensitivity, it adds no real threat to the pound. Exchange regulations in the outer sterling area largely prevent sales of sterling liabilities against dollars or other non-sterling currencies; sales can only be against sterling-area currencies. Hence, any net reduction of private balances within the bloc is matched simply by a corresponding net increase of official balances – which, as we have just noted, are not likely to be used to speculate against the pound. Accordingly, we may assume that there is no significant threat of volatility from this source either.

Regrettably, the same cannot be said for the balances of non-sterling-area non-official holders, which, as we can see in Fig. 7.1, tend to fluctuate much more in the short run than either of the other two series. These liabilities have got to be assumed to pose a significant threat of sensitivity to changes of sentiment – a quite serious threat at that, since the changes of sentiment need not concern solely the pound. An international currency that is widely held privately is prone to speculation not only *against* its own parity, but also *in favour of* other

[1] Richard N. Cooper, 'The Balance of Payments', in Richard E. Caves and Associates, *Britain's Economic Prospects* (Washington: Brookings Institution, 1968) p. 1986, n. 80.

currencies' parities. If some particular currency is expected to appreciate, speculators may want to buy it. But to move into one currency they must move out of another. It follows that the more widely a money is held, the more likely it is to be sold. And since sterling is one of the most widely held of all moneys, it is consequently one of the most liable to this kind of 'backwash' effect. In 1957, for instance, speculators betting on a revaluation of the Deutschmark accidentally sparked off a run on the pound which had nothing at all to do with the underlying state of the British balance of payments at the time (which was sound).[1] Similarly, in other recent years, like 1961, 1968 and 1969, pressures on sterling tended to develop in the backwash of speculation in favour of the Deutschmark.

How serious is the threat from this source? Fig. 7.1 shows that non-sterling private balances declined sharply three times in the years 1965–1969. Each decline was roughly in line with general changes in confidence. More importantly, in each instance funds were withdrawn at roughly the same rate. In 1966 holdings dropped by 22 per cent in two quarters; in 1967–8, by 36 per cent in three quarters; and in 1968–9, by 17 per cent in two quarters. Taken together, these three experiences suggest a potential rate of liquidation of at least 8–9 per cent per quarter, and possibly as much as 10–12 per cent.

This accords with what we know about the composition of these balances (Table 7.3D). Most are current and deposit accounts. In the opinion of many experts in London, this is sufficient reason for *disregarding*, rather than worrying about, any risk of further withdrawals of non-sterling private balances. By the end of 1969, according to this view, the general lack of confidence in sterling had 'squeezed the sponge dry'; holdings were presumably already reduced to a 'hard-core' minimum of working and trading balances. And certainly it must be admitted that if these really *were* all genuine working balances, there would hardly be much danger of further reduction or liquidation in the short run. However, as *The Economist* has pointed out, this is truly a vain and forlorn hope:

> The British authorities . . . trust that non-sterling countries' holdings of sterling are down to a level where they could not easily be further depleted. . . . This latter hope is a vain one. It is still very easy, as well as tempting, to dump sterling whenever rumours fly.[2]

[1] See, e.g., 'The Debate on Sterling', *Planning*, XXIV 421 (Apr 1958) 76–7.

[2] *The Economist*, 26 Apr 1969, p. 70. Experts in London do not have a very good record of estimating the hard-core 'natural working level' or 'reasonable

The Committee on Invisible Exports suggests that in fact only 25 per cent of current and deposit accounts are working balances, the other 75 per cent investments in the United Kingdom;[1] and in chapter 5 I have agreed that from an operational point of view this does not seem an unreasonable estimate. I have also agreed (in Chapter 5) that the same ratio can probably be applied to the other types of liabilities as well. This means that as much as 75 per cent of the total of non-sterling-area private balances may be assumed to be investments in Britain – and hence potentially liquifiable assets. Of course, not all 75 per cent could be easily liquidated in the short-term – say, in one or two quarters – even if their holders wanted to try. Some investments are much less liquid than others: such a rate would not be plausible. Indeed, even a rate of 8–9 per cent per quarter may be too high today; perhaps the sponge *was* squeezed nearly dry by the end of 1969. But on the other hand certainly a rate at half that level – say, 5 per cent per quarter – seems not at all implausible. In fact, on the whole it seems a rather conservative estimate of the threat of speculation from this source.

We conclude, then, that of all the sterling balances, only those privately held outside the sterling area pose any significant threat of sensitivity to short-term changes of sentiment.[2] At end-1969 these holdings totalled some £546 million. A potential rate of liquidation of 5 per cent per quarter would thus mean, in the event of a weakening of confidence in sterling, an outflow of roughly £25 million per quarter – £100 million in a year. This seems to be the approximate dimension of the additional balance-of-payments constraint for Britain presently caused by potential volatility of the sterling balances themselves.

---

minimum' of sterling balances. Especially notorious in this respect is the research staff of the Bank of England. See, e.g., 'Overseas Holdings of Sterling', a memorandum submitted by the Bank of England to the Radcliffe Committee, reprinted in A. R. Conan, *The Rationale of the Sterling Area* (London: Macmillan, 1961) pp. 62–7 (esp. paras 5 and 7).

[1] Committee on Invisible Exports, *Britain's Invisible Earnings* (London: British National Export Council, for the Financial Advisory Panel on Exports, 1967) pp. 190–1.

[2] This accords with the view of other writers on the subject. See, e.g., Klein, op. cit., pp. 947–51; A. R. Conan, *The Problem of Sterling* (London: Macmillan, 1966) pp. 84–7; Roy Harrod, 'The Role of Sterling', *District Bank Review*, no. 160 (Dec 1966) pp. 6–9; Richard Fry, 'Sterling in Europe – A British View', *The Banker*, cxvii 493 (Mar 1967) 217; J. R. Cadman, 'Sterling, the U.K. and Europe', *Westminster Bank Review* (Feb 1967) p. 36; and Richard N. Cooper, op. cit., p. 186.

Other speculative movements

It is difficult to say anything at all precise about the possibility that, apart from their own (limited) potential volatility, the sterling balances might induce or aggravate speculative movements of other types of funds.[1] Here we are getting rather deep into the realm of economic and financial psychology. Certainly it seems *plausible* that adverse speculation is apt to develop more quickly, probably also to involve larger sums, than it would otherwise. The overhang of liabilities certainly does make Britain's international liquidity position *look* more precarious. As we can see from Table 7.4, the ratio of U.K. total liabilities to total gold and dollar reserves was, and still is, extraordinarily high – between 4:1 and 6:1 in most post-war years, and still higher in 1969 (approximately 7:1). Indeed, even if we restrict the measure to those liabilities that are clearly related to the international roles of the pound (thus excluding international organisations and non-sterling-area official holders), the ratio is never lower than 3:1; and even if we exclude sterling-area official holders as well, using a measure of private balances only, the ratio just once falls barely below unity. In most recent years private balances alone have been nearly double available reserves. Certainly figures like these are sufficient to engender insecurity on the part of other holders and users of sterling – and hence to prompt additional speculation at times of weakening confidence. The difficulty is that it is not very easy to demonstrate just how important this incremental effect might be. The estimate in this section must be assumed to be subject to a rather wide margin of error.

The incremental effect of the sterling balances could conceivably take one of two forms. In the first place, it could materialise as an outflow of specifically British money: British residents might flee their own currency directly. Alternatively, it could materialise as an increase of 'leads and lags' in British trade and payments. The latter of these possibilities constitutes a real threat for Britain. The former, on the other hand, under present circumstances has very little practical significance.

British residents are not free to sell sterling assets against dollar or other non-sterling securities. Transfers of portfolio capital outside the sterling area must go through the so-called 'investment-currency market',[2] which is effectively self-balancing. (That is, funds for

[1] Richard N. Cooper, op. cit., p. 186.

[2] See 'The U.K. Exchange Control: A Short History', *Bank of England Quarterly Bulletin*, vii 3 (Sep 1967) 256, 258. The investment-currency market is more popularly known as the investment-dollar market.

Table 7.4

Three Alternative Measures of the International Liquidity Position of the United Kingdom, 1945–69
(amounts in £ millions)

	Gold and convertible currency reserves[a]	Total sterling liabilities		Sterling liabilities related to the international functions of sterling		Private sterling liabilities	
		Total	Ratio to reserves	Total	Ratio to reserves	Total	Ratio to reserves
1945	610	3,602	6·0	2,760	4·5	837	1·4
46	664	3,690	5·6	2,807	4·2	918	1·4
47	512	3,970	7·8	2,639	5·2	820	1·6
48	457	3,650	8·0	2,523	5·5	789	1·7
49	603	3,835	6·4	2,539	4·2	782	1·3
1950	1,178	4,242	3·6	3,071	2·6	962	0·8
51	834	4,396	5·3	3,170	3·8	918	1·1
52	659	3,974	6·0	2,930	4·4	911	1·4
53	899	4,196	4·7	3,211	3·6	1,008	1·1
54	986	4,390	4·5	3,454	3·5	1,194	1·2

Year							
1955	757	4,286	5·7	3,378	4·5	1,112	1·5
56	799	4,345	5·4	3,276	4·1	1,036	1·3
57	812	4,183	5·2	3,154	3·9	1,028	1·3
58	1,096	4,235	3·9	3,213	3·0	1,220	1·1
59	977	4,503	4·6	3,472	3·6	1,307	1·3
1960	1,154	4,811	4·2	3,763	3·3	1,734	1·5
61	1,185	4,890	4·1	3,492	3·0	1,395	1·2
62	1,002}	4,535	4·5	3,555	3·6	1,499	1·5
62		4577,	4·6	3,520	3·5	1,705	1·7
63	949	4,859	5·1	3,795	4·0	1,858	2·0
64	827	5,409	6·5	3,895	4·7	1,948	2·4
1965	1,073	6,016	5·6	3,906	3·6	1,995	1·9
66	1,107	6,401	5·8	3,808	3·4	1,953	1·7
67	1,123	6,689	6·0	3,638	3·2	1,902	1·7
68	1,009	7,671	7·6	3,418	3·4	1,768	1·8
69	1,053	7,356	7·0	3,716	3·5	1,679	1·6

[a] In 1949 and 1967 reserves were written up after devaluation. In 1966 and 1967 there were transfers from the Government's dollar portfolio to reserves (respectively, £316 million and £204 million).

Sources: *Bank of England Quarterly Bulletin*; and Central Statistical Office, *Economic Trends.*

investments outside the sterling area must be obtained from investors who liquidate non-sterling securities.) Consequently, *net* outward speculation against the pound is impossible outside the sterling area. Within the sterling area, by contrast, residents are relatively free to transfer capital whenever they like.[1] But even outward speculation in this form poses few risks for Britain. For the most part it results simply in an increase of private and/or official sterling-area balances, and these, as we know, do not themselves tend to be used in a speculative fashion. A risk is posed only if a free market develops somewhere in the outer sterling area which British residents can use to circumvent exchange regulations at home. In the 1950s two important leaks of this kind developed – the notorious Kuwait and Hong Kong gaps – but eventually each was successfully closed by the British authorities.[2] At present there appear to be no serious gaps in the sterling-area network of controls.[3] Accordingly, there seems to be little practical scope for a direct flight from the pound by British residents.

On the other hand, there seems to be considerable scope for an increase of leads and lags in British trade and payments. Leads and lags involve short-term variations in the timing of impact of commercial transactions on the exchange market and the balance of payments. Leads are concerned with arrangements by importers that tend to accelerate payments of foreign exchange due in respect of purchases. Lags are concerned with arrangements by exporters that tend to retard receipts in respect of sales.

> To put it more briefly, leads hasten the adverse effects of imports on the exchange of the importing country, while lags delay the favourable effects of exports on the exchange of the exporting country. The longer the leads the sooner imports produce their adverse effect. The longer the lags the later exports produce their favourable effect.[4]

[1] The word 'relatively' must be stressed here. Since 1961, and especially since 1966, some restrictions have been placed on capital transfers even within the sterling area. Ibid., pp. 257–60; and below.

[2] John Cooper, op. cit., pp. 217–18; Peter B. Kenen, *British Monetary Policy and the Balance of Payments, 1951–1957* (Cambridge, Mass.: Harvard University Press, 1960) pp. 150–2; and below.

[3] It is known that several minor leaks in the network do exist, but their potentiality is judged to be distinctly limited. See, e.g., *Sunday Times*, 17 Nov 1968, p. 25, and 9 Feb 1969.

[4] Paul Einzig, *Leads and Lags* (London: Macmillan, 1968) p. 9. See also 'Leads and Lags in Overseas Trade', *Bank of England Quarterly Bulletin* I 2 (Mar 1961) 18.

Leads and lags may be increased for any number of reasons, but undoubtedly the most important reason is anticipation of changes in parities or spot exchange rates.[1] A variety of arrangements is involved, including in particular four basic practices.[2] Assume that depreciation of the local currency is anticipated. Traders may:

1. Change the timing of their purchases and sales abroad. Importers may advance their foreign orders; exporters may postpone their foreign sales.

2. Change the timing of their payments for imports and receipts for exports. Importers may put forward their payments for goods invoiced in foreign currencies; exporters may delay the receipt for payments for goods invoiced in foreign currencies, or the disposal of the foreign-currency proceeds once received.

3. Change the choice of currency in which their imports and exports are financed. Importers and exporters, foreign as well as resident, may choose to finance their business transactions locally rather than abroad. This has the effect of accelerating net foreign payments and retarding net foreign receipts.

4. Change the purchase and sale of spot or forward exchange in connection with covering the exchange risk on their commercial transactions. Resident importers with foreseeable commitments in foreign currency may advance their purchases of the necessary exchange, whether in the spot or forward market; foreign exporters due receipts in local currency may advance their forward sales. Resident exporters due receipts in local currency may postpone their forward sales; foreign importers with foreseeable commitments in local currency may postpone their purchases, whether in the spot or forward market. These various arrangements have the effect of reducing the net demand for local currency, both spot and forward, relative to net supply.

In Britain, increases of leads and lags are limited to a certain extent by exchange-control regulations. British importers, for instance, are restricted in their ability to lead conversion of sterling into dollars or other foreign exchange: payment is not permitted until the goods are actually ready to be shipped.[3] Similarly, British exporters are restricted in their ability to lag conversion of foreign-exchange receipts into sterling, and both importers and exporters are restricted in their ability

---

[1] Einzig, op. cit., chap. 3.
[2] Ibid., chaps 4–6, 8.
[3] 'The U.K. Exchange Control: A Short History', loc. cit., p. 259.

to switch the financing of their business transactions between London and centres abroad.[1]

But even so, the scope for leads and lags affecting Britain is considerable. Britain is still (with the United States and West Germany) one of the three main trading nations of the world: imports currently run at a rate of nearly £7 billion a year (f.o.b.), exports at a rate well above £6 billion a year (f.o.b.). There are certainly substantial opportunities here for British traders to change the timing of their purchases and sales, if not the timing of their conversions. Moreover, Britain is still (with the United States) one of the two main centres for the financing and coverage of trade. Thus there are also substantial opportunities for foreigners trading with Britain, if not for British importers and exporters themselves, to switch their commercial financing to London, or to change the timing of their spot or forward transactions in pounds. And finally, it is important to remember that Britain is still the pivot of the sterling area – in particular, that the British gold and dollar reserve is still the central pool of the system. This means that the U.K. is affected by leads and lags not only in its own trade and payments; it is affected by leads and lags in the trade and payments of all the overseas sterling-area countries as well. This increases even further the scope for adverse movements.

Considering the manifold possibilities for leads and lags in Britain's case, it is not surprising that when estimates of the scope for adverse movements are essayed, generally they turn out to be fairly astronomical. Andrew Shonfield, for instance, has reckoned that the figure annually 'is probably of the order of several thousand million pounds'.[2] Peter Oppenheimer has suggested £1500 million in a quarter 'to indicate possible orders of magnitude'.[3] And Paul Einzig has placed the figure at £200 million in a week, enough, in his opinion, to explain the sterling devaluations of both 1949 and 1967: 'On both occasions sterling was devalued largely because of heavy and persistent selling pressure caused by increases in leads and lags.'[4]

---

[1] 'Leads and Lags in Overseas Trade', loc. cit., p. 21.
[2] Shonfield, op. cit., p. 151.
[3] Peter M. Oppenheimer, 'Forward Exchange Intervention: The Official View', *Westminster Bank Review* (Feb 1966) p. 2, n. 1.
[4] Einzig, op. cit., p. 100. For additional estimates, see 'London's Overseas Credits', *The Banker*, cviii (Feb 1958) 80; and John E. Nash, 'U.K. Policy and International Monetary Reform', in Harry G. Johnson and John E. Nash, *U.K. and Floating Exchanges*, Hobart Papers, No. 46 (London: Institute of Economic Affairs, 1969) p. 52.

On the face of it, estimates such as these may not appear too un-reasonable. However, there is a problem: they find very little support in the available statistics. The data themselves do not allow for direct identification of the magnitude of leads and lags in the British balance of payments. It is necessary therefore to rely on partial and indirect measures instead – and even these are not really reliable.[1] Two possible measures are presented in Table 7.6: the 'balancing item' in the balance of payments, and sterling claims on non-sterling private holders. These are available only on a quarterly basis: movements within quarters therefore cannot be readily identified. The series are shown for the years 1965–9, in order to facilitate comparison with the quarterly changes in sterling liabilities shown in Table 7.3 and Fig. 7.1. For what they are worth, the two measures demonstrate that there is little solid evidence of increases of leads and lags at times of weakening confidence in sterling – at any rate, certainly not on anything like the scale vari-ously suggested.

The balancing item in the statistical record of the balance of pay-ments is interpolated to equate the observed balance of current and long-term capital with observed monetary movements. Since it is affected by differences of timing between entries 'above the line' and their impact 'below the line', the item is sometimes thought to be a useful indirect measure of that part of leads and lags resulting from changes in the timing of payments and receipts. But it is not really a reliable measure, because it is affected by a host of other considerations as well. By definition, the balancing item covers *all* of the incalculable errors and omissions in the payments account:[2] in view of the fact that many of these may happen to be changing at the same time as the timing of payments and receipts, it would be unreasonable to expect it to give any clear indication of leads and lags.[3] This is borne out by Table 7.5. Neither in mid-1966 nor again in either late 1967–early 1968 or late 1968–early 1969, when non-sterling-area private holdings were rapidly being withdrawn, is it possible (except in the first quarter of

---

[1] See Samuel I. Katz, 'Leads and Lags in Sterling Payments', *Review of Economics and Statistics*, xxxv 1 (Feb 1953) 75–9; and *Sterling Speculation and European Convertibility: 1955–1958*, Essays in International Finance, No. 37 (Princeton: International Finance Section, 1961) pp. 6–9.

[2] In the United States balance of payments, the balancing item in fact is labelled, simply, 'errors and omissions'.

[3] 'Leads and Lags in Overseas Trade', loc. cit., pp. 22–3; and Einzig, op. cit., pp. 151–5.

1969) to detect in the balancing item any significant increase in out-flows of funds.

Sterling claims on non-sterling private holders include all the various forms of trade credit – advances and discounts, commercial bills, pro-

Table 7.5

Two Alternative Partial Measures of Leads and Lags in the United Kingdom Balance of Payments, 1965–9
(in £ millions)

		Balance-of-payments balancing item[a]	Sterling claims on non-sterling-area private holders[b]
1965	I	− 1	635
	II	+ 49	640
	III	+ 1	638
	IV	+ 38	669
1966	I	+ 57	664
	II	− 27	694
	III	+ 38	696
	IV	− 69	743
1967	I	+ 133	750
	II	+ 82	771
	III	− 105	789
	IV	+ 71	794
1968	I	− 129	851
	II	− 26	946
	III	− 8	988
	IV	− 3	1041
1969	I	+ 181	1120
	II	− 76	1168
	III	− 102	1204
	IV	+ 179	1274

n.a. Not available.

[a] Outflow + ; inflow − .

[b] Includes advances and overdrafts, commercial bills and promissory notes, and acceptances.

Source: *Bank of England Quarterly Bulletin.*

missory notes and acceptances. Accordingly, the total is sometimes thought to be a useful measure of that part of leads and lags resulting from changes in the choice of currency of financing: if importers and exporters are switching the locale of their trade financing from non-sterling centres to London in anticipation of a depreciation of the pound, that fact should be reflected in a net increase of claims outside the sterling bloc. But this too is not really a reliable measure, because it too is affected as well by a host of other considerations. For instance, interest rates may be changing at the same time, or even the volume of business transactions in general. It would therefore be unreasonable to expect any clear indication of leads and lags from this source either. This also is borne out by Table 7.5. True, in all three instances of weakening confidence in sterling, the total of foreign-trade credits increased. However, none of the increases was very large, and all were broadly in line with the secular upward trend of the series over the five-year period as a whole (which in turn was broadly in line with the secular upward trend of United Kingdom trade).

Thus, it seems safe to assume that astronomical estimates of leads and lags such as those by Shonfield *et al.* are unrealistic. But at the same time, despite the absence of firm confirmation of their existence in the data, it seems equally unrealistic to assume that there are no leads and lags at all. The opportunities for varying the timing of impact of commercial transactions are simply too numerous to be ignored. The question is: what is a *plausible* estimate? A decade ago the Radcliffe Committee suggested a figure of £90–£100 million.[1] In the absence of anything better, I suggest using the same figure. Admittedly, this is just a guess; a wide margin of error must be conceded. But at least the figure has the virtue of being conservative. As always, I prefer to err on the side of overstated benefits or understated costs, rather than the reverse.

Before leaving this subject, it is important to emphasise one additional point – specifically, that the scope for leads and lags in the British balance of payments does *not* depend on the roles of sterling as an international quotation or transactions currency. True, the pound is widely used in invoicing and discharging contracts. But these functions have no direct effect at all as far as the timing of impact of commercial transactions is concerned. Even if sterling were to cease being used for such purposes, the manifold possibilities for leads and lags would remain:

> In itself the fact of a change in the currency of invoicing, unlike a change in the currency of financing, need not affect the timing of payments by importers to exporters. Nor does it affect the moment when the currency of the importers' country comes to be sold against the currency of the exporters' country. If as a result of a change agreed upon between the two trading partners, the goods

[1] *Report of the Committee on the Working of the Monetary System*, Cmnd 827 (Aug 1959) p. 236.

come to be payable in the exporter's currency instead of in the importer's currency as hitherto, all that happens is that now it is the latter who carries out the necessary foreign exchange transaction instead of the former. From the point of view of exchange rates or of official reserves it does not make the slightest difference whether it is the U.K. importer who buys dollars or the U.S. exporter who sells sterling.[1]

To be sure, there might be some indirect effect if less trade were to be denominated and settled in pounds, but it is impossible to say what that effect might be. As Roy Harrod has concluded: 'It is anyone's guess.'[2] The point, essentially, is that it does not matter at all what currency is used for these purposes. What really matters is the position of Britain as a great world trader and financial centre. The possibilities for leads and lags are so numerous because the volume of British trade is so large, and because the mechanisms of the City of London are so opportune:

> It is indeed the very efficiency of the international banking and credit facilities available in London which makes matters worse for sterling in these periodic crises of confidence. It makes it so easy for the foreign trader to speculate against sterling.[3]

And where do these periodic crises of confidence originate? As already suggested, in the overhang of sterling liabilities. I began this discussion with the point that leads and lags may be regarded as an incremental effect of the sterling balances: the potential volatility of foreign holdings engenders insecurity on the part of other users, thus prompting additional speculation at times of weakening confidence. In other words, the threat of the overhang has two aspects, one direct (sensitivity of holdings), one indirect (leads and lags): both intensify the constraint of the balance of payments for Britain. I now conclude by returning to the same point, for we know from the previous discussion that of all the sterling balances, only those privately held outside the sterling area, consisting largely of investments in the United Kingdom, pose any real danger of volatility. Therefore, it would appear that both aspects of the constraint have their source in but a single function of sterling: the function of asset currency. This means that the problem of attributing the cost of the constraint is anticipated. Our only prob-

---

[1] Einzig, op. cit., pp. 50–1.

[2] Roy Harrod, *Dollar–Sterling Collaboration: Basis for Initiative* (London: Atlantic Trade Study, 1967) p. 32. See also Einzig, op. cit., pp. 51–9.

[3] Shonfield, op. cit., p. 152. See also Richard N. Cooper, op. cit., pp. 186–7.

lem now – admittedly a formidable one – is to estimate the magnitude of that cost. That is what we shall be attempting to do in the next section of this chapter.

II. THE COST OF THE TRADE-OFFS

Each of the two aspects of the threat of the overhang has been estimated at a rate of about £100 million. Neither figure is necessarily very accurate, but the two at least have the merit of being indicative of probable orders of magnitude. Together they add up to £200 million, which is, broadly speaking, the additional constraint for Britain ensuing from the asset-currency function of sterling. That is, £200 million is the additional amount by which, at any time, the balance of payments could potentially deteriorate (on an exchange-market basis) if for one reason or another confidence in the pound were to weaken. This is the amount of additional improvement in the balance of payments that the authorities must achieve, by means of available economic and social policies, if a loss of reserves of such magnitude is to be avoided.

In the short run, of course, the payments crisis could be financed: the additional improvement could be achieved by borrowing from abroad – from the International Monetary Fund or from the major central banks. In fact, this is what the British did on a massive scale between 1964 and 1968. However, in the longer run credits must be repaid; and they cannot simply be repaid from funds returning after the crisis is past. That has too much of an appearance of taking money from one pocket merely to put it into another – robbing Peter to pay Paul. Credits lose their credibility unless they are backed up by policies of real adjustment. The improvement in the balance of payments must be genuine, otherwise funds may not come back at all.

How is the additional improvement in the balance of payments to be achieved? The United Kingdom has taken on a number of important policy commitments in the world bearing on its foreign-exchange position.[1] Most importantly, these include: (1) a commitment to maintain full employment and maximum growth at home; (2) a commitment to preserve relatively unrestricted freedom of current-account transactions abroad; (3) a commitment to export capital to the rest of

[1] Richard N. Cooper, op. cit., pp. 153–6.

the world; (4) a commitment to maintain an extensive diplomatic and
military role in the world; and (5) a commitment to preserve the roles
of sterling as an international currency. Assuming for our purposes that
the last objective remains fixed, it follows that Britain's paramount
commitment is to sustain the credibility of its convertibility pledge: if
sterling's international status is to be preserved, the terms of convertibility must not be allowed to fall into doubt (see Chapter 2). Thus both
exchange control and currency devaluation are ruled out as possible
adjustment policies – except as a very last resort.[1] Short of that, additional improvement in the balance of payments can be achieved only
by compromising some or all of Britain's four *other* policy objectives.
The authorities must either (1) depress employment and growth at
home; (2) restrict freedom of current-account transactions abroad; (3)
restrain capital outflows; or (4) reduce overseas diplomatic and military
commitments. These effectively define the range of available options.
Under ordinary circumstances, the authorities are necessarily limited
to just these four choices of policy.

Analysis of the cost implied by each of these alternative choices will
be simplified because of the pioneering work by Richard N. Cooper in
the 1968 Brookings Institution study of *Britain's Economic Prospects.*[2]
Approaching the U.K. balance of payments as a problem of economic
policy, Cooper quantified the potential impact on Britain's foreign-
exchange position of several different courses of action. These included
a rise of the unemployment rate; the imposition of a surcharge on
imports of manufactured products; an across-the-board reduction of
private capital outflows; an across-the-board reduction of foreign aid;
a reduction in the Government's military expenditures overseas; and a
devaluation of the pound. In effect, his calculations showed all the
relevant trade-offs among objectives with respect to a general improvement of the balance of payments. The trade-offs for an improvement
of £200 million in a year are shown in Table 7.6.[3] We see that an

[1] As we know, the U.K. has devalued three times as a last resort over the course
of the century. The separate costs of devaluation are considered in the last section
of this chapter.
[2] Cooper, op. cit., pp. 147–97.
[3] Ibid., p. 196. Cooper's summary shows his calculations of the trade-offs with
respect to an improvement of £100 million in a year. I have adjusted his figures
for an improvement of twice that amount.
In addition, I have specifically adjusted his calculation of the trade-off for a
reduction of private capital outflows. Cooper reckoned that for a payments
improvement of £100 million, a reduction of £110 million would be required.

improvement on this scale could be achieved only by a rise of 0·68 per cent in the rate of domestic unemployment, or by a surcharge rate of 8 per cent on the import of foreign manufactures. Alternatively, if the authorities prefer to avoid these two courses of action, then they would instead have to reduce either private capital outflows by £224 million, foreign aid by £318 million, or overseas military expenditures by £286 million; or they would have to devalue by approximately 3 per cent. Of course, not all of the burden of adjustment need fall on any single item. Various combinations (partial trade-offs) are possible also.

These estimates are valuable. To be sure, they must be handled with caution. Cooper himself is appropriately modest about his results: 'the calculations made here are crude and in one sense border on being presumptuous'.[1] But at the same time it must be acknowledged that the calculations are of high quality, and based on the best available information. They are reasonable and not at all misleading. There seems little cause, therefore, not to use them for the analytical purposes at hand. They will be helpful in estimating the alternative costs implied by the asset-currency constraint. The following discussion will be limited to just three of the courses of action listed in Table 7.6: a rise of unemployment; a surcharge on imports; and a restriction of private capital outflows. These three all translate directly into potential losses of national income. I exclude reductions of foreign aid or overseas military expenditures because these are too bound up with political considerations to yield useful measures of economic cost. The contingent costs of devaluation will be examined separately in the last section of this chapter.

This figure was based on Professor Reddaway's *interim* study of the effects of British overseas investment, published in 1967, which had estimated that for every £100 million of new capital outflow, British exports rise (on average) by about £9 million. (Thus 91:100 = 100:110.) However, after Cooper wrote, Reddaway published his final report (1968), increasing the estimated rise of exports to £11 million. Cooper's calculation must therefore be increased to £112 million (89:100 = 100:112) – or £224 million for a £200 million improvement of the balance of payments. See W. B. Reddaway in collaboration with J. O. N. Perkins, S. J. Potter and C. T. Taylor, *Effects of U.K. Direct Investment Overseas: An Interim Report* (Cambridge: Cambridge University Press, 1967) p. 122; and W. B. Reddaway in collaboration with S. J. Potter and C. T. Taylor, *Effects of U.K. Direct Investment Overseas: Final Report* (Cambridge University Press, 1968) p. 342.

[1] Cooper, op. cit., p. 195.

Table 7.6

Alternative Methods of Improving the British Balance of Payments by £200 Million[a]

Course of action	Size of policy change
Rise of unemployment rate	0·68 percentage points
Imposition of import surcharge on manufacturers[b]	8 per cent
Across-the-board reduction of private capital outflows	£224 million
Across-the-board reduction of foreign aid	£318 million
Reduction of overseas military expenditures	£286 million
Devaluation of the pound[c]	2·82 per cent

[a] Per year, in terms of transactions levels of 1966. 'Medium-term' effects, after a period of adjustment.

[b] Assumes no foreign retaliation.

[c] Assumes other currencies devalued are limited to those devalued in November 1967.

Source: Richard N. Cooper, 'The Balance of Payments', in Richard E. Caves and Associates, *Britain's Economic Prospects* (Washington: Brookings Institution, 1968) p. 196.

Deflation

Ever since the inter-war period Britain has placed heavy emphasis on full employment as a central objective of national economic policy. However, at the same time it has not escaped the notice of successive British Governments that domestic deflation is a convenient means of achieving an improvement, when it is needed, in the balance of payments. In the United Kingdom both monetary and fiscal policies can be employed flexibly to influence aggregate output and employment, and through them aggregate imports and exports. Cooper estimates that the trade-off between unemployment and the payments balance is of the order of 0·1 additional percentage points of the former for roughly every £29 million improvement of the latter.[1] For £200 million of improvement, approximately 0·68 additional percentage points of unemployment would be required. What would this mean in terms of national income forgone?

[1] Cooer, op. cit., pp. 156–62.

As a rule, short-term fluctuations in employment tend to understate the corresponding fluctuations in gross income and output. That is, in the short term the rate of employment of labour typically varies by less than the corresponding rate of employment of total capacity. There are several reasons for this.[1] The most important explanation is that the rate of utilisation of labour tends to change simultaneously. Some workers, in production as well as administration, are regarded by their employers as a kind of overhead: their number is neither reduced when there is a temporary decline in output, nor raised when there is a temporary increase; instead, they simply work at a more or less leisurely pace. Additional factors include changes in the length of the working week and changes in the number of marginal workers entering or leaving the labour force.

The precise relationship between unemployment and output is not easy to identify. Frank Paish has suggested that a variation in the rate of unemployment is associated with a variation in gross output (sign changed) multiplied by a factor of five.[2] However, this seems an extraordinarily high figure; at any rate, Paish's evidence is sketchy and not very convincing. Much more complete and convincing is the evidence from two full-scale empirical investigations, one an international comparison by Brechling and O'Brien, the other a U.K. study by Godley and Shepherd.[3] Both sources produce a virtually identical estimate of a factor of two. That is, they both agree that changes in gross output in Britain typically are about double the corresponding (opposite) changes in the rate of unemployment.

This means that an increase of roughly 0·68 percentage points of unemployment will be associated with a loss of approximately 1·36 per cent of real national output. In Britain in 1968 gross domestic product (which is the most comprehensive measure of the output of the economy) stood at £36,267 million. 1.36 per cent of that is £493 million. This is indicative of the amount of national income that would have to be foregone if deflation were the alternative chosen to achieve an additional £200 million improvement in the balance of payments.

---

[1] See, e.g., Cooper, op. cit., pp. 157–8; and F. W. Paish, *Studies in an Inflationary Economy* (London: Macmillan, 1962) p. 318.

[2] Ibid., p. 319.

[3] Frank Brechling and Peter O'Brien, 'Short-Run Fluctuations in Manufacturing Industries: An International Comparison', *Review of Economics and Statistics*, XLIX 3 (Aug 1967) 277–87; and W. A. H. Godley and J. R. Shepherd, 'Long-Term Growth and Short-Term Policy', *National Institute Economic Review*, no. 29 (Aug 1964) pp. 26–38. But cf. Richard N. Cooper, op. cit., p. 160, n. 26.

Trade restriction

The United Kingdom has a long tradition of liberal commercial policy. Indeed, it was not until the inter-war period that British imports came to be seriously restricted at all. In the post-war period Britain has been a leader in the multilateral movement to reduce barriers to trade, participating actively in the liberalisation programme of GATT, the O.E.C.D. and EFTA. In addition, in 1961 Britain accepted a commitment to keep all current-account transactions free from exchange restrictions under Article VIII of the I.M.F. Articles of Agreement. But on the other hand, in November 1964 the new Labour Government took a step unilaterally to raise barriers to trade, by imposing a surcharge of 15 per cent on imports of most manufactured products. Such imports amounted to about £1·6 billion in 1964, roughly one-third of total imports at the time. However, despite appearances, the step was not the beginning of a reversal of Britain's traditionally liberal trade policies: it was not taken for ostensibly protectionist purposes. Rather, the balance of payments was in crisis, and the new Government recognised that trade restriction was one of the alternative means available for achieving an improvement on external account.

Some forms of trade restriction during a payments crisis are perfectly legal under current international arrangements.[1] Unfortunately, the Labour Government's surcharge was not one of them, and as a result the step evoked strong verbal reactions from other countries – especially from Britain's partners in EFTA. Although no direct retaliation to the surcharge was forthcoming, the foreign backlash was undoubtedly sufficient to hasten its ultimate demise. In April 1965 the levy was reduced to 10 per cent (announced the preceding February), and in November 1966 it was finally eliminated altogether (announced the preceding May).

There is still disagreement regarding the effectiveness of the surcharge. When it was first announced, it was expected to reduce imports by about £300 million a year. But according to the most systematic estimate to date, by Johnston and Henderson, imports were in fact probably reduced by only £156 million through the end of

---

[1] For example, both the General Agreement on Tariffs and Trade (Article 12) and the Stockholm Convention establishing the European Free Trade Association (Article 19) sanction the use of import quotas for balance-of-payments purposes.

1965, and by £72 million in 1966, both in terms of 1958 prices.[1] Converting to 1964 prices suggests a reduction of £130 million during the year 1965 (excluding the last quarter of 1964, which is included in the £156 million) and of £80 million in 1966.[2] However, Johnston and Henderson probably underestimated the effectiveness of the surcharge, to the extent that the full amount of the tax was not reflected in the price paid in Britain for manufactured imports. The surcharge was known to be temporary. Accordingly, many foreign exporters, wanting to maintain their position in the British market, may have absorbed some of its themelves. As Cooper points out, this possibility is supported by the fact that import unit values, which had been rising steadily during the several years before 1965, stopped rising in 1965 and 1966 despite continued price increases in exporting countries. By adjusting for this possibility, Cooper increases the estimated effectiveness of the surcharge.[3] His calculation of the trade-off between a control of this kind and the payment balance (on the assumption of no direct foreign retaliation) is of the order of approximately one additional percentage point of the former for every £25 million improvement of the latter. For £200 million of improvement a surcharge of 8 per cent would be required.

A surcharge on this order – or indeed any trade control at all – is bound to create an efficiency loss incidentally by protecting import-competing industries. The misallocation of resources is the cost of the improvement in the balance of payments. The magnitude of the cost will depend on the flexibility of output and demand in the economy, on the structure of prior trade restrictions, and especially on the nature of the new trade restriction. In general, the more selective barriers to imports are, the greater are the distortions that are introduced into the domestic price system. Conversely, the more uniform a new barrier is, the smaller is the loss of income that will ensue.[4] Labour's surcharge in 1964 was applied uniformly to virtually all imports competing with manufacturing industries in Britain. We may assume, therefore, that the cost of the surcharge, or of any control like it, represents broadly

---

[1] John Johnston and Margaret Henderson, 'Assessing the Effects of the Import Surcharge', *Manchester School of Economic and Social Science*, XXXV 2 (May 1967) 89–110.

[2] Richard N. Cooper, op. cit., p. 167.

[3] Ibid.

[4] Richard N. Cooper, *The Economics of Interdependence: Economic Policy in the Atlantic Community* (New York: McGraw-Hill, for the Council on Foreign Relations, 1968) p. 252.

the *lower* limit of the range of potential efficiency losses from trade restriction.

There has been surprisingly little empirical research by economists into the efficiency losses of trade restrictions. However, what little work has been done suggests that in developed economies such losses tend to be very small for uniform tariffs or surcharges – certainly lower than the corresponding losses of income that are necessitated by deflations of equivalent impact on the balance of payments.[1] At the theoretical level this suggestion has been confirmed by Harry Johnson. Using a simplified but highly plausible model, he calculates

> that both the total gains from international trade and the cost of protection are likely to be relatively small in the large advanced industrial countries, owing to their relatively flexible economic structures, probably high elasticities of substitution among the goods on which this consumption is concentrated, and relatively low natural dependence on trade.[2]

We can use Johnson's calculations to estimate the cost for Britain of an 8 per cent surcharge on manufactured imports. As it happens, the British do not have a relatively low natural dependence on trade: in fact, imports run at between 16 and 17 per cent of gross national product. But on the other hand, it happens that like other large advanced industrial countries they do have a relatively high degree of flexibility in both output and demand. If we assume that the elasticities of substitution in production and consumption are each unity, we find that the efficiency loss created by an 8 per cent surcharge amounts to not more than one-third of 1 per cent of free-trade output.[3] Of course, we have no idea what free-trade output might potentially be, but as an approximation we may instead take the most comprehensive statistical measure available of actual output – namely, gross domestic product. In 1968, one-third of 1 per cent of G.D.P. was roughly £120 million. This is indicative of the *minimum* amount of national income that would have to be forgone if a uniform surcharge were the alternative chosen to achieve an additional £200 million improvement in the balance of

[1] Richard N. Cooper, *The Economics of Interdependence*, pp. 249–52, 257–9. Existing empirical work on the efficiency losses from trade restriction is summarised by Harvey Leibenstein, 'Allocative Efficiency *vs.* "X-Efficiency"', *American Economic Review*, LVI 3 (June 1966) 392–4.

[2] Harry G. Johnson, 'The Costs of Protection and Self-Sufficiency', *Quarterly Journal of Economics*, LXXIX 3 (Aug 1965) 371.

[3] This is composed of a consumption cost of approximately 0·09 per cent (calculated from Johnson, Table IA, p. 361) and a production cost of approximately 0·24 per cent (from Table II, p. 365).

payments. If more selective forms of trade restrictions were chosen (e.g. differential levies or import quotas), the cost would be correspondingly greater.

Capital restriction

Britain has historically been a large exporter of long-term capital on private account (Chapter 4), though over the years the nature of the outflow has changed radically. Throughout the nineteenth century, and indeed even as late as the 1920s, investments abroad were predominantly in the form of fixed debt, mainly bonds. Since the Second World War, on the other hand, portfolio investment has declined in comparative importance, becoming subordinated to direct investment, where British residents have a controlling interest in the foreign operation. Table 7.7 shows capital outflows (including re-invested earnings) after 1958, the period for which such detailed data are available. The 'oil and miscellaneous' category is mostly oil, and also mostly direct investment. It is clear that while direct investment has been growing substantially, there have actually been net liquidations of portfolio investments in most years. Purchases of new securities issued in London by members of the sterling area have continued on a modest scale (averaging, after redemptions, approximately £5 million a year from 1960 to 1968), but these have been more than offset by sales of outstanding securities.

Private capital exports are a key element in sustaining the credibility of an international currency's convertibility, since (unless they are grossly unprofitable) they help to maintain the issuing country's international solvency. Even so, for many years successive British Governments have maintained strict controls on the outward movement of funds.[1] The country's foreign-exchange position has been considered too precarious to leave investors unfettered. Outside the sterling area direct investments have been administratively controlled, and portfolio investments have been limited by the requirement, already mentioned, that they go through the investment-currency market. Since 1965 these restraints have actually been tightened.[2] And indeed, even

[1] 'The U.K. Exchange Control: A Short History', loc. cit., pp. 245–60.

[2] However, currently an exception is made, under certain conditions, for direct investors and investment trusts to borrow Euro-dollars abroad for the purpose of investment outside the sterling area. The exception does not extend to individuals interested in non-sterling portfolio investments.

within the sterling area, where traditionally capital outflows are supposed to be unrestricted, recently certain new limitations have been imposed. In 1957, for instance, in order to close the Kuwait and Hong Kong gaps, the authorities prohibited British purchases of dollar or other non-sterling securities from overseas sterling-area residents. Similarly, in 1966, in order to strengthen further the balance of payments during the great crisis, a so-called 'voluntary' programme was instituted to limit direct investments in the 'developed sterling area' – defined as comprising Australia, Ireland, New Zealand and South Africa. In previous years these four countries apparently had accounted for the bulk of British investment in the sterling area.[1]

Table 7.7

United Kingdom Private Long-term Capital Outflows, 1958–68[a]
(in £ millions)

	1958	1959	1960	1961	1962	1963	1964	1965	1966	1967	1968
Direct	144	196	250	226	209	236	263	308	276	281	429
Portfolio			−37	−28	−39	+5	+3	−92	−82	+52	+218
Oil and miscellaneous	166	107	109	115	72	79	133	140	110	124	89
Total	310	303	322	313	242	320	399	354	304	457	736

[a] Outflow + ; inflow − .

Source: Central Statistical Office, *United Kingdom Balance of Payments 1969*.

All of this does not leave much room for further restriction of capital exports. Even if at some point the authorities should need to turn another screw, they may well find it difficult to locate one – unless they are willing to contemplate virtually a complete embargo on new investments abroad. But even before that point is reached, a prior consideration intervenes, at least in so far as the overseas sterling area is concerned: further restrictions could endanger the very foundations of the system. It is well known that the outer member's privileged access to British capital is one of the few threads still holding the sterling bloc together:

> The kernel of the sterling area arrangement, in so far as any arrangement formally exists, is a *quid pro quo*: that Britain should give the overseas sterling countries broadly free access to the London capital and money market, and impose no exchange control on outward payments to them – in exchange for which these countries will generally keep their external reserves at the Bank of England, rather than in dollars or in gold. . . .
> The fear is that, if Britain ever rescinded its part of the bargain, the sterling

---

[1] John Cooper, op. cit., p. 162.

area countries could cause massive disturbances by liquidating their balances in London and demanding dollars and gold that Britain could not pay.[1]

Nevertheless, suppose Britain *must* temporarily turn on the screw, further restricting private investments overseas. What is the income cost of this kind of restriction? On balance, portfolio investments abroad have been in a process of liquidation, rather than increasing, over the post-war period. Accordingly, to estimate the cost of capital restriction we may concentrate exclusively on direct investment. This was, likewise, Cooper's procedure in estimating the balance-of-payments trade-off for a reduction of capital outflows. Also like Cooper's, the calculation here will be based on Professor Reddaway's research into the various effects of British direct investment overseas.[2]

As I described in Chapter 5, Reddaway estimated that foreign assets on average produce an operating return to British investors of 6 per cent on the total of capital invested. Table 7.6 indicates that investments abroad must be reduced by £224 million if the balance of payments is to be improved by £200 million, which means that a return stream of earnings equal to some £13 million a year would have to be forgone as a result. Discounted at the domestic 'opportunity' cost of 3 per cent suggested by Professor Reddaway, this represents a total loss to Britain of some £433 million. This is the order of magnitude of the cost of capital restriction to the British economy, should that alternative be chosen to achieve the additional improvement on external account.

Summary

Three alternative costs implied by the asset-currency constraint have been estimated. Rounding to the nearest quinquevalent, these are:

Deflation	£495 million.
Trade restriction	£120 million (minimum).
Capital restriction	£435 million.

[1] *The Economist*, 19 Feb 1966, p. 721. In 1966, following the announcement of the voluntary programme affecting the developed sterling area, the fear was almost realised. Many sterling-area countries saw the programme as the thin edge of a wedge. It is reported that New Zealand definitely threatened to withdraw its reserves from London. See John Cooper, op. cit., p. 230.

[2] See pp. 172–3, n. 3 above, and Chapter 5.

Obviously, all three policy options are potentially quite costly to Britain. The least costly appears to be a uniform trade restriction such as an import surcharge. However, it is enough simply to recall the violence of the outcry that followed the imposition of Labour's 15 per cent surcharge in 1964 to realise how unlikely it is that that option will ever be adopted again. The rules of the international trade game today make it much more acceptable to use selective controls – specifically, import quotas – than uniform levies.[1] On the other hand, there are few legal restraints of any kind on the use of capital controls; and apart from domestic electoral considerations, there are no limits at all to the degree of deflation that may be exerted. Thus, in the event of a weakening of confidence in sterling and a deterioration of the balance of payments, the Government is likely first to resort to deflation or capital controls or import quotas, rather than to another surcharge on the 1964 model. In other words, in the event that the contingent cost of the asset-currency constraint becomes an actual cost, it is more likely to be near the upper than the lower limit of the estimated range.

III. THE COST OF EXCHANGE GUARANTEES

Devaluation of an international currency is ordinarily unthinkable. As Chapter 1 emphasised, convertibility at a fixed rate of exchange is a necessary condition for any national currency to begin being used for international purposes; once it is being used for international purposes, convertibility at a fixed rate of exchange must remain credible. Hence devaluation is ruled out as a possible means of adjustment. Under normal circumstances the authorities are limited to a choice of *other* policies for improving the balance of payments. However, circumstances are not always normal, and consequently international currencies are sometimes devalued after all. Sterling has been devalued three times in the twentieth century – in 1931, 1949 and 1967 – and it is not at all inconceivable that it could happen again. It is not at all inappropriate, therefore, to think about the ordinarily unthinkable. In this final section we shall briefly consider the potential costs of another devaluation for Britain. Specifically, these are the contingent costs of exchange guarantees, formal or informal.

[1] See p. 176, n. 1 above.

Formal guarantees

Under the terms of the Basle reform, Britain formally guaranteed to maintain the dollar value of most official sterling reserves of sterling-area countries, with no counterpart concession by members apart from their commitment to maintain a Minimum Sterling Proportion in their reserves. These were obviously generous terms – some might think almost too generous. However, at the time the arrangement was nego-tiated the British had little choice in the matter. Their backs were to the wall. As I have emphasised before, the 1967 devaluation shocked the overseas members, many of whom suffered severe windfall losses on their sterling assets. In the second quarter of 1968 they began seriously to move their reserves out of London. Britain, faced with the prospect of a new and truly serious run on the pound, apparently responded by offering to negotiate some kind of exchange guarantee against future losses.[1] The confidential talks were then initiated which resulted in the reform announced in September.[2]

Because the guarantee is so generous, it is certain to cost the British dearly if they are ever compelled to devalue again. They have agreed to make a payment in sterling to each overseas member to restore the dollar value of the guaranteed portion of its reserves. Regrettably, we cannot know precisely what the cost to Britain might be, because the published statistics do not reveal just what amount of reserves is actually covered in the arrangement. However, we do at least have an official approximation. In an oral answer to a parliamentary question on Budget Day, 1969, the Financial Secretary to the Treasury esti-mated that at end-1968 the total amount of sterling guaranteed was 'of the order of £1750 million'.[3] Interestingly, this is more than the total of liquid liabilities to sterling-area official holders reported outstanding at the time by the Bank of England in its *Quarterly Bulletin* (£1650 million). But the discrepancy is easily explained. The Basle reform

[1] Apparently the possibility of compensation for 1967 devaluation losses was never seriously considered, even though a precedent for at least partial reimburse-ment had been established at the time of the devaluation in 1949. See Livingstone, op. cit., p. 64.

[2] It is perhaps symptomatic of how pressed the British were, that as early as June, Hong Kong, a crown colony nominally under British rule, was able to extract an effective guarantee for up to half of its sterling reserves. See *The Economist*, 8 June 1968, p. 78; and *Bank of England Quarterly Bulletin*, VIII 3 (Sep 1968) 236. [3] *Hansard*, 14 Apr 1969.

guarantees official sterling reserves *as defined by the associated bilateral agreements between the United Kingdom and overseas-sterling-area countries.* For this purpose the agreements include, within the definition of reserves, some funds which in the published British statistics are treated as long-term capital.[1]

Richard Cooper calculates that the trade-off between devaluation and the balance of payments is 1·41 per cent of the former for every £100 million additional improvement of the latter. Thus for £200 million of improvement on external account, a devaluation of roughly 3 per cent would be required (Table 7.6). But in such an event £1750 million worth of sterling reserves would also have to be written up by a like amount – namely, by £52·5 million. This is indicative of the contingent devaluation cost today of the formal guarantee provided under the terms of the Basle reform. On the assumption that total overseas sterling-area reserves are likely to rise over time – and therefore sterling reserves as well – it is in fact a minimum estimate.

The cost of the guarantee is attributable exclusively to the pound's use for official purposes. It is the price Britain must potentially pay to ensure the stability of sterling-area reserve liabilities. (It is also a measure of the minimum price Britain will now be willing to pay, by other means, in order to avoid any new devaluation of the pound.) As between the medium-of-exchange and store-of-value functions, the cost divides in proportion to the ratio of working balances (use as an intervention currency) to investment balances (use as a reserve currency) in the total. I have already suggested (in Chapter 5) how that ratio may be determined. Working balances may be assumed to include all bank deposits, plus 25 per cent of all other short-term liabilities; liabilities recorded as long-term in the British statistics may be assumed to be all investment balances. This yields a ratio of a little more than 1:2.[2] The contingent devaluation cost of sterling's use as an intervention currency today is approximately £20 million; of its use as a reserve currency, approximately £35 million.

---

[1] *Exchanges of Notes and Letters Concerning the Guarantee by the United Kingdom and the Maintenance of the Minimum Sterling Proportion by Certain Overseas Sterling Area Governments,* Cmnd 3834 (Nov 1968); and *Exchanges of Despatches and Letters Concerning the Guarantee by the United Kingdom and the Maintenance of the Minimum Sterling Proportion by Certain Overseas Sterling Area Governments,* Cmnd 3835 (Nov 1968).

[2] Working balances = bank deposits (£259 million) + 25 per cent of other published short-term liabilities (343). Investment balances = 75 per cent of the other published liabilities (1030) + liabilities recorded in British statistics as long-term (118). Ratio = 603:1148 = a little more than 1:2.

Informal guarantees

Beginning in 1964 and continuing until devaluation in 1967, the British Government intervened actively in the forward-exchange market to support the forward price of the pound.[1] The authorities understood that the forward market was an important indicator of expectations with respect to the spot rate for sterling. A drop in the forward rate would be widely interpreted as a signal of declining confidence in the pound; if not reversed, it would frequently lead to cumulative waves of adverse and destabilising speculation. (A drop in the forward rate would of course also lead to cumulative outward movements of arbitrage funds). Therefore, the Government decided to intervene to keep the rate ever from dropping in the first place. In the process, obviously, it artificially cheapened the cost of forward cover for private transactions in general. In other words, the authorities effectively provided private sterling transactors with an informal exchange guarantee, in the form of a kind of officially subsidised insurance.

In principle, official intervention in the forward market can be very advantageous – so long as there is no devaluation of the currency involved.[2] The authorities moderate speculative influences and promote market confidence, and indeed can even earn a profit, in the form of the discount below spot price on forward purchases. This is the price that private transactors must pay for their informal exchange guarantee. In the case of Britain between 1964 and 1967, the forward discount varied generally between 0·5 and 2·0 per cent on a per annum basis – pure profit for the British Government.

Unfortunately, in Britain's case there was also a devaluation. Accordingly, on 18 November 1967 the authorities found themselves with a mass of outstanding commitments to buy pounds at a rate considerably higher than the new spot price. These commitments are now known to have cost the Government a total of £356 million as they were gradually unwound in 1967 and 1968.[3]

This is a lot of money. However, it does not provide a true picture

[1] John Cooper, op. cit., pp. 51–7.

[2] The advantages and disadvantages of official forward intervention are summarised by Peter M. Oppenheimer, 'Forward Exchange Intervention: The Official View', loc. cit., pp. 2–13; and Henry H. Goldstein, 'Forward Exchange Intervention: Another View of the Recent British Experiment', *Westminster Bank Review* (Aug 1966) 2–14.

[3] Central Statistical Office, *United Kingdom Balance of Payments 1969.*

of the cost of the informal guarantee. In the years before devaluation the authorities were earning a profit from their activities in the forward-exchange market. The cost estimate ought to be adjusted to take account of that fact. Altogether, the Government was in the business of forward intervention for three years. What we need to know is how large that volume of business was. At the time of devaluation the Government's outstanding commitments must have been in the vicinity of £3 billion (assuming an average loss rate of 11-12 per cent).[1] Unfortunately, this figure cannot be taken as an accurate index of official activity in the forward market between 1964 and 1967, since the amount is inflated by the massive waves of speculation which engulfed the authorities just prior to devaluation. A better index has been provided by John Spraos, who estimates that at end-September 1966 official commitments amounted to £1·5-£2·0 billion.[2] We can use this figure. If we assume that over the three years prior to devaluation the volume of the Government's business was broadly constant at about that level,[3] and if furthermore we assume that during the period the forward discount on sterling averaged out to about 1 per cent per annum, then we may conclude that profits prior to devaluation added up to something like £45-£60 million. Subtracting this from the estimated loss from devaluation suggests a net cost of forward intervention of the order of approximately £300 million.

Whatever the actual magnitude of the cost, the British Government apparently considered it sufficiently great to refrain from similar activity in the future. Since devaluation there has been no sign of significant official intervention to support the forward price of the pound. Discouraged and disillusioned by the 1967 experience, the authorities no longer intend to provide private sterling transactors with an informal exchange guarantee. Therefore, we may be permitted to ignore this contingent cost of devaluation in the remainder of Part Two. However, looking forward to Part Three, it is worth while to

[1] Immediately after devaluation *The Economist* suggested that commitments outstanding on the day of devaluation amounted to no more than £1·2-£1·5 billion (25 Nov 1967, p. 867). But this figure is clearly too low: on that basis the Government's devaluation loss could not have been more than half of what in fact has been officially reported.

[2] John Spraos, 'Some Aspects of Sterling in the Decade 1957-66', in Robert Z. Aliber (ed.), *The International Market for Foreign Exchange* (New York: Praeger, 1969) p. 163.

[3] This is not an implausible assumption. It would account for *The Economist's* post-devaluation estimate of £1·2-£1·5 billion.

remember that the cost of forward intervention is a *net* cost: it includes not only the devaluation loss on outstanding commitments (if and when there is a devaluation), but also all of the profits earned from supporting the rate prior to devaluation. The longer the intervals between devaluations, the greater the profits to offset the cost of devaluation itself. Indeed, if the intervals are long enough, over time the Government could actually make money from the business.

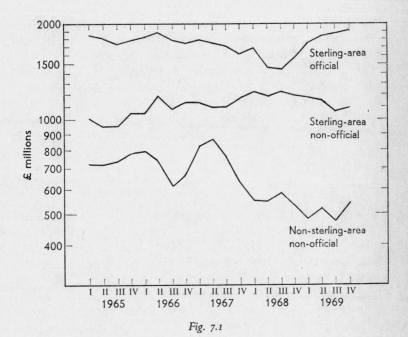

Fig. 7.1

8 Reserves and a Unit of Account

Two potential effects of the international use of sterling remain to be discussed: the effect of supplying reserves to the rest of the world; and the effect of supplying a unit of account for the purpose of expressing par values (see Chapter 2). Our discussion may be kept brief, for owing to the gradual shrinkage over the years of the pound's international functions, by today neither of these effects is any longer of much practical significance for Britain.

I. SUPPLYING RESERVES

The incomes effect of supplying reserves (which may be either benefit or cost) presupposes that there is foreign official accumulation of the international currency. The point is obvious: plainly, unless reserves are in fact supplied, there can be no effect from this source. Nevertheless, the point must be made, for it explains why this effect is now of negligible significance for Britain – because, as already emphasised (in Chapters 4 and 5), the country has long since ceased to be a source of net reserve growth for other countries. Only during the Second World War was there any substantial build-up of official sterling balances; at that time the British undoubtedly did experience an income effect from supplying reserves. However, since the war genuine net accumulation of the pound for official store-of-value purposes has left off completely. The result is that for the United Kingdom today the effect of supplying reserves is just a thing of the past.

To be sure, since the Second World War there has been a significant build-up of sterling balances in the hands of official holders *outside* the sterling area. This can be seen clearly in Table 8.1 (adapted from Table 5.3). After a gradual decline by about £300 million between 1945 and 1964, liabilities to non-sterling-area monetary authorities increased enormously in the next five years, by almost £1 billion, to a grand total

Table 8.1

United Kingdom Sterling Liabilities to Official Holders, 1945–69
(in £ millions)

	Sterling area	Non-sterling area			Sterling area	Non-sterling area
1945	1923	842		1960	2029	499
46	1889	857		61	2097	440
47	1819	943		62)	2056	375
48	1734	729		62)	1815	451
49	1757	720		63	1937	437
1950	2109	594		64	1947	523
51	2252	660		1965	1911	629
52	2019	477		66	1855	938
53	2203	474		67	1736	1511
54	2260	460		68 I	1815	1885
1955	2266	439		II	1531	1720
56	2240	400		III	1506	1891
57	2126	384		IV	1650	2171
58	1993	399		69 I	1847	2084
59	2165	326		II	1921	1774
				III	1977	1779
				IV	2037	1517

Source and notes: as for Table 5.3.

Table 8.2

*United Kingdom Sterling Liabilities to Non-Sterling-Area
Official Holders, 1964–9*
(in £ millions)

		Total	North America	Western Europe	Other
1964		523	97	260	166
1965		629	239	225	165
1966		938	347	394	197
1967		1511	775	555	181
1968	I	1885	996	717	172
	II	1720	820	741	159
	III	1891	970	770	151
	IV	2171	1183	890	98
1969	I	2084	1146	854	84
	II	1774	1089	602	83
	III	1779	1117	588	74
	IV	1517	903	546	68

Source: *Bank of England Quarterly Bulletin.*

of some £1½ billion at the end of 1969. However, as emphasised in Chapter 5, none of these increases represented genuinely voluntary net acquisitions of an international currency; none went to the group of official institutions in Latin America, Scandinavia and other non-sterling areas where the pound is still used occasionally for intervention or reserve purposes. (Indeed, as Table 8.2 shows, total balances owed to such holders actually declined by £98 million.) All went rather to official institutions in North America and Western Europe, and represented the counterparts of credits acquired in consequence of Britain's various swap arrangements during the great balance-of-payments crisis of those years. Precisely for that reason they cannot be regarded as reserve accumulation in the traditional sense. 'To count each sterling assets in reserves is about as appropriate as it would be, say, for a business firm to include its accounts receivable in its cash.'[1] Having been acquired in exchange for assistance in support of the pound, these new sterling balances were not immediately marketable assets. They could not be readily used by their holders, where necessary, to finance balance-of-payments deficits elsewhere; they could not be treated as additions to ordinary reserves. Accordingly, there could be no income effect of supplying reserves, and hence no benefit or cost to reflect back to Britain.

Only *within* the sterling area, where the pound still functions as an international currency for official purposes, can official holdings of sterling be regarded as reserve accumulation in the traditional sense. However, in fact net accumulation of sterling reserves by sterling-area countries ended with the Second World War. Of course, since the war many individual members have voluntarily accumulated sterling reserves – sometimes in quite substantial volume. But their acquisitions have been more than offset by the actions of other members who have chosen instead to run down their holdings in London. As Table 8.1 shows, for the group as a whole sterling reserve balances have actually stagnated over the post-war period to date. Between 1945 and 1964 there was virtually no net change; since 1964 there has been a net increase of only some £90 million. Accordingly, here too for Britain there could no longer be any income effect of supplying reserves to the rest of the world.

---

[1] Milton Gilbert, *The Gold–Dollar System: Conditions of Equilibrium and the Price of Gold*, Essays in International Finance, No. 70 (Princeton: International Finance Section, 1968) p. 5.

II. SUPPLYING A UNIT OF ACCOUNT

The income effect of supplying a unit of account (which also may be either benefit or cost) presupposes that there are foreign currencies pegged to the international currency. Again, the point is obvious: plainly, unless the money is in fact employed for expressing par values, there can be no effect from this source. Nevertheless, this point too must be made, for it explains why this effect too is now of negligible significance for Britain – because, also as already emphasised (in Chapter 4), for most countries the pound has long since ceased to serve as an international accounting unit. The shrinkage of this function has paralleled the shrinkage of sterling's world in general. The result is that for the United Kingdom today this effect too is largely just a thing of the past.

To see by just how much the pound's unit-of-account function has shrunk, we may compare the devaluation experiences of 1931, 1949 and 1967. Devaluation of an international currency such as sterling provides the ultimate test of the extent to which this role is performed, because it obliges other governments to reconsider their own par values in the light of the change. Governments whose currencies are genuinely pegged to the international currency will wish to maintain the fixed relationship by devaluing *pari passu*; governments whose currencies are not pegged to it, on the other hand, need make no alteration at all. Thus we can see how much this role is performed by observing how many currencies are devalued parallel to the international currency. True, the test is scarcely definitive. Some governments whose currencies are not pegged to the international currency may nevertheless devalue *pari passu* in order to protect their competitive trading positions in world markets; similarly, some governments whose currencies are pegged may nevertheless seize the opportunity to alter their rates of exchange vis-à-vis the international currency, also for commercial reasons. Even so, with a little caution, the comparison may still be made.

The devaluation experience of 1931 has already been described in Chapter 4. Britain left the gold standard on 21 September. Gold convertibility was suspended, the sterling exchange rate was left free to fluctuate, and other governments were obliged to decide whether to follow suit or to remain tied to gold (or, if they wished, to some other international currency). A very substantial number of countries – some immediately, some only after a considerable lag – elected to remain pegged to the pound. These included of course not only all of Britain's overseas dependencies. They included as well the independent British 'dominions' (Canada excepted), many European states (Estonia, France, Greece, Ireland, Latvia, Portugal, the Scandinavian countries, Turkey and Yugoslavia), and several other nations scattered about the face of the globe (Argentina, Egypt, Iran, Iraq, Japan and Thailand).[1] In the 1930s, the population of currencies using sterling as a unit of account obviously was quite large.

After 1939, however, that population shrank markedly, and by 1949, when the pound was devalued again (on 18 September, by 30·5 per cent), it was confined essentially to the membership of the now-formal

Table 8.3

*Non-Sterling-Area Countries that Devalued
Following Devaluation of Sterling, September 1949*

Country	Percentage of devaluation	Country	Percentage of devaluation
Austria	30·6	Indonesia	30·2
Belgium[a]	12·3	Israel	30·5
Canada	9·1	Italy	8·0
Denmark	30·5	Luxembourg	12·3
Egypt	30·5	Netherlands[a]	30·2
Finland	30·4	Norway	30·5
France[a]	38·6	Portugal[a]	13·0
Germany	20·6	Sweden	30·5
Greece	33·3	Thailand	20·0

[a] Including dependent territories overseas.

Source: International Monetary Fund, *Annual Report, 1950*.

sterling area. Every one of Britain's dependencies, and with one exception (Pakistan) every one of the independent members of the sterling area, followed the pound down with devaluation of equal percentage. But by this time few others were still using the sterling yardstick. True, many non-sterling-area countries also devalued when Britain did (see Table 8.3), also usually by the same percentage, but most did so explicitly for commercial reasons, in order to maintain their competitive trading positions, and not because they were pegged to the

[1] League of Nations, *International Currency Experience* (1944) chap. 3; and W. A. Brown, Jr, *The International Gold Standard Reinterpreted, 1914–1934*, vol. II (New York: National Bureau of Economic Research, 1940) chap. 30.

pound.[1] Only Egypt and Israel, both recent members of the sterling area, seemed still to be using sterling as a unit of account.[2]

By 1967, when the pound was devalued a third time (on 18 November, by 14·3 per cent), the population of currencies pegged to sterling had shrunk even further. Not one non-sterling-area country devalued specifically in order to maintain a fixed relationship to the pound.[3]

Table 8.4

Sterling-Area Countries that Devalued Following
Devaluation of Sterling in 1967

Country	Percentage of devaluation
Hong Kong	5·7
Fiji	8·95
Cyprus	
Gambia	
Gibraltar	
Guyana	
Irish Republic	
Jamaica	
Malawi	
Malta	14·3
Mauritius	
Southern Yemen	
Sierra Leone	
West Indian countries other than Bahamas	
Other United Kingdom dependent territories	
New Zealand	19·45
Ceylon	20·0
Iceland	24·6

Source: International Monetary Fund, *Annual Report, 1968.*

[1] See International Monetary Fund, *Annual Report, 1950*, chap. 2. Three other countries not shown in Table 8.3 – Argentina, Paraguay and Uruguay – undertook the equivalent of devaluation by instituting sweeping revisions in their existing multiple exchange-rate systems. However, their reasons too were explicitly commercial, having nothing to do with sterling's role as a unit of account.

[2] Egypt had withdrawn from the sterling area in 1947. Israel had been excluded in 1948 following the termination of Britain's mandate in Palestine.

[3] Six non-sterling-area countries did devalue following sterling in 1967: Brazil (15·7 per cent), Denmark (7·9 per cent), Israel (14·3 per cent), Macao (5·7 per cent), Nepal (24·75 per cent) and Spain (14·3 per cent). However, all did so explicitly for commercial reasons. See International Monetary Fund *Annual Report, 1968*, pp. 96–7.

Even more significantly, neither did many sterling-area countries. All
the larger members of the bloc, such as Australia, India, Kuwait,
Pakistan and South Africa, refrained from altering their par rates; and
so too did many of the smaller members, such as the Bahamas, Jordan,

Table 8.5

*United Kingdom Trade with Countries Still Using Sterling
as a Unit of Account in 1967*

(in £ millions; final row in percentages)

	U.K. exports to:	U.K. exports from:
Cyprus	18·9	12·0
Fiji	4·4	7·9
Gambia	2·8	3·3
Gibraltar	3·4	0·4
Guyana	12·5	9·5
Irish Republic	195·9	204·8
Jamaica	25·2	21·6
Malawi	7·2	10·7
Malta	15·6	3·2
Mauritius	5·8	20·2
Southern Yemen	6·8	7·9
Sierra Leone	9·8	26·2
West Indian countries other than Bahamas	49·0	62·4
Other United Kingdom dependent territories	36·1	25·5
	393·4	415·6
World	5,210·4	6,441·6
U.K. trade with unit-of-account countries as a percentage of U.K. trade with world	7·6 per cent	6·5 per cent

Sources: Board of Trade, *The Commonwealth and the Sterling Area*; and International Monetary Fund, *Direction of Trade*.

Libya, Malaysia, Nigeria and Singapore.[1] Just the few countries and
dependencies listed in Table 8.4 elected to follow the pound down, and
even of this small group some apparently did so primarily for commercial reasons rather than because they were pegged to sterling. The

[1] Also, it is important to remember that sterling-area membership had shrunk
between 1949 and 1967, owing to the departures of Iraq (1959), Rhodesia (1965)
and Burma (1966). None of these altered their par rates in 1967.

evidence suggests that this was undoubtedly true of Ceylon and New Zealand; it was probably true of Hong Kong and Iceland as well. We can be certain only of the remainder – Fiji (which, for commercial reasons, seized the opportunity to alter its rate of exchange vis-à-vis the pound) and that little band which elected to maintain a fixed relationship to sterling. Just these currencies were still using the pound as a unit of account as late as 1967.

With so few currencies still involved, clearly the income effect for Britain was not apt to be considerable. The devaluation of 1967 was not made any less effective because of this handful of countries. In all, the group accounts for only about $7\frac{1}{2}$ per cent of British exports, and for only about $6\frac{1}{2}$ per cent of British imports (see Table 8.5). On the export side, it is unlikely that there was any offset at all following devaluation, since in any event these countries do not generally compete directly with British products. And likewise on the import side the offset was undoubtedly slight, since anyway the demand for the type of products that these countries sell to the U.K. – mainly foodstuffs, beverages and crude material – tends as a rule to be comparatively price-inelastic. We may conclude, therefore, that in 1967 there was no significant income effect for Britain from supplying a unit of account. For similar reasons, we may be certain that there will be no such effect again in the near future either.

9 Summary

THE time has now come to summarise the empirical analysis of sterling's international roles. In the last four chapters we have examined all of the potential benefits and costs originally enumerated in Table 2.2. We have found that some effects, however important they were once, today are no longer of any practical significance for Britain. These include both the advantage of 'flexibility' (Chapter 7) and the indirect effects of supplying reserves and a unit of account (Chapter 8). Only four effects are still real and operative: the 'seigniorage' benefit and interest cost of the sterling balances (Chapter 5), the City's invisible earnings (Chapter 6), and the disadvantage of 'constraint' (including the contingent cost of exchange guarantees: Chapter 7). Of these, three of the four (the first, second and fourth) are attributable to more than one use of the pound; the second, the City's overseas income, depends essentially on just the one use as a transactions currency. Three of the four (the first, second and third) are specific and continuing effects of sterling's international status; the fourth, the constraint disadvantage, is a contingent effect. The allocations and estimated magnitudes of all four effects are catalogued in Table 9.1.

The table reproduces the format of Table 2.2, omitting, however, the unit-of-account functions at the two levels of transactions, which cause neither gains nor losses for Britain today; and also omitting the several effects of sterling's status which are now no longer of any practical significance. Four functions of the pound remain. Specific effects of these functions are indicated by absolute numbers, contingent effects by parentheses. The allocations and estimated magnitudes are those derived in Chapters 5–7. Once again, the reader is warned against a spurious illusion of unattainable refinement. I believe that these results are the best that could be obtained under the circumstances, but I make no claim for a very high degree of precision. The figures must be assumed to give no more than a rough idea of rank order of magnitude.

Within these limitations it is interesting to note that, of the four remaining roles shown in Table 9.1, only one appears to result in a net benefit for Britain today. This is the transactions-currency role, which yields a considerable gain in the form of seigniorage benefit plus the overseas income of the City, only fractionally offset by the interest payments attributable to sterling's use as a private exchange inter-mediary. As for the other three functions, none of these yields any net gain at all: they are all losers on balance. The biggest loser by far seems to be the asset-currency role. Interest charges for this role may be

Table 9.1

Allocation and Estimated Magnitudes of the Benefits and Costs of Sterling
(in £ millions)

Function	Medium-of-exchange		Store-of-value	
Level of transactions	Transactions currency:		Asset currency:	
	Benefit:		Benefit:	
	Seigniorage	45	Seigniorage	10
PRIVATE	The City's invisible			
TRANSACTIONS	earnings	40		
	Cost:		Costs:	
	Interest payments	30	1. Interest payments	15
			2. Constraint dis-advantage	(120–495)
	Intervention currency:		Reserve currency:	
	Benefit:		Benefit:	
	Seigniorage	20	Seigniorage	35
OFFICIAL				
TRANSACTIONS	Costs:		Costs:	
	1. Interest payments	20	1. Interest payments	45
	2. Exchange guarantee		2. Exchange guarantee	
		(20)		(35)

Source: Chapters 5–7.

smaller than for either role at the level of official international trans-actions, but the contingency cost is most certainly greater. As I em-phasised in Chapter 7, my estimate of the constraint disadvantage is deliberately conservative; moreover, I argued that should this con-tingency cost become an actual cost, it is more likely to be near the upper than the lower limit of the postulated range. There can be little doubt, therefore, that it is this international role of sterling – the use as private store of value – which is potentially most costly for the British.

Logically, the contingency costs in the table ought to be recorded with a probability factor attached, to indicate how *likely* it is that they will become actual costs. Unfortunately, this is impossible: it would be no more than guesswork. But one thing *is* certain: speculative runs on the pound occur much more frequently than devaluations. This means that the asset-currency constraint is more likely to come into force – and to come into force much more often – than the exchange guarantee on official sterling-area balances. Not only is the contingency cost of the asset-currency role greater than at the level of official transactions; so too is the probability that it will become an actual cost.

This might be thought to imply that the asset-currency role should be eliminated. Indeed, the results in Table 9.1 might be thought to imply that at least three of the pound's four roles should be eliminated: apart from the private transactions function, none of the pound's roles brings any net benefit to Britain today. But this would be fallacious reasoning. Eliminating any of the functions of sterling calls for a monetary reform of one kind or another, and any reform, as we know (Chapter 3), would generate its own costs and benefits. Whether any of the pound's roles should be eliminated, therefore, depends on its own cost as *compared with the net cost of any conceivable reform*. If it seems likely that each conceivable reform will be more costly than the role(s) the reform is intended to eliminate, then obviously it would not be in Britain's interest to make any change at all. It pays the British to change only if there is some reform that will cost less than sterling's present status.

PART THREE

The Future of Sterling as
an International Currency

10 The End of Sterling?

PROPOSALS for the reform of sterling divide basically into two classes, according to whether or not it is thought that the currency should cease once and for all to serve as international money. One class would eliminate all of the international roles of the pound: the cycle that started with the globalisation of sterling, and continued with its regionalisation, would now be completed by a return to total 'domestication'. Henceforth, as before the cycle began, the pound would serve only national monetary functions; it would survive only as a purely domestic currency. The other class of proposals would merely modify the pound's international roles: the currency would still be used for at least some international purposes. Proposals to 'domesticate' sterling will be considered in the present chapter. Less dramatic reforms will be taken up in the following two chapters. The conclusions of the analysis will be summarised at the end of Chapter 12.

I. AN AGNOSTIC POSITION

Should sterling be domesticated? Should it cease to serve altogether as international money? That is the common objective of a wide variety of reforms proposed over the years from all points of the spectrum of professional opinion.[1] It is the objective, for instance, of schemes projected from time to time to fund the sterling balances by means of a long-term loan from, variously, the United States, the E.E.C. countries, the Group of Ten, the membership of the O.E.C.D., the Commonwealth countries or sterling area, or the International Monetary Fund.

---

[1] Many of these proposals are discussed by Christopher McMahon, *Sterling in the Sixties*, Chatham House Essays, No. 4 (London: Oxford University Press, for the Royal Institute of International Affairs, 1964) chap. 7; and Susan Strange, *The Sterling Problem and the Six*, European Series, No. 4 (London: Chatham House and P.E.P., 1967) chap. 6.

Equally, it is the objective of schemes sometimes proposed which would integrate the British currency with some others, usually either with the American dollar or with the Common Market currencies. In either event, sterling holdings would be replaced by an alternative asset-reserve medium, and the pound presumably would no longer be used for any international purposes. Britain would be left with a consolidated long-term liability in place of the present mass of short-term debts.

Likewise, sterling could be domesticated in conjunction with a world-wide increase of the official price of gold. If the revaluation of gold were great enough, the United Kingdom could use its own windfall profits, plus some of the profits of others, to liquidate all outstanding sterling balances. Or the U.K. could switch to a floating rate for the pound, and in this way discourage the use of the currency for international purposes. Reform along either of these lines has frequently been proposed. Alternatively, the British might simply default on their obligations, by repudiating or confiscating the overhang of short-term liabilities. Action along these lines has not been seriously suggested. Still, it is a weapon that everyone recognises the British could be forced to use *in extremis*. It would certainly ensure the end of sterling as an international currency.

The relative merits of these alternative reforms will be discussed at length in the remainder of the present chapter. My position will be agnostic. I shall argue that none of the reforms can be seriously recommended as a genuine policy option for Britain. So far as the British are concerned, sterling *cannot* be fully domesticated. It may be quite desirable to *modify* the international roles of the pound; that we shall see in the next two chapters. But it does not seem advantageous to try to *eliminate* them altogether. The U.K. will be better off if sterling continues to serve as international money, at least in partial form.

The defect of these various reform proposals is that, basically, they are all quite unrealistic. If the U.K. is to wind up its international-currency business, someone must pay the cost of liquidation – either the British themselves or someone else. Schemes to fund the sterling balances, or to integrate the pound with some other currency, anticipate that the British would bear most of the burden. But given the size of outstanding balances, this, I submit, is an unrealistic expectation. Over the relevant time horizon the cost to Britain would actually be greater than the current cost of sterling as an international currency. It is not in the country's interest to press for reform along these lines.

Of course, the British would be happy to have someone else pay the cost of liquidation if it could be arranged. This helps to explain the interest often aroused in the U.K. for proposals for gold revaluation, or a floating rate for the pound, or even default on the sterling balances. But these alternatives too, I submit, are unrealistic under current political and economic circumstances. The illusion that others can be made to pay is spurious; and besides, these proposals all have other critical deficiencies which seriously diminish their attractiveness as genuine policy options. In the real world, they are all non-starters.

II. MAKING THE BRITISH PAY

A variety of proposals

Proposals to fund the sterling balances began in 1945 – almost as soon as the huge overhang of balances itself came into existence as a result of Britain's overseas wartime expenditures.[1] In the quarter-century since, all kinds of variations on this theme have been played. One is the I.M.F. variation: the balances would be taken over by the Fund in exchange for its own gold-guaranteed liabilities; and Britain would be left with a single consolidated long-term debt to be repaid gradually over a fixed period to maturity. This was the proposal, for instance, of Alan Day in his evidence submitted to the Radcliffe Committee in 1958;[2] and in its Report a year later the Committee itself indicated qualified approval of the suggestion.[3] Robert Triffin advocated I.M.F. funding in his *Gold and the Dollar Crisis*.[4] In 1965 the idea received official support from the Italian Finance Minister at the annual meeting of the International

[1] Richard N. Gardner, *Sterling–Dollar Diplomacy*, rev. ed. (New York: McGraw-Hill, 1969) pp. 205–7; and Fred Hirsch, *Money International*, rev. ed. (London: Penguin Books, 1969) pp. 489–93.

[2] A. C. L. Day, 'The World Liquidity Problem and the British Monetary System', in Committee on the Working of the Monetary System, *Principal Memoranda of Evidence* (1960) pp. 75–6.

[3] *Report of the Committee on the Working of the Monetary System*, Cmnd 827 (Aug 1959) paras 660, 678.

[4] Robert Triffin, *Gold and the Dollar Crisis* (New Haven: Yale University Press, 1960) pt 2, chap. 4.

Monetary Fund.[1] In 1958 it was advocated by a subcommittee of the United States Congress.[2]

Alternatively, the sterling balances could be funded by a gold and dollar loan from other industrialised countries – from, say, the Group of Ten or the membership of the O.E.C.D. The loan could be arranged either directly or through the Bank for International Settlements. This variation was also mentioned by the Italian Finance Minister in 1965.[3] A third variation was mentioned parenthetically by Professor Day – a long-term loan arranged on a European–Commonwealth basis. Sterling balances would be exchanged for the liabilities of a European–Commonwealth bank created expressly for this purpose.[4] A fourth variation might be a loan arranged on a purely Commonwealth (or purely sterling-area) basis.

Proposals to integrate sterling with other currency systems are more recent in origin, beginning really just in the early 1960s, following Britain's first application to join the European Economic Community. Here, according to some observers, was an unparalleled opportunity for the U.K., with help, to wind up its unilateral role in the international-currency business. Somehow the Six would be persuaded to co-operate in the liquidation of the pound. They might, for instance, help the British pay off the sterling balances by means of a long-term gold and dollar loan – a fifth variation on the funding theme. Alternatively, they might take over and manage the business themselves, promoting their own currencies as substitute asset-reserves media; or they might run the business jointly with Britain on the basis of a merged European currency – the 'Europa', perhaps. As a result of any of these, the pound itself would be eliminated as international money, and Britain would be left simply with a consolidated debt to its Common Market partners.[5]

---

[1] International Monetary Fund, *Summary Proceedings of the Twentieth Annual Meeting of the Board of Governors, 1965*, p. 41.

[2] *Next Steps in International Monetary Reform*, Report of the Subcommittee on International Exchange and Payments of the Joint Economic Committee of the Congress (Washington, 1968) p. 6.

[3] I.M.F., *Summary Proceedings, 1965*, p. 41. See also Robert Triffin, 'Sterling, Europe and World Monetary Reform', in *Sterling: European Monetary Cooperation and World Monetary Reform* (London: Federal Trust for Education and Research, 1968) pp. 27–8; and C. H. Villiers, 'Proposals for a European Currency', in *European Monetary Co-operation* (London: Federal Trust for Education and Research. 1969) pp. 6–7.   [4] Day, op. cit., p. 75.

[5] The possibility of a joint E.E.C.–sterling initiative is discussed by McMahon, op. cit., pp. 98–100; Strange, op. cit., pp. 51–3; and Maxwell Stamp, 'Sterling

France's repeated vetos of British attempts to join the E.E.C. have by no means destroyed enthusiasm in the U.K. for Common Market membership. However, they have had the effect of turning attention to other options as well – and in particular, to the option of some kind of North Atlantic Free Trade Area (NAFTA).[1] This would be based essentially on a trade partnership between Britain and the United States. In addition, it would almost certainly include Canada and most of the other members of the present European Free Trade Association (EFTA), and perhaps Japan, Australia and New Zealand also. As in the Common Market alternative, so here too, in the opinion of some observers, may be an opportunity for the U.K., with help, to wind up its unilateral role in the international-currency business.[2] Somehow Britain's NAFTA partners – and most especially the United States – might be persuaded to co-operate in the pound's liquidation. Like the Six, they could help fund the sterling balances by means of a long-term loan, or the United States could take over the business directly, or the partners could manage the business jointly on the basis of a common NAFTA currency.

All of these various reform proposals share the same fundamental objective. They aim to domesticate sterling – to terminate its status as an international currency once and for all. But, in fact, it is not at all clear that this objective would actually be accomplished by any of them. They all concentrate exclusively on the store-of-value function of the pound: they provide for eliminating the overhang of outstanding liabilities. However, this is not the only function of international money, as we know. There are the medium-of-exchange and unit-of-account functions as well – and none of the reforms makes any specific provisions for these roles at all. Tacitly, the proposals seem to assume that if asset and reserve balances of sterling are eliminated, the pound

---

and the Common Market', *The Banker*, CXVI 490 (Dec 1966) pp. 850–2. The latest proposals along these lines were made by Louis Camu, 'The Future of Monetary Cooperation in Europe', in *Sterling: European Monetary Cooperation and World Monetary Reform*, pp. 40–1; and by Robert Triffin, *The Fate of the Pound* (Paris: The Atlantic Institute, 1969) pp. 24–9; and 'Monetary Aspects of the Accession of Britain to the Common Market', in Edgar Pisani *et al.*, *Problems of British Entry into the E.E.C.: Reports of the Action Committee for the United States of Europe*. European Series, No. 11 (London: Chatham House and P.E.P., 1969) pp. 61–5,

[1] See, e.g., Maxwell Stamp Associates, *The Free Trade Area Option: Opportunity for Britain* (London: The Atlantic Trade Study, 1967).

[2] See, e.g., R. F. Harrod, *Dollar–Sterling Collaboration: Basis for Initiative* (London: The Atlantic Trade Study, 1967) chap. 5.

will no longer be used for transactions or intervention purposes either, or for invoicing or expressing par values. But this is a dubious assumption, to say the least.

In Chapter 1, I demonstrated that there is no unique relationship of dependence between, on the one hand, either the medium-of-exchange or unit-of-account roles of international money, and on the other hand its function as store of value. A currency may be used for accounting purposes simply in so far as it is practical; and for settlement purposes simply in so far as it is credibly convertible and attractive as a means of reducing transactions costs. Neither role requires as a necessary condition that the currency be used as a store of value too. In practice, therefore, both roles may well be maintained even if the currency ceases to serve as an asset of reserve medium. Indeed, in the case of the pound, use as an exchange intermediary might actually be expanded, once sterling balances are funded, since elimination of the overhang would be bound to enhance the credibility of Britain's foreign-exchange convertibility pledge.

Thus, it is not enough just to focus on the store-of-value function of the pound, if the objective really is to terminate sterling's status completely as an international currency. We must pay attention to the other roles as well. The various proposals to fund sterling or to integrate it with other currencies are seriously deficient in this respect. However, it is a deficiency that can be easily remedied. It is not too difficult to conceive of the kinds of supplementary foreign-exchange control measures that would suffice to discourage use of the pound as medium of exchange and unit of account also. In the following discussion I shall assume that such supplementary devices are in fact implied by each of the reform proposals presently under consideration.

An impossible burden of debt

Politically, these various reform proposals could hardly be more diverse. Some, like the NAFTA option, would perpetuate Britain's 'special relationship' with the United States; others, like the E.E.C. alternative, would terminate it. Funding sterling balances on a Commonwealth or sterling-area basis would maintain Britain's world-wide post-colonial ties and commitments; funding on an O.E.C.D. or Group of Ten basis would imply a 'little Britain' role in world affairs. Funding through the I.M.F. would suggest a more congenial attitude toward supranational economic management than any of the other variations.

Conversely, in their economics the proposals could hardly be more uniform. They are essentially similar in both means and effects; only their details are different.[1] For present sterling holders, the pound would be replaced by an alternative asset-reserve medium. For Britain, the present mixed bag of short-term liabilities would be replaced by a single consolidated debt of fixed maturity, to be repaid over a long period and at an agreed annual rate.

Superficially, the attractions of this kind of approach appear great. The problem of sterling would be solved once and for all. By a quick stroke of financial surgery, the sterling balances would be consolidated and excised, and a source of uncertainty in international monetary affairs removed. The cure would be neat, clean and final. And yet it is impossible, in my opinion, to recommend the cure to the patient, for it is not in Britain's own interest. In addition to an already massive load of outstanding fixed-term obligations (quite independent of the sterling balances), the British would be called upon to shoulder a new burden of fixed debt considerably in excess of what it presently costs to maintain the pound as an international currency. From the U.K. point of view, this kind of comprehensive reform just does not pay.

At the end of 1969, the total of sterling liabilities outstanding to all foreigners stood at approximately £7400 million. Of this, the total of liabilities closely related to the traditional roles of the pound – including all private holdings, plus the official holdings of overseas sterling-area countries – stood at approximately £3700 million (Table 5.4). At least this latter amount would have to be consolidated if sterling were to be completely funded or integrated with another currency.[2] This would mean a minimum long-term borrowing expressed in dollars

---

[1] Not that details are unimportant: however, they do not significantly affect the logic of the present discussion. The most important detail, of course, is who will make the long-term loan to Britain. Other considerations include: in what currency will the loan be made? at what interest rate? in what currency will holders of sterling be 'repaid'? and what conditions will attach to the new asset-reserve medium replacing the sterling balances? See, e.g., A. R. Conan, 'Restructuring the Sterling Area', *The Banker*, cxviii 507 (May 1968) 433–6; and Malcolm Crawford, 'Funding the Sterling Balances', *The Banker*, cxviii 509 (July 1968) 607–8.

[2] In addition, probably the balances of non-sterling-area official holders and of international organisations (excluding the U.K. subscription to the I.M.F.) would be consolidated as well. However, these additional balances are excluded from the

(since the loan would inevitably carry an exchange guarantee in dollars, if not in gold) of something close to $9 billion.

Table 10.1

United Kingdom Known Outstanding Foreign Debt, End-1969
(in $ millions)

	To be repaid in 1970	in 1971	1972 onwards	Deadline for complete repayment
United States	168	170	3787	
Lend-Lease[a]	10	10	444	2004
Line of credit[a]	65	65	2837	2000
Economic Cooperation Administration[a]	12	14	221	1983
Mutual Security Agency[a]	1	1	38	1987
Export–Import Bank[b]	80	80	247	1973–6
Canada[a]	19	19	828	2000
Portugal[a]	12	12	17	1973
Germany[c]	22	17	–	1971
Deutsche Bundesbank (April 1968)[d]	–	–	50	1972
Deutsche Bundesbank (August 1969)[d]	–	–	125	1979
International Monetary Fund				
May 1965 drawing	400	–	–	1970
June 1968 drawing	–	–	1400	1971–3
June 1969 drawing[e]	–	–	1000	1974–5
Total	621	218	7207	

[a] Debts incurred during the Second World War or early post-war years.
[b] Credit for purchase of U.S. military aircraft and missiles.
[c] Residual debit balance in European Payments Union.
[d] Offset loans for British military expenditure in Germany.
[e] Includes initial drawing of $500 million, plus three subsequent quarterly instalments totalling an additional $500 million (including a final instalment of $150 million in March 1970).
Source: *The Economist*, 3 Jan 1970, p. 41.

By any standard, this would be an immense burden of fixed debt. For Britain it would be almost too much to bear. Effectively, it would more than double the country's known outstanding fixed debts overseas. These are detailed, as of the end of 1969, in Table 10.1. In addition, at end-1969 Britain still owed substantial sums which were not officially disclosed, including drawings on central-bank swap facilities

present discussion in order to facilitate comparison with the benefits and costs estimated in Part Two of this study.

unofficially reckoned to be of the order of £1300 million ($3·1 billion);[1] and also drawings on the 1968 Basle sterling facility, which could have been as high as $1·5 billion in early 1969.[2] The U.K. has already been experiencing difficulty in servicing these various debts. The I.M.F. stand-by arranged in June 1969, for instance, was designed not to increase the total borrowing available to Britain, but merely to enable the country to postpone for between two and five years the repayment of the final instalments of Britain's 1965 credit from the Fund. The $500 million immediately drawn was used at once to pay off some of the Bank of England swap drawings from other central banks, which were all overdue.[3]

An additional burden of fixed debt of nearly $9 billion would thus come at a rather inopportune moment in British financial history. Table 10.2 provides some figures to illustrate the order of magnitude of the potential cost to Britain of a debt of these dimensions. Costs are calculated on an average annual basis, on the assumptions that (*a*) amortisation instalments would be of equal size; and (*b*) interest would be paid on the balance outstanding before each payment is made. A 10 per cent per annum rate of interest is the highest that Britain's creditors could reasonably be expected to charge. If the British were given only ten years to repay, this would mean annual instalments averaging well over half a billion pounds a year; even if they were given a hundred years, average instalments would be in excess of £200 million annually. Of course, the cost would be correspondingly lower if the interest charge were reduced. But even at the nominal rate of just $2\frac{1}{2}$ per cent per annum, and given a hundred years to repay, the U.K. would have to meet instalments averaging some £84 million a year. Even this is no mean figure.

These illustrative figures may be contrasted with the fact that at

---

[1] *The Times*, 3 Jan 1970, p. 11. At end-1968, U.K. central-bank swap drawings were officially reckoned at £2000 million ($4·8 billion) by the International Monetary Fund. See I.M.F., *Annual Report, 1969*, p. 65.

[2] *The Times*, 15 Feb 1969, p. 13. According to the Bank of England, some of this amount was repaid in the first quarter of 1969, 'because of the increase in the sterling balances of sterling area countries during the fourth quarter of 1968'. *Bank of England Quarterly Bulletin*, IX 2 (June 1969) 143. At mid-year 1969 Britain still owed $600 million under the earlier 1966 Basle sterling facility (liquidated at the time of the 1968 announcement), all of which was due to be repaid by 1971. The first of eight quarterly instalments of this debt – $75 million – was made in September 1969. See *The Times*, 3 Oct 1969, p. 21.

[3] *The Times*, 3 July 1969, p. 19.

Table 10.2

Potential Average Annual Cost to the United Kingdom of Funding the Sterling Balances: Alternative Estimates[a]
(in £ millions)

Repayment period	Annual repayment of principle (1)	Average annual interest cost				Average total annual cost			
		2·5% (2)	5% (3)	7·5% (4)	10% (5)	2·5% (1)+(2)	5% (1)+(3)	7·5% (1)+(4)	10% (1)+(5)
10 years	372	51	102	153	204	423	474	525	576
25 years	149	48	97	145	194	197	246	294	343
50 years	74	47	95	142	190	121	169	216	267
100 years	37	47	94	190	188	84	131	177	225

[a] Based on sterling balances clearly related to the international roles of the pound, including all private holdings plus the official holdings of overseas sterling-area countries. At end-1969 these totalled £3716 million. For the assumptions underlying the calculations, see the accompanying text.

present the British actually gain on balance, rather than lose, excluding contingent effects (see below), from the continued use of sterling as an international currency. Recall the benefits and costs summarised in Chapter 9 (Table 9.1). Interest payments amounting to approximately £110 million a year were found to be more than offset by the sterling-related earnings of the City and of overseas investments, estimated together at about £150 million a year. This net benefit would be lost if the pound were to become a purely domestic currency; it would become a cost item instead, *in addition to* the cost of amortisation and interest. Accordingly, it seems clear that a funding of the sterling balances simply would not be in the British interest. It does not matter how generous repayment terms might be. Britain's creditors could agree to wait two or three generations, or even more, to be fully repaid on their loan; they could even agree to forgo interest altogether. (Such generosity is difficult to imagine.) The U.K. still stands to gain more under present currency arrangements.

The reason why should be evident. Under present arrangements the bulk of the sterling balances are really rather stable. As I demonstrated in Chapter 7, only a relatively small proportion of the total tends to show any significant degree of downward volatility in the short term. Moreover, in the longer term outstanding balances are more likely to rise than to fall, as expanding international transactions and global wealth steadily increase the demands of sterling users for an exchange intermediary and store of value (offset only by a tendency on the part of users to switch from the pound to other international currencies). So long as the pound continues to function as international money, therefore, most sterling balances probably never will have to be repaid at all (on a net basis). However, if the sterling balances are funded, *all* of them, in effect, must be repaid: liabilities, most of which are tantamount to obligations of *indefinite* maturity and payment terms, would be transformed into a consolidated debt of *fixed* maturity and payment terms. Britain would now have to finance amortisation payments as well as the cost of interest – besides losing the sterling-related e arning of the City and of overseas investments. No wonder this alternative tends to be so expensive.

Because of this, it is sometimes suggested that the debt created by any form of funding operation should be made perpetual and non-redeemable rather than of fixed maturity. This idea is most often heard in connection with the I.M.F. variation on the funding theme.[1]

[1] See McMahon, op. cit., p. 105; and Triffin, *The Fate of the Pound*, p. 27.

Interest would be payable by the U.K. to the Fund, which would in turn pay interest to the one-time sterling holders who now hold a new type of I.M.F. obligation; but nothing at all would be required of the British in the form of amortisation of the outstanding principle. In effect, Britain's presently indefinite liabilities would be transformed formally into a consolidated obligation with a fixed maturity of infinity – into a kind of foreign-exchange 'Consol', as it were.

Naturally, this idea ought to appeal to the British. But it is not a very realistic idea. The I.M.F. as currently constituted is in no position to accept liability for some £3½ billion worth of convertible balances without new backing. It would need a grant of comparable magnitude from the remainder of its full international membership. Unfortunately, it is difficult enough to imagine Britain's potential creditors *lending* an amount like this for forty to a hundred years or more; it is virtually impossible to conceive of them actually *giving* such a sum away.

Alternatively, the Fund might be given the authority to issue *inconvertible* obligations in place of the sterling balances. However, this too is virtually impossible to conceive of. True, the I.M.F. now has the authority to issue special drawing rights which, from its point of view, are in fact, if not in name, inconvertible obligations. (That is, the Fund itself incurs no liabilities when S.D.R.s are created.) But the important point about S.D.R.s is that *every* country gets a share of the allocation, in proportion to its current quota in the Fund. Everyone gets a slice of the cake: there are no special beneficiaries (except, perhaps, to the extent that Fund quotas themselves are suspected of being somewhat unrepresentative of the economic weight of various countries).[1] But if on the other hand the Fund were to create additional inconvertible obligations (e.g. a supplementary issue of S.D.R.s) specially for the purpose of replacing the sterling balances, there would be only *one* immediate beneficiary – the United Kingdom itself. In effect, the British would be getting a free grant to pay off all of their short-term foreign liabilities. Once again, generosity on such a scale is difficult to imagine.[2] Among other reasons, Britain's potential creditors fear the

[1] To minimise any such suspicions, the first activation of the S.D.R. scheme in 1970 was linked with a general increase of Fund quotas – including large selective increases for those members whose economic strength was previously thought to be under-represented. Britain accepted the smallest quota increase of any I.M.F. member – to $2·8 billion, just under 10 per cent of the total ($28·9 billion).

[2] As a matter of fact, whenever the idea of using S.D.R.s for the purpose of replacing the sterling balances is discussed, it is ordinarily assumed that the

precedent that would be established by a funding of this kind: other countries might be tempted similarly to run up massive short-term debts, and then appeal to the I.M.F. to be bailed out. All idea of 'discipline', much favoured by central banks, would be vitiated.

To be sure, there would be nothing to prevent the British from using their *regular* allocation of S.D.R.s for the purpose of replacing the sterling balances. The amendment of the I.M.F. Articles of Agreement incorporating the S.D.R. scheme specifically permits any participant, 'in agreement with another participant', to use its S.D.R.s 'to obtain an equivalent amount of its own currency held by the other participant'.[1] Accordingly, in the long run all of Britain's short-term liabilities could be paid off in this way. But it should be noticed just how long in this event the long run would actually be. The first activation of the S.D.R. scheme, voted in 1969, provided for an allocation of $3·5 billion of S.D.R.s in the first year 1970, and $3 billion in each of two subsequent years – in all, $9·5 billion over a three-year period. At the same time, the U.K. quota in the Fund in 1969 amounted to just a little over 10 per cent of the total; after the general and selective increases scheduled for 1970, this proportion in fact fell to just below 10 per cent. Accordingly, the British share of the first three annual allocations will not come to more than $1 billion. At this rate it would take Britain over a quarter of a century to fund just the sterling balances closely related to the traditional roles of the pound – to say nothing of other sterling balances or of the country's additional $8 billion worth of fixed-term foreign debt. And this makes no allowance at all for adding to reserves or for financing potential payments deficits. Clearly, this approach takes us far beyond the time horizon relevant to the question at hand. The problem of sterling requires much more immediate attention than that.

Until now I have ignored the matter of the contingency costs of the

---

supplementary issue to the U.K. would take the form not of a grant but rather a *loan*. See, e.g., *The Times*, 30 Sep 1968, p. 22; 8 July 1969, p. 21; and 29 Sep 1969, supplement, p. i. This, however, is even less generous: in fact, it merely updates the I.M.F. variation on the funding theme, the problems of which have already been enumerated.

[1] Article XXV, Section 2(*a*)(i). According to one observer, this has all along been an important secondary purpose of S.D.R.s. 'It has only been kept in the background by the scheme's principal authors ... in order not to prejudice general acceptance of the new units. . . .' Peter Jay, 'I.M.F. Must Find Firm Ground', *The Times*, 29 Sep 1969, supplement, p. i. See also J. O. N. Perkins, *International Policy for the World Economy* (London: Allen & Unwin, 1969) pp. 93–4.

pound's international functions, which derive principally from the volatility of private non-sterling-area balances plus the incremental impact of these on other short-term movements into and out of Britain (see Chapter 7). These costs, as we know, may be quite considerable (Table 9.1). If we take them also into consideration, it is possible that the burden of funding the pound or integrating it with another currency will not appear so unattractive after all. However, in the next chapters we shall see that there are less expensive ways of dealing with this particular problem of the threat of the overhang. The British need not assume such an immense additional burden of debt simply in order to avoid the contingent costs of sterling.

For that matter, they need not assume such an immense burden of debt in order to avoid any of the specific costs of sterling either. There are less expensive ways of dealing with this problem also. Funding has its advantages, but not when applied to the total of sterling balances outstanding. As I have suggested, not all of the country's liabilities need to be funded. A partial funding might actually be more in Britain's own interest, even though leaving at least some balances intact. I shall return to this point in the next chapters. It is one of the main reasons for my belief that the U.K. would be better off if the pound continues to be used for at least some international purposes.

III. MAKING SOMEONE ELSE PAY

I mentioned earlier that funding or integrating with another currency are not the only methods for achieving a total domestication of the pound. Other reforms are also possible which, from Britain's point of view, would have the additional advantage of appearing to require someone other than the British to help pay some or all of the cost of liquidation. These include proposals for gold revaluation, a floating rate for the pound, or default on the sterling balances. However, none has much merit as a policy option for the U.K. It is not so easy to shift the burden of the sterling problem. There are no easy solutions.

Gold revaluation

Gold revaluation frequently used to be urged as a solution of the general problem of international liquidity. If global reserves were inadequate, it was argued, then it was advisable to raise the official price of gold vis-à-vis all national currencies. This would not only increase the value of existing gold stocks; it would also induce dishoarding from private gold hoards, and would stimulate greater production from the mine fields of South Africa and elsewhere. Not surprisingly, the South African Government was among the most vocal proponents of this approach to international monetary reform. However, in other countries the idea received little official support. Governments recognised the inherent deficiencies of the approach: in the short run, revaluation would be inflationary and highly inequitable; in the longer run, it would fail to provide for the steady growth of global reserves which was generally thought to be desirable. Nevertheless, for a time the idea generated considerable political controversy, thanks especially to the personal attitudes and utterances of Charles de Gaulle. However, eventually the whole issue grew somewhat obsolete – once official and private gold markets were separated by the two-tier price system in 1968, and then the I.M.F.'s new special drawing rights started coming into existence. Today revaluation is not considered a serious or relevant policy option.

In the United Kingdom the approach used to receive support in a number of quarters, especially in the financial Press. It was realised that although a rise of the official price of gold would be a multilateral operation designed to remedy a genuinely world problem, none the less Britain could expect to be one of the most important incidental beneficiaries. With reserves held mainly in gold and liabilities denominated mainly in sterling, the country stood to profit from any revaluation of monetary stocks. The idea was that the windfall gain could then be used to liquidate some part of the overhang of sterling liabilities – at the expense, it should be noted, of sterling holders (who would lose by holding sterling rather than the appreciating asset, gold').[1]

Indeed, if the windfall gain were great enough, it could have been used to fund *all* of the sterling liabilities. By this means, gold revaluation might have been a convenient *deus ex machina* for the total domestication of sterling (all at the expense of sterling holders). But of course for this purpose Britain's gold reserve alone, while large, was just not large enough. For example, at the end of 1969 U.K. monetary gold stocks stood at £613 million. At the same time the minimum amount

[1] The gold-revaluation approach to the sterling problem is discussed by McMahon, pp. 91–3, and Strange, pp. 53–4.

of sterling balances outstanding to be funded (including all private holdings, plus the official holdings of overseas sterling-area countries) stood at some £3700 million[1] – a ratio of approximately 6:1. In order to pay off all of these liabilities by itself, Britain would have required a sixfold increase in the official price of gold (a rise of 500 per cent). This would have been far beyond anything even remotely dreamed of by the various advocates of revaluation. More commonly, they used to think of a doubling of the gold price, or at most perhaps a tripling. Yet anything as small (relatively) as this simply would not have been enough. Britain's own revaluation gain would not have sufficed to finance a liquidation of all the sterling balances.

Therefore, if a total domestication of sterling were the objective, it would have been necessary to mobilise not only Britain's own revaluation gain, but also the gains of other major gold-holding countries as well. Suppose the price of gold had been only doubled. Other countries would still have gained enough to make a loan to the British sufficient, together with Britain's own profit, to fund all outstanding sterling liabilities. The pound could thus have become a purely domestic currency, and Britain would have been left simply with a single consolidated long-term debt. Jacques Rueff was especially prominent in advocating this kind of solution for the problem of the sterling balances.[2]

Certainly this kind of solution had the advantage of simplicity. Like the straightforward funding schemes already discussed, it would have removed the sterling problem once and for all, neatly and cleanly. However, also like the other schemes, it would have saddled the British with a burden of fixed debt that would be immense by any normal standard. The gold revaluation solution shared the same basic defect of the other funding proposals. To illustrate, suppose again that the gold price had been doubled at the end of 1969. Britain's own revaluation gain would have amounted to only £613 million (equal to the size of the U.K. monetary gold reserve). But since minimum balances to be consolidated amounted to some £3700 million, a loan of roughly £3100 million ($7½ billion) would have been required

---

[1] This amount does not include the official holdings of non-sterling-area countries and the I.M.F., almost all of which carry a gold-value guarantee. See below.

[2] See, e.g., Jacques Rueff, 'The Gold Standard', in Francis Cassell (ed.), *International Monetary Problems* (London: Federal Trust for Education and Research, 1965) pp. 35–41.

from other major gold-holding countries, out of their own windfall profits, in order to liquidate all of the outstanding sterling balances. Once again, extreme generosity would have been required on the part of Britain's creditors in order to hold down the annual cost of servicing such a debt. Otherwise, once again the reform just would not have been in Britain's own interest.

A floating rate for the pound

What about letting the pound float? This alternative is often urged as a solution for the overall problem of sterling.[1] Several advantages are claimed for it, in particular with respect to the process of balance-of-payments adjustment. If the rate for the pound were absolutely free to move, adjustment supposedly could be accomplished simply through variations in the price of foreign exchange. Accordingly, international reserves would be unnecessary to defend Britain's external economic position; consequently, the balance of payments supposedly would be removed as a constraint on independent domestic economic and social policies – and with it the threat of the overhang of sterling liabilities. Another advantage often claimed is that the rate for the pound could be unpegged unilaterally. It would not be necessary to wait for the rest of the world to agree to a co-ordinated move in the direction of multi-lateral exchange-rate flexibility.

Whether the decision were unilateral or not, a floating rate in all likelihood would eventually terminate sterling's status as an international currency. Conceivably, of course, that might not happen: the pound might continue to be used for at least some international purposes. For example, as in the 1930s some countries in the sterling area might continue to peg their own exchange rates to the pound, treating sterling in effect (rather than the dollar or gold) as their ultimate unit of account. Likewise, some private transactors might continue to use the pound as exchange intermediary and accounting unit, perhaps also even as a store of value. Indeed, if the move to exchange-rate flexibility were general, private demand for sterling could actually be

[1] See, e.g., Harry G. Johnson, 'The Case for Flexible Exchange Rates, 1969', in Harry G. Johnson and John E. Nash, *U.K. and Floating Exchanges*, Hobart Papers, No. 46 (London: Institute of Economic Affairs, 1969) pp. 34–7; and *The Economist*, 30 Nov 1968, pp. 15–16; and 17 May 1967, pp. 16–17. Also, for a discussion of this alternative, see McMahon, pp. 59–60, and Strange, pp. 54–6.

increased. This was suggested, for instance, by James Meade, writing in
1955:

> On this score we can, I think, be more optimistic about the future of sterling
> under a general system of fluctuating exchange rates. For . . . a general system
> of fluctuating exchange rates should lead to all sorts of developments in which
> transactions between countries whose currencies are expected to be peculiarly
> liable to fluctuation will be expressed in terms of the currencies of third
> countries. The City of London with its traditions and its continuing strengths
> in this kind of business might well provide some of the most important services
> of this kind to traders and others in the rest of the world. . . .[1]

However, in the years since 1955 the development of the Euro-
currency market has demonstrated the error of Professor Meade's
early reasoning. The services of the City do not depend much on the
demand for sterling as international money (Chapter 6); in fact, the
Euro-market demonstrates that so far as private transactors are concerned, the dollar is currently a much more popular asset and exchange
intermediary than the pound. Likewise, at the level of official transactions, events have shown that sterling has long since ceased to serve
widely as an international accounting unit (Chapter 8). Accordingly,
it seems clear that if the pound were allowed to float, undoubtedly it
would soon lose whatever significance it still retains as an international
currency. Most sterling holders would almost certainly begin to sell off
their balances, in order to switch into dollars or other more stable
asset-reserve media. Use of the pound for international purposes would
shrink to a minimum.

A wholesale liquidation of sterling balances would mean a lower
foreign-exchange rate for the pound. In turn, from the U.K. point of
view, this might be thought to imply the additional advantage of
shifting some part of the cost of the pound's liquidation from the
British to their creditors overseas. In fact, though, this advantage is
more apparent than real. Today, the largest part of sterling liabilities
outstanding are covered by exchange guarantees of one kind or another.
Drawings on the I.M.F. have always carried the Fund's usual gold-
value guarantee. Now, in addition, liabilities incurred as part of central-
bank swaps are also protected against a depreciation of the pound.
Similarly, under the terms of the 1968 Basle reform, liabilities to
official sterling-area holders (except for a portion equal to 10 per cent

---

[1] James E. Meade, 'The Case for Variable Exchange Rates', *The Three Banks
Review* (Sep 1955) p. 27.

of total reserves) are now subject to a guarantee expressed in dollar terms – though this, to be sure, is conditional upon each country maintaining a Minimum Sterling Proportion in its reserves (Chapter 7). Only privately owned sterling balances still carry no formal guarantee of any kind. At the end of 1968 these amounted to less than £1700 million – less than a quarter of the total of all balances outstanding (Table 5.3).

In actual practice, therefore, only a small proportion of sterling liabilities could be fully liquidated simply by allowing the pound rate to depreciate. Most would still have to be paid off at their outstanding gold or dollar value – meaning, obviously, that they could not be paid off at all without a massive long-term loan from abroad. In other words, once again Britain would have to be saddled with an immense burden of fixed-term debt (payable, moreover, at fixed rates of exchange); once again, extreme generosity would be required on the part of the country's creditors in order to make the consolidation of obligations worth while. The solution contains the same basic defect as all other variations on the funding theme.

Nor is this the only defect of the floating-rate solution: there are other deficiencies as well. Absolute exchange-rate flexibility would not necessarily accomplish all that is claimed for it as a balance-of-payments adjustment mechanism. On the contrary, adjustment might actually be more difficult than it is now if private speculation in the exchange markets turned out to be destabilising rather than stabilising. Moreover, a floating rate might actually prohibit rather than promote foreign trade and investment, by emphasising uncertainties about the near-term future. Forward markets can compensate for the risks of single transactions; but they cannot compensate for the absence of a fixed frame of certainty in the medium run which is so essential to the calculation of traders and investors.[1] There is no need to rehearse all of the objections to flexible exchange rates here; they have been elaborated enough elsewhere.[2] Suffice it to say that they are serious – sufficiently serious, in my opinion, to rule out the idea altogether as a genuine policy option. The approach receives hardly any support at all in official or banking circles.

[1] Charles P. Kindleberger, *Europe and the Dollar* (Cambridge, Mass.: The M.I.T. Press, 1966) pp. 117–23.

[2] See, e.g., Fritz Machlup and Burton G. Malkiel (eds), *International Monetary Arrangements: The Problem of Choice*, Report on the Deliberations of an International Study Group of 32 Economists (Princeton: International Finance Section, 1964).

Many of the deficiencies of freely flexible exchange rates would be corrected by alternative proposals for either 'wider bands' or 'crawling pegs' – or some combination of the two.[1] These approaches receive considerably more support in official and banking circles. However, as far as the sterling balances are concerned, the same defect remains: funding would be required on a scale that would burden Britain with the same impossible load of fixed long-term debt (payable at fixed rates of exchange). Therefore, in so far as the problem of the sterling balances is concerned, the same objections apply to these variations as well.

Default

One last alternative to consider is default. The U.K. could, by uni-lateral action, just repudiate or confiscate all of its foreign liabilities. This would immediately spell the end of sterling as an international currency: no one would ever voluntarily accumulate wealth in the form of pounds again; and in turn this would discourage the currency's use for transactions and accounting purposes as well. This would also be the simplest way of making someone else pay the cost of liquidation. The losses would be borne directly by the individuals and govern-ments who, trusting the convertibility pledge of the British Govern-ment, have until now continued to hold the pound for asset or reserve purposes.

However, it is obvious that sterling holders are hardly likely to accept such losses without a fight. More probably, they would attempt to recoup the cost of liquidation by any means available. Consequently, by its unilateral action the U.K. would be exposing itself to the risk of all manner of retaliation from abroad. For example, British exports might be boycotted or subjected to discriminatory restrictions; like-wise, imports might be withheld at the source or embargoed. For a country as dependent on trade as Britain is, a commercial war could be disastrous. Alternatively, British foreign assets and investments might themselves be repudiated or seized. The U.K. is a creditor nation inter-

---

[1] See, e.g., George N. Halm, *The Band Proposal: The Limits of Exchange Rate Variations*, Special Papers in International Economics, No. 6 (Princeton: Inter-national Finance Section, 1965); John H. Williamson, *The Crawling Peg*, Essays in International Finance, No. 50 (Princeton: International Finance Section, 1965); and James E. Meade, 'Exchange-Rate Flexibility', *The Three Banks Review* (June 1966) pp. 3–27.

nationally: total assets overseas exceed total liabilities by nearly £2000 million.[1] The country stands to lose much more than it might gain from any cut-throat competition of this sort.

For precisely these reasons, no one seriously proposes default as a deliberate policy measure for Britain. It would be suicidal. To be sure, as I suggested at the start of this chapter, it is an action that the U.K. could be forced to *in extremis* – say, by the heavy burden of its outstanding fixed debts, or by a severe and prolonged crisis of the balance of payments, or by a general breakdown of the international monetary system. Under such conditions there might be no alternative to a repudiation of the country's liabilities. However, this would represent the ultimate failure of policy, not a conscious choice among options. So long as other alternatives are available, default must be rejected as a solution for the problem of sterling as an international currency. The potential risks and costs are just too great to contemplate.

[1] At the end of 1968, the total foreign assets of the United Kingdom, including both long-term and short-term items, official as well as private, amounted to £18,235 million. At the same time, total liabilities amounted to £16,260 million. Central Statistical Office, *United Kingdom Balance of Payments 1969*, pp. 44–6.

11 The Basle Facility of 1968

I F sterling cannot be fully domesticated, then it must continue to be used for at least some international purposes. Britain has no choice but to remain in the international-currency business. The real issue for the British is not whether the pound should be liquidated; I have argued that so far as they are concerned, it should not be. The problem is, rather, whether the pound ought to be modified – to what extent and by what means. Should sterling continue to serve as fully developed money for both private and official international transactions, or should some of its roles be eliminated? Should it function on a global scale or a regional scale? Should reform be unilateral or multilateral? These are the questions we shall be concerned with in the final chapter of this study.

The logical starting-point for any reform of sterling is the so-called Basle facility of 1968 (see Chapters 4 and 7). This arrangement, to-gether with the associated bilateral agreements between Britain and the overseas sterling-area countries, established several important prece-dents in the history of the pound as an international currency. None can be ignored in any future modification of sterling's status. I shall begin, therefore, in this chapter with an examination of the 1968 reform, and then consider in Chapter 12 possible changes in each of the separate roles of the pound. The conclusions of the analysis will be summarised at the end of Chapter 12.

I. AN AMBIGUOUS LANDMARK

When the Basle reform was announced in September 1968, many observers jumped to the conclusion that the domestication of sterling was at hand. It was presumed to be only a matter of time before the pound would cease altogether to perform any international functions. 'The purpose of the scheme is the gradual withdrawal of sterling from its reserve role', *The Times* reported bluntly;[1] and *The Economist*, equally forthrightly if not a bit more nostalgically, described it as 'the end of the old sterling area'.[2] But *was* this the end? Certainly the arrangement was a landmark – indeed, a watershed – in the history of sterling; and certainly in the long run it could really lead to a gradual withdrawal of functions. But in the shorter run, and particularly in immediate impact, Basle was far from the end of an international money. In fact, its ultimate implications were quite ambiguous. As Richard Gardner has recently remarked: 'Was this a step toward perpetuating or terminating the sterling area? One could not be sure. . . .'[3]

Consider some of the details of the arrangement. The stand-by credit arranged through the Bank for International Settlements was supposed to be available to finance net withdrawals of private and/or official sterling-area balances, with repayments due between 1973 and 1977. In effect, the stand-by was a medium-term funding facility. However, in all it amounted to just \$2 billion – less than one-third of the total of liabilities to the overseas sterling area outstanding at the time. This was hardly sufficient to fund the whole mass of sterling-area balances. Of course, it could have been a start in that direction. But then, what about the balances held outside the sterling bloc? No provision at all was made for these liabilities: the roles of the pound outside the region were completely unaffected by the scheme.

Similarly, the term of the B.I.S. credit facility, as well as of the associated bilateral agreements between Britain and the overseas sterling-area members, amounted to just three years (plus the additional two-year renewal option). This was hardly sufficient time for the end of anything, let alone the decades-old sterling area – though once again, of course, it could have been a start in that direction.

Most importantly, there was the provision for the Minimum Sterling Proportion (M.S.P.) – the necessary condition for overseas members' eligibility for the exchange guarantee promised by the United Kingdom. This was hardly consistent with an ambition ultimately to terminate the sterling area. On the contrary, it seemed rather more

[1] *The Times*, 9 Sep 1968, p. 1.

[2] *The Economist*, 7 Sep 1968, p. 65.

[3] Richard N. Gardner, *Sterling–Dollar Diplomacy*, rev. ed. (New York: McGraw-Hill, 1969) p. lx. See also Harry G. Johnson, 'Financial and Monetary Problems: Britain and the E.E.C.', in H. G. Johnson, J. Pinder, D. Swann and M. A. G. van Meerhaeghe, *Economics: Britain and the E.E.C.* (London: Longmans, 1969) p. 29.

consistent with a desire to perpetuate it. The exchange guarantee provided an incentive for overseas members to continue to use the pound for reserve and intervention purposes; the M.S.P. provided an assurance that they would in fact do so. The effect could well be to *maintain*, rather than eliminate, the international functions of the pound – at least at the level of official transactions within the sterling region.

The U.K. Government itself has apparently been of two minds on the subject. Roy Jenkins, Chancellor of the Exchequer at the time the Basle arrangement was negotiated, was reported to be determined to end sterling's status as an international currency; 'an anachronism from a different world', he is said to have called it before a meeting of Labour Party M.P.s.[1] Yet when the Treasury's own White Paper on the scheme was issued in October 1968, it took another attitude entirely:

> Sterling's role in the international monetary system has not expanded over recent years. In proportion to world reserves and world trade it has indeed contracted, and in 1968 it has contracted in absolute terms also. *But it will continue in the future as a major part of the international monetary system.*[2]

Thus, Professor Gardner seems to be quite correct: one *cannot* be sure. The most that can be said with certainty about the Basle arrangement is that it was a *reform* of sterling. What its ultimate meaning will be has yet to be decided.

II. THREE PRECEDENTS

As a reform of sterling, the Basle scheme established three important precedents. These were first, the exchange guarantee itself; second, the principle of limitation on the rate of withdrawal of sterling balances (the M.S.P.); and third, the funding to sterling balances on a partial and self-qualifying basis. All three provide an organic basis on which to build further reforms in the future.

The exchange guarantee

The idea of an exchange guarantee for the sterling balances was an old one: observers for years had urged the British Government to con-

---

[1] *The Times*, 20 May 1969, p. 21.
[2] *The Basle Facility and the Sterling Area*, Cmnd 3787 (Oct 1968) p. 7. Emphasis supplied.

sider it as a means of countering the ever-present threat of the over-hang.[1] Some balances, as we know, have always been potentially vola-tile in the short term; in addition, their very existence has tended to induce or aggravate speculative movements of other types of funds (Chapter 7). The reason, of course, was the fear of devaluation. By comparison with holders of dollars or gold, holders of pounds stood to sustain a windfall loss if the parity of sterling were to have been lowered. Their international purchasing power would have been reduced. Consequently, they tended to flee from the pound at every crisis of confidence. But according to the proponents of exchange guarantees, all that would have been changed had the U.K. agreed to maintain fully the exchange value of its liabilities in the event of de-valuation. Then, if parity had happened to be lowered, sterling holders could have been expected to be compensated *in toto* for their losses. Accordingly, they would no longer have had any incentive to flee in moments of strain. So far as they would have been concerned, devalua-tion would be an irrelevant issue. As a result, the overhang of balance itself would finally have been stabilised.

The advantages of an exchange guarantee, proponents argued, were therefore obvious. By agreeing to the idea, the U.K. could in some circumstances avoid a devaluation of the pound – or at least reduce the extent or postpone the date of devaluation – since it would not then be necessary to lower the sterling parity solely because the central reserve was threatened by speculative capital outflows. On the other hand, if devaluation were judged to be the appropriate balance-of-payments policy in a given situation, it could be initiated effectively without the usual air of crisis and weakening confidence. These were strong arguments. Nevertheless, successive British Governments tradi-tionally opposed the idea of a guarantee on principle – on several principles, in fact.[2]

In the first place, the Government doubted whether a guarantee

---

[1] See, e.g., A. C. L. Day, 'What Price the Sterling Area?', *The Listener*, LVIII 1495 (21 Nov 1957) 846; J. O. N. Perkins, 'The World Dollar Problem and Sterling', *Economic Record*, XXXIV 67 (Apr 1958) 44–7; Perkins, *The Sterling Area, the Commonwealth and World Economic Growth* (Cambridge: Cambridge University Press, 1967) pp. 85–9; and John Cooper, *A Suitable Case for Treatment: What to do about the Balance of Payments* (London: Penguin Books, 1968) pp. 231–6.

[2] Christopher McMahon, *Sterling in the Sixties*, Chatham House Essays, No. 4 (London: Oxford University Press, for the Royal Institute of International Affairs, 1964) pp. 58, 93–4.

could be made sufficiently *credible*. Other governments had been known to renege on similar commitments: the United States, for instance, had abrogated gold clauses in 1933. Who would accept that the United Kingdom might not, at some moment of strain, attempt to do likewise? Besides, Britain's short-term liabilities were already far in excess of its gold and dollar reserves: cover was already inadequate. A promise to compensate sterling holders might therefore just not be believed.

As a matter of fact, it is true that guarantees must be credible to be effective. However, it is not true that they are automatically subject to suspicion merely because of some dusty historical analogies. The British Government did itself little good by always casting prospective doubt on its own integrity. And as for the matter of inadequate cover, this was simply a red herring. A commitment to compensate sterling holders in the event of devaluation would not have required the British actually to pay them off in gold or dollars. On the contrary, it would have required them only to *maintain the value* of sterling holdings in terms of gold or dollars – in other words, to write up the exchange worth of balances in proportion to any devaluation that might occur. This was a different matter entirely. Since most sterling balances tended never to leave the U.K. at all (on a net basis), little additional pressure would have been exerted on the central reserves (though of course the overhang of liabilities would have been increased). With its terms clearly understood, a guarantee could easily have been believed. (Certainly the Basle guarantee has been believed.)

A second Government objection to the idea of a guarantee was that full compensation would actually give sterling holders a greater real value for a devaluation than they had had previously, in terms of what they would then be able to buy in the U.K. or in other currencies devalued *pari passu* with the pound. In effect, full compensation would be 'over-compensation': the purchasing power of sterling holders would in fact be increased.

Technically, this argument was quite correct. To counter it, proponents of a guarantee sometimes suggested that compensation be partial instead of total – or, alternatively, that sterling holders forgo or remit some part of their interest earnings.[1] However, in fact this was beside the point. The real issue was what the purchasing power of

[1] See, e.g., Perkins, *The Sterling Area, the Commonwealth and World Economic Growth*, pp. 86–7; and Richard N. Cooper, '*The Balance of Payments*', in Richard E. Caves and Associates, *Britain's Economic Prospects* (Washington: Brookings Institution, 1968) pp. 194–5.

sterling holders would have been if, rather than remaining in pounds prior to a devaluation, they had switched into gold or dollars or some other non-devaluing currency. By that comparison their purchasing power would be no greater as a result of full compensation by the U.K. They would not be receiving 'over-compensation'; they would simply be avoiding a windfall loss (which would otherwise be a windfall gain for Britain).

Does this mean that there is no valid argument for partial compensation (or for its equivalent, partially forgone interest)? Not at all. There *is* a valid argument, but it must be based on different considerations. Rates of interest in London generally tend to be higher than in most other financial centres. Consequently, net yields on sterling balances generally tend to be significantly higher than returns on most other assets-reserve currencies – and certainly higher than on gold, which pays no interest and for which in addition there are storage costs. Central banks and others customarily draw a rigid distinction between current income on the one hand and capital gains and losses on the other. However, this is essentially an accounting convention: in economic terms current earnings and capital revaluations are identical in so far as their impact on the balance sheet are concerned. The British can thus legitimately insist on regarding them as functional equivalents. In the event of devaluation, for instance, they might deduct from the sum of compensation to overseas creditors an amount equal to some or even all of the excess yield on sterling balances previously earned. Or, alternatively, since the former approach could lead to flights from sterling just prior to any suspected devaluation, the U.K. might, in return for a guarantee of full compensation, ask overseas creditors to forgo or remit some or all of their current excess of interest earnings. Either alternative would be partial compensation in a technical sense; but both would be full compensation in an economic sense. Over the long term, by comparison with holders of dollars or other asset-reserve media, sterling holders would sustain no loss of international purchasing power. They would be no worse off than anyone else because of devaluation. But neither would they be any better off than anyone else because of the high interest rates they happened to be earning in Britain.

The final Government objection to the idea of a guarantee was, simply, that it would be too expensive. True, it would cost nothing so long as the sterling parity remained unchanged; but if on the other hand the pound were devalued, then the cost would be substantial.

This argument too obviously was correct – yet it too was beside the point. The contingent cost of compensation could not be considered in isolation. The real issue was to compare that cost with the contingent cost of the constraint disadvantage of sterling's asset and reserve roles, since the latter cost, itself quite substantial, would be diminished if not wholly eliminated by the initiation of an exchange guarantee. Viewed in this light, the potential expense of compensation was not nearly so great as the British Government traditionally maintained.

Actually, despite its objections in principle, in practice the British Government was not nearly so consistent in its opposition to the idea. In fact, guarantees were gradually extended, first to one category of balances, then to another, so that by the time of Basle the proportion of liabilities that had still not been subject to compensation at one time or another was really comparatively small. The precedent established in September 1968 was more one of manner than of substance.

For instance, as long ago as 1944 the British agreed at Bretton Woods to the principle that all I.M.F. drawings, as well as subscriptions, carry a gold-value guarantee. Similarly, in 1949, following the first post-war devaluation of the pound, the country undertook to pay compensation totalling £75 million on sterling balances held outside the sterling area under various bilateral payments agreements. And in 1958 it accepted the requirement of a guarantee for central-bank holdings in the European Monetary Agreement. In 1963 this last was limited to working balances only, but at about the same time the principle of guarantee was adopted as an integral part of the network of swap facilities then being constructed by the major central banks. Most interestingly, in 1964 the U.K. began to experiment with intervention in the forward-exchange market, providing *private* sterling holders with what amounted to an *informal* exchange guarantee, in the form of a kind of officially subsidised insurance. However, as noted in Chapter 7, this experiment was terminated after the second post-war devaluation in 1967.

Thus, by 1968 Britain had already had a variety of experience with different forms of exchange guarantees. What was new about the Basle arrangement was that, for the first time, the principle of compensation was introduced formally *as a reform of sterling*. This had not been true of previous arrangements. Guarantees under the I.M.F., the E.M.A. and the inter-central-bank swap network had all been incidental to the functioning of the pound as an international currency; their primary purpose had been simply to ensure short-term support, whenever necessary, for the British balance of payments. Likewise, the informal guarantee provided by forward intervention was supposed to be designed for balance-of-payments purposes only; no intention to reform the roles of sterling was ever acknowledged. But as we know, the guarantee promised at Basle was most definitely supposed to be part of a reform of the roles of sterling – at least at the level of official transactions within the sterling region. This was a radical departure indeed.

As a matter of fact, in the opinion of some observers the departure was perhaps rather *too* radical. The terms of the guarantee were much too generous, it was said; some additional counterpart concession ought to have been extracted from the sterling-area countries (apart from their single commitment to maintain an M.S.P. in their reserves). As one Member of Parliament expressed it:

> All save a small proportion of sterling balances which are retained will in future be guaranteed against exchange rate fluctuations, while continuing to enjoy an exorbitant rate of interest. It is rather as if the Government had offered holders of War Loan both a guarantee of the current yield on their holdings and a floor price at the present market level. There is not much incubus-shedding about that.[1]

Indeed, there *is* not much incubus-shedding about that. I agree that from Britain's point of view the terms of the guarantee *were* too generous. However, I also believe that in principle the general case for guarantees is a strong one. Furthermore, it is important to remember, as I pointed out in Chapter 7, the situation in which the particular guarantee included in the Basle package was negotiated. In 1968 the British had their backs to the wall; they had little choice in the matter. In 1973, on the other hand, by which time the arrangement must be renegotiated (assuming the two-year renewal option is exercised in 1971), the situation hopefully will be somewhat different. The British should not be negotiating in quite the same atmosphere of crisis. Consequently, they should have more choice about the terms of any further guarantees in the future. A useful precedent has now been established; in my opinion it would be a waste not to build on it. But as I shall indicate below, it seems to me that the British can reasonably argue for a better deal for themselves.

---

[1] John Bruce-Gardyne, in a letter to the editor of *The Times*, 19 Nov 1968, p. 25. See also Paul Bareau, 'Sterling after Basle', *The Banker*, CXVIII 512 (Oct 1968) 871–3; and *The Economist*, 14 Sep 1968, pp. 17–18.

The Minimum Sterling Proportion

I have emphasised that in principle (though not always in practice) the British Government was traditionally opposed to the idea of any guarantee of the exchange value of sterling liabilities. Yet in the opinion of many observers it was hardly possible either, as the only alternative, simply to ignore the threat of the overhang. It was not enough merely to offer attractive interest rates and hope for the best: some other means had to be found for countering the risk of flights from the pound. One alternative often suggested was that the U.K. negotiate some form of limitation on the rate of withdrawal of balances.[1] Either some portion of outstanding liabilities might be blocked; or else a ceiling might be imposed on the amount by which they could be drawn down in any single year. Once again, the advantage would be the stabilisation of the ever-threatening overhang.

However, the British Government was traditionally opposed to this idea also.[2] Any limitation on the rate of withdrawal of balances, it was argued, would cast doubt on the credibility of Britain's convertibility pledge, which was so essential to the continued functioning of the pound as an international currency. Indeed, it would run counter to the entire tenor of British exchange policy, which before 1958 was directed toward enhancing the convertibility of sterling, and after 1958 toward preserving it. A step of this kind would be just too detrimental to foreign confidence.

Nevertheless, in 1968 a step of this kind was taken, with the introduction of the Minimum Sterling Proportion. This provision – the *quid pro quo* for the new exchange guarantee from the U.K. – clearly limited the rate of withdrawal of balances by overseas sterling-area governments. In effect, it turned the clock back to the late 1950s, when sterling-area members still customarily maintained a generally constant percentage of their official reserve-assets in London. After about 1961, by contrast, members began to diversify out of pounds: the percentage of sterling in their reserves declined, though until devaluation in 1967 their balances in absolute amount remained fairly steady;

---

[1] See, e.g., A. C. L. Day, 'Solving the Sterling Problem', *Financial Times*, 2 May 1958, p. 8; and Andrew Shonfield, *British Economic Policy since the War* (London: Penguin Books, 1958) p. 286.

[2] See, e.g., *Report of the Committee on the Working of the Monetary System*, Cmnd 827 (Aug 1959) para. 660.

after devaluation, even in absolute terms, overseas reserve balances began to decline (Chapters 4 and 7). The M.S.P., however, put a stop to all that. Henceforth overseas reserve balances may decline only in proportion to decreases of total reserves of a sterling-area member (assuming the member desires to remain eligible for the British exchange guarantee). As a matter of fact, they must actually rise if the member's total reserves are rising. Overseas sterling-area governments may no longer diversify out of sterling at will.

Significantly, foreign confidence was not shaken by the M.S.P. provision; on the contrary, it was reinforced. True, some overseas sterling-area governments were a bit unhappy about the limitation on the transferability of their sterling reserves.[1] But they soon realised that the limitation was more apparent than real. In fact, the only constraint on their behaviour was that they use sterling in fixed proportion with other reserve assets (gold, dollars, etc.) in the settlement of payments imbalances. This was hardly a major inconvenience. Moreover, even they could see that it was in their common interest to stabilise a portion of the overhang of British liabilities. For Britain, therefore, the threat of sudden withdrawals was reduced: from the British point of view the precedent was an extremely useful one. I see little reason why it should not be possible to extend the principle in the future.

Funding

A third alternative means of countering the threat of the sterling overhang was the idea of funding. Various proposals along these lines have already been outlined in the previous chapter. Needless to say, these suggestions too were traditionally opposed by the British Government. Its customary reasoning was summarised cogently by Malcolm Crawford:

> The Treasury and the Bank of England have been far from eager to pursue ideas of funding overseas holdings of sterling. Their (unpublished) thinking has been roughly this: the sterling balances have posed a potential threat to Britain's reserves, and this threat may even at times have prevented the Government from pursuing rational policies, for fear of a run on sterling; but we do not now have a choice between having the sterling balances or not having them – it is a question rather of relatively more or less onerous terms on which they (or a part of them) could be disposed of. It would make little

[1] See, e.g., *The Economist*, 7 Sep 1968, p. 65.

sense to exchange balances, which may well remain intact, for an obligation to make fixed repayments over a period of years – especially at a time when we already have heavy fixed-term repayment obligations falling due for several years ahead. And anyway, the magnitude of the problem made it a pipe dream.[1]

I agree of course with the Government's reasoning: funding *is* a pipe dream if the idea is to consolidate *all* of the overseas holdings of sterling. Essentially this was the position I argued at length in the previous chapter. But what about the alternative idea of a partial funding of sterling liabilities? That, I suggested, might actually be more in the British interest. After all, why *not* leave untouched those balances which may well remain intact anyway? Let sleeping dogs lie. There is no need to liquidate liabilities that are already tantamount to obligations of indefinite maturity. On the other hand, there are, as we know, also numbers of creditors who may well wish to run down some or all of their sterling holdings, if not immediately, then at the first hint of crisis. These are truly obligations of definite (short-term) maturity – liquidations that must in any event be financed. But in that case why *not* make use of a longer-term loan, in order to stretch out the structure of the country's external debt? The balance of advantage would be all in Britain's favour.

Unfortunately, the idea of partial funding hits a snag on the problem of identification. Just how can one tell which balances are likely to remain intact and which are not? In a 1966 debate Robert Roosa put the question to Fred Hirsch. Hirsch answered it in the only way possible:

> Well, put that way, you never can tell. You never can identify the potentially troublesome balances in advance, any more than you can ever identify in advance which particular banking depositor is going to rush to the door first. You cannot tell; all you can say is that there are these nervous banking depositors and at any given time they are in danger of all storming the door at once. And the very fact that they are in danger of all storming the door, even if they do not actually get there, worries other people, and adds to the trouble of the situation. This is not fancy; it is very recent London history. Therefore, what I think one must do is have an open-ended possibility for any of these banking depositors. ...Personally, I would make this entirely voluntary and open-ended; and in that way, to use your terms, create a self-qualifying situation.[2]

[1] Malcolm Crawford, 'Funding the Sterling Balances', *The Banker*, CXVIII 509 (July 1968) 608.

[2] Robert V. Roosa and Fred Hirsch, *Reserves, Reserve Currencies, and Vehicle Currencies: An Argument*, Essays in International Finance, No. 54 (Princeton: International Finance Section, 1966) p. 6.

Significantly, this is precisely the principle that was incorporated into the Basle arrangement of 1968. Although offered an incentive to remain in sterling (the exchange guarantee), sterling-area members retained the right to run down their holdings if they so wished; and the $2 billion stand-by facility was arranged to finance any consequent net withdrawals from London.[1] At long last, despite previous British Government opposition, the precedent of funding was established. However, no drawings on the credit facility need ever be made unless sterling holdings are in fact withdrawn, and no holdings will ever be run down except on a genuinely voluntary basis. Thus funding in fact was established in terms that were both partial and self-qualifying. Here was a third precedent on which to build organically in the future.

---

[1] In this respect the, 1968 Basle arrangement was quite different from the 1966 stand-by facility which preceded it (see Chapter 5). That facility 'was limited in size and was clearly intended not to finance a permanent reduction in the sterling balances but only to offset fluctuations'. *The Basle Facility and the Sterling Area,* p. 3.

12 The Reform of Sterling

WE may now get down to the issue posed at the outset of this study (and paraphrased at the beginning of the previous chapter): should sterling be reformed – to what extent and by what means? At present, the pound performs all six monetary functions of an international currency.[1] It is a fully developed international money at both levels of transactions, albeit mainly on a regional rather than a global scale. Of the six functions, two – those of quotation currency and of unit of account for expressing par values – generate neither gains nor losses for the United Kingdom. Accordingly, these two roles may be ignored in the discussion which follows: it hardly matters whether they are modified in the future or not. On the other hand, it matters a great deal whether any of the pound's four other roles are modified or not, since they all do generate gains or losses for the U.K. Indeed, as we know, their effects are substantial (Chapter 9). These roles cannot be ignored.

I. LEVEL OF OFFICIAL TRANSACTIONS

At the level of official international transactions, the pound functions both as intervention currency and reserve currency. Use for these purposes is restricted to the sterling area alone, and has been since the end of sterling's period of globalisation in 1931. Outside the bloc the pound is held by central banks largely to accommodate the British balance of payments, rather than from choice (Chapter 5).

No argument can be made for *reviving* the roles of the pound outside the sterling region. There is just no incentive for it – either from the

---

[1] This includes of course the function of unit of account for expressing par values, which has diminished since the Second World War but has not quite disappeared. A few countries (plus Britain's dependencies) still do peg their currencies to the pound (see Chapter 8).

point of view of non-sterling countries or from the point of view of the British themselves. As I argued in Chapter 1, a currency is not likely to be adopted generally for intervention purposes unless it already is used widely for transactions purposes. The pound, though, outside the sterling area, is not used widely at all as a transactions medium; the dollar is therefore rather more convenient than sterling as an intervention medium. Likewise, the dollar is rather more convenient than sterling as a reserve medium, principally because it is more directly (and credibly) gold-convertible. Non-sterling countries would have an incentive to accumulate pounds voluntarily only if they were given the same exchange guarantee as sterling-area countries.[1] However, for this the *British* have no incentive. True, in the short run voluntary acquisitions abroad would generate seigniorage benefits at home. But in the longer run they would inevitably burden Britain with the same net costs as have previous accumulations. A renaissance of sterling as a global intervention and reserve currency would not be in Britain's interest.

What about a renaissance of sterling as a *regional* intervention and reserve currency? The same argument applies here also: there are no incentives for this possibility either. As I argued in Chapter 4, the mutual ties of trade, finance and politics on which the sterling area was originally based have gradually withered away in recent decades. It is therefore unlikely that many overseas members would now welcome an effort to reverse the trend toward diversification of their international monetary relationships. Nor would it be in Britain's interest to sponsor such an effort. In the longer run the net cost would inevitably be high.

From Britain's point of view, the preferable alternative would be to sponsor a gradual *reduction* of the sterling-area roles of the pound. Total elimination is out of the question. However desirable domestication might appear – whether by funding or by any of the other means discussed in Chapter Ten – over the relevant time horizon its cost would be even higher than the cost of the pound's official functions at present. In this regard the British have no choice: these roles must continue. But on the other hand, they need not continue at the same rate: they could be reduced. In this regard the British *do* have a choice. Partial elimination of sterling's intervention and reserve functions would not be at all impracticable, and could actually generate significant

---

[1] At present, the only non-sterling countries benefiting from a U.K. exchange guarantee are the handful of major powers participating in the network of inter-central-bank swaps.

savings for the U.K. The costs of these functions are unlikely to disappear, but they could be minimised. The basic for reform would of course be the Basle arrangements of 1968.

The Basle arrangement has worked remarkably well. The flight from the pound by sterling-area official holders in 1968, which had been gathering steam from the first quarter, after September was very quickly curtailed by the M.S.P. provision: effectively, much of the threat of the overhang of liabilities was fully neutralised. Even more importantly, the exchange guarantee actually created an incentive for a return flow of funds. By the end of the first quarter of 1969, sterling-area reserve balances in London were already greater than they had been a year earlier. Few calls have had to be made on the stand-by credit arranged through the B.I.S. As *The Economist* noted after the arrangement's first half-year:

> The authorities believe that they have most of all to thank the Basle agreement for sterling's healthier look (this gave Britain a medium-term $2 billion credit to counter fluctuations in the sterling balances of sterling area countries). Not only has it made the bad periods for sterling more short-lived, because holders of these balances have not wanted to rush their money away from London at the first sign of trouble, but it has actually made it more attractive for them to hold sterling and they have responded.[1]

Obviously, nothing succeeds like success. Accordingly, I believe that nothing ought to be done to reverse the gains that have been wrought by the Basle arrangement. In my opinion, the stand-by credit and associated bilateral agreements between the British and overseas sterling-area members ought to be renewed when their term expires in 1971; if possible, in order to maximise its effectiveness, the whole scheme should be made into a permanent rather than an *ad hoc* feature of the overall sterling system. This would minimise the burden for Britain of the official roles of the pound (which, I have argued, they have no choice but to continue anyway). However, in at least two respects I feel that changes in the Basle scheme are possible that would be more to Britain's advantage. One modification concerns the terms

---

[1] *The Economist*, 5 Apr 1969, p. 57. In fact, the authorities have been so pleased with the arrangement's effectiveness that they have begun to suggest that perhaps the same principles ought to be applied to the entire world monetary system as a whole. Roy Jenkins made a proposal along these lines at the 1969 annual meeting of the International Monetary Fund. See *The Times*, 1 Oct 1969, p. 21; and *The Economist*, 4 Oct 1969, p. 83.

of the exchange guarantee on sterling-area reserve balances; the other concerns the nature of the funding facility provided through the B.I.S.

I have already suggested that so far as the British are concerned, the terms of the Basle exchange guarantee are rather too generous. Overseas sterling-area countries now enjoy both stable capital value and exceptionally high interest rates on their balances. Yet no *quid pro quo* was extracted from them in return, apart from the M.S.P. provision, and that, I have argued, is hardly much of an inconvenience. In my opinion, the outer members could reasonably be expected to pay a much higher price for their guarantee than they do now. The additional concession ought to be negotiated before the arrangement is renewed in 1971.

Conceivably, the concession might take the form of an agreement for partial rather than full compensation in the event of another sterling devaluation. This would have the effect of reducing the contingent costs of the official roles of the pound: if sterling were devalued, the British would pay less. But note also that unless sterling were in fact devalued, the British would derive no benefit at all from the concession, whereas outer members would meanwhile continue to enjoy a riskless asset earning high rates of interest. In other words, outer members would continue to get something (security) for nothing. From Britain's point of view, this would not be the best possible deal. The best possible deal would take the form of the alternative to direct partial compensation – namely, a concession of interest on sterling-area reserve balances in London. Member-countries would agree to forgo or remit a designated portion of their interest earnings. This would have the effect of reducing the *current* costs of the official roles of the pound.

What form should the interest concession take? A whole variety of arrangements may be imagined. Perhaps the easiest one to implement would simply build on the precedent already established by the M.S.P. Under the terms of the Basle scheme, sterling-area countries must now hold a minimum proportion of their total reserves in sterling. I propose that, in future, they be obliged in addition to invest a fixed proportion of their sterling holdings in non-interest-bearing British Government securities. This might be called the Minimum Non-interest Sterling Proportion (M.N.S.P.). Outer members wishing to remain eligible for the exchange guarantee would have to maintain an M.N.S.P. as well as an M.S.P.

Like the M.S.P., the M.N.S.P. could be determined for each country mutually through a process of bilateral negotiation. It could not be set too high; if members were to be unable to earn as much on sterling as on alternative reserve assets (viz. dollars), they would have little incentive to continue using the pound at all. But it could not be set too low either if it is to be worth while for the British. Ideally, it might be established as a variable ratio in relation to the moving average of the differential of representative interest yields between London and (say) New York. For example, if at a given time representative interest rates in New York were only half as high as in London, the M.N.S.P. might be set at 50 per cent. If rates were then to rise to a level 75 per cent as high as in London, the M.N.S.P. could be reduced to 25 per cent; if, on the other hand, they were to decline to just 25 per cent of London's rates, then the M.N.S.P. could be raised to 75 per cent; and so on. Probably the ratio would have to be adjusted to include some premium of interest earnings on sterling, as a supplementary incentive to sterling-area members not opt out of the system. But this would not be asking too much of the British: even then they would be able to save considerably on what it now costs to maintain the pound as an intervention and reserve currency.

The stand-by credit provided through the B.I.S. was another useful precedent established by the Basle agreement. I propose that this too should be extended beyond 1971, also if possible on a permanent rather than an *ad hoc* basis.

Conceivably, the B.I.S. facility might be replaced by a similar stand-by from the International Monetary Fund. This could provide for supplementary issues of S.D.R.s when needed to finance withdrawals of sterling-area balances; to match these issues, the U.K. would assume a longer-term debt to the Fund.[1] The two alternatives are equivalent in so far as the British are concerned: there is no *a priori* reason for preferring one over the other. However, whichever approach is chosen, it ought to include as well an easing of repayment terms for Britain. The present B.I.S. facility is only medium-term in duration: any drawings made during the first three years are supposed to be fully repaid between the sixth and tenth years (1973–7). From the British point of view this is an uncomfortably short repayment period,

---

[1] Similar suggestions have been put forward by Geoffrey Bell, 'Can the U.K. Get More Time to Pay its Debts?', *The Times*, 17 July 1969, p. 25; and by Peter Jay, 'The I.M.F. Must Find Firm Ground', *The Times*, 29 Sep 1969, supplement, p. i.

coming on top of an already very heavy load of fixed debts due in the next few years (Chapter 10). Consequently, in so far as the British are concerned, it would be preferable to lengthen the terms of any re-negotiated facility as much as possible. A repayment period of fifteen to twenty years might not be an unrealistic goal to aim for. This would certainly have a significant impact in reducing the average annual cost of any funding of official balances that does occur.

II. LEVEL OF PRIVATE TRANSACTIONS

At the level of private international transactions, the pound still func-tions on a global scale for both transactions and asset purposes. Of course, it is only inside the sterling area that the currency is used really widely; there it predominates. Outside the bloc it is just one of several international moneys. Indeed, to the extent that the pound is still used at all outside the region, it is mainly because of its convenience as a medium for doing business with residents within the limits of the sterling area.

On balance, the global *transactions* role of the pound appears to be beneficial rather than costly for the U.K. True, interest charges on private working balances are quite high, amounting to an estimated £30 million a year at present. But the related earnings of the City, and of overseas investments, are even higher – almost three times as high, in fact (Table 9.1). Accordingly, there hardly seems to be any reason for disturbing this particular function of sterling. On the contrary, there seems to be good reason for preserving it. In my opinion, British policy ought to be directed toward the maintenance of the pound's role as a transactions currency.

Furthermore, in my opinion the object of policy ought to be to maintain this role not merely on a regional scale but, to the extent that it remains today, on a global scale. This would not require Britain, for instance, to restore exchange-control authorisation for sterling credits on third-country trade; on a world-wide basis the pound cannot hope to compete with any success against the more popular dollar. But it would require Britain to protect the convenience non-sterling-area residents now find in using sterling to do business with residents within the bloc. Not only would this preserve all of the net social gain

FS I

to Britain accruing from the pound's medium-of-exchange function for private transactions. It might in addition help in minimising the net losses from this and other functions at the level of official international transactions. I have argued that the British have no choice but to maintain in some form sterling's official functions within the sterling area. The more widely the pound is used as a private exchange intermediary, the more likely it is that sterling-area governments will continue to find it attractive as an intervention currency too; and in so far as this in turn makes the currency a more practical store of value as well, it should ensure continued use as a reserve medium also. In other words, the prospective cost of funding official balances could well be reduced if sterling remains widely used for private transactions purposes.

How can British policy help to maintain the transactions role of the pound? Sterling is already highly attractive as a means of reducing transactions costs, at least within the sterling region. Though it no longer predominates globally, the U.K. is still the single most important country in sterling-area trade; and in addition, its financial facilities are still among the best available anywhere. Little can be done within the sterling region to enhance the currency's transactions attractiveness further. On the other hand, much might be done to enhance the other condition necessary to its medium-of-exchange function – namely, convertibility. Britain today does not credibly satisfy this requirement of an international money. After two devaluations in a generation, the country's pledge of convertibility at a fixed rate of exchange elicits little faith anywhere. Moreover, this is no longer a matter of concern only to non-sterling-area residents; now that all but a few member-countries have stopped pegging their currencies to the pound, residents within the bloc have to be concerned as well. The credibility of Britain's convertibility pledge must be enhanced. It is not necessary to convince private transactors that the pound will never be devalued. That would be unrealistic: in a dynamic world, the possibility of a third devaluation (or more) must realistically be conceded. It is only necessary to convince transactors that they need not *worry* about devaluation. This can be accomplished by providing them with some kind of exchange guarantee.

The Basle arrangement established the precedent of an exchange guarantee for the purposes of reforming sterling, though of course that guarantee was intended for official sterling-area balances only. The British Government has always opposed the principle of compensation for private holders, indeed even more adamantly than it traditionally opposed guaranteeing official holders. The latter, the authorities sometimes seemed prepared to concede, perhaps actually might have had a case. A claim to compensation could conceivably have been based on the argument that because of ties of law, loyalty or politics, official holders were already observing an informal obligation not to convert their pounds into other currencies for speculative reasons. (In fact, this was just the lever the sterling-area countries used to obtain the Basle guarantee in 1968.) Private holders, by contrast, have never felt themselves under any such obligation. They presumably invest in the pound mainly for reasons of convenience or yield. Their exchange risks, in so far as these are not covered in the forward market, are an integral part of their overall business calculations. For them, therefore, an exchange guarantee would be an unwarranted bonus – or so the British Government has always maintained.

Nevertheless, between 1964 and 1967 the Government did in fact provide private transactors with a kind of exchange guarantee – in the form of officially subsidised insurance in the forward-exchange market. As I described in Chapter 7, this experiment was discontinued after the devaluation in 1967 and is apparently not to be resumed. However, in my opinion that decision is a mistake. Certainly it is true that the policy of forward intervention resulted in very sizeable losses to the Government, owing to the mass of commitments outstanding on the day parity was actually lowered. Forward intervention does have a cost. But it is also true that over the years prior to devaluation, as a partial offset to this cost, the Government had earned a considerable profit from supporting the forward rate. Forward intervention has a benefit as well.

This benefit could be regained if the policy of forward intervention were resumed. I propose that it should be resumed. Except in the event of another devaluation, the policy would not cost Britain at all; moreover, even if parity must eventually be lowered again, cumulative profits (assuming the interval to the next devaluation is sufficiently long) could well be enough to make the devaluation loss, in effect, self-financing. And in the meantime, the credibility of Britain's convertibility pledge would be enhanced by the informal exchange guarantee provided through the forward market, thus helping to maintain the private transactions role of the pound. As a result, the net social gain of this monetary function could continue to accrue to Britain.

By contrast with its transactions role, the pound's global *asset* role appears to be costly for the U.K. on balance rather than the reverse. Indeed, at present it is the *most* expensive of any of sterling's uses, specifically because of the contingent cost of the constraint disadvantage (Table 9.1). Accordingly, there hardly seems any reason for preserving this particular function on its present scale, unless its contingent cost could be very significantly reduced.

The contingent cost of the asset-currency constraint has two aspects: first, the potential volatility of foreign holdings of sterling; and second, the effect of this sensitivity in prompting additional speculation (leads and lags) at times of weakening confidence. Both aspects have a common source: the overhang of sterling balances privately held outside the sterling area, consisting largely of investments in the United Kingdom. Only these pose any real danger of volatility in the short term (Chapter 7). Therefore, only these need concern us here. Nothing at all need be done about private asset holdings within the sterling area.

True, sterling-area private-asset holdings do cost the British a small amount of interest annually, but this is more than offset by the continued seigniorage benefit of related investment earnings in the bloc. The important point about these holdings is that they traditionally show little sensitivity to temporary changes of sentiment. They do not add to the balance-of-payments constraint for Britain. To be sure, there may well have been some increase in the sensitivity of sterling-area private balances since the devaluation of 1967, owing to the windfall losses suffered at the time by many holders. However, as I noted in Chapter 7, even if this has occurred, it adds no real threat to the pound. Sterling-area joint exchange-control regulations ensure that any net reduction of private balances within the bloc will be matched simply by corresponding net increases of official balances, and the probability of a matching decrease of official balances is limited by the exchange-guarantee and M.S.P. provisions of the 1968 Basle arrangement. Consequently, very little drain of reserves is likely to result. Moreover, the stand-by credit facility provided through the B.I.S. is available to meet any net drains that might ensue (though of course at a cost). Accordingly, it does not seem necessary to do anything about the asset-currency role of the pound within the sterling area.

On the other hand, it does seem necessary to do something about this role *outside* the sterling area. One idea might be to preserve the role while attempting to reduce its contingent cost. However, this does not appear a very promising approach. Essentially, this was the approach of the British Government between 1964 and 1967, when it was following its policy of active intervention in the forward market. By providing a cheap, informal guarantee for private transactions, the authorities hope to forestall massive withdrawals at moments of weakening confidence. Unfortunately, in this respect the policy was less than totally successful. Certainly it helped to maintain the attractiveness of the pound as a private exchange intermediary. But it was unable to prevent occasionally quite substantial outflows from London. Non-sterling-area residents still found it profitable to speculate against the pound whenever there was the simultaneous possibility of speculating *in favour* of some other currency (e.g. the Deutschmark). Indeed, this was an inevitable consequence of the pound's role as a private store of value: so long as it continues to be widely used extra-regionally as an asset currency, sterling must always remain subject to this kind of 'backwash' effect (see Chapter 7). Official support of the forward rate can do nothing about it.

If the contingent cost of the pound's asset-currency role outside the sterling area cannot be reduced significantly, then the role itself must be eliminated. This is the avenue of approach that I recommend. However, in turn this raises a difficult question: how is it possible to reconcile this objective with the simultaneous objective, recommended earlier, of maintaining the pound's extra-regional transactions-currency role (to the extent that this latter remains today)? The answer, I believe, is to be found in two of the precedents established by the 1968 Basle arrangement – the M.S.P. provision and the principle of funding on a partial and self-qualifying basis.

Essentially, to reconcile these two objectives it is necessary to identify, within the total of non-sterling-area private balances in London, the line between working balances and investment balances. To eliminate the asset-currency role of the pound outside the sterling region, non-resident investment balances must be liquidated once and for all. But if the transactions-currency role is to be maintained, working balances must be allowed to remain. How can we identify the line between the two?

A priori, we probably *cannot* identify the line between the two. On an aggregate basis, the distinction between working balances and investment balances can rarely be decided with any degree of precision. (The analysis in Part Two ought to be sufficient proof of that proposition.) Only the individual owners of the balances can really know for sure. Therefore, what I propose is that the owners themselves be given the responsibility for deciding. That is where the principle of self-qualification comes in. To begin with, the British Government should negotiate to broaden the terms of the 1968 Basle stand-by (or the I.M.F. substitute for it mentioned earlier) to permit drawings to cover net withdrawals of private non-sterling-area as well as sterling-area balances. This would effectively extend the precedent of partial funding in order to minimise the cost of liquidating the pound's extra-regional asset-currency role. The Government should then establish a time limit within which non-sterling-area residents would be required to liquidate all of their investment balances held in London. The period specified would of course have to be long enough – one or two years, say – to permit investors to sell off their sterling assets with a minimum of capital loss. But the owners of the balances themselves would have full authority to decide which of their holdings are investments and which are really for working purposes. In effect, eligibility for funding would be determined on a genuinely self-qualifying basis.

To ensure that all investment balances will in fact be sold off, the Government should also announce that from the end of the period specified, all remaining non-sterling-area private balances in London will be subject to limitations on their rate of withdrawal outside the sterling area. Holdings would still be freely transferable within the bloc. Sales outside the area, however, would now be limited. This is where the principle underlying the M.S.P. provision comes in. Probably it would not be feasible to apply the same provision exactly: what assets would the minimum proportion apply to? But it should be possible to apply the same *principle* exactly. For instance, the Government could simply limit the rate of withdrawal outside the bloc to some fixed percentage of the outstanding total in any given period – 10 per cent in a quarter, say, or perhaps 50 per cent in a year. For larger totals a smaller authorised percentage might apply; for smaller totals, a larger percentage. Alternatively, consecutively smaller percentages of withdrawal might be authorised in successive time periods. Requirements of this kind would be sure to induce non-area residents to liquidate all of their holdings in London that are not absolutely essential to current or prospective business in the bloc. On the other hand, they would not necessarily have any dampening effect at all on the continued use of sterling for transactions purposes. Therefore, despite the details of this proposal, the pound should probably remain a convenient medium for doing business with residents of the sterling area.

III. CONCLUSIONS

To summarise, I have argued here in Part Three that so far as the British are concerned, it would be best if sterling were to continue in the future as in the past to serve as international money, at least in partial form (Chapter 10). I come to this conclusion not because the currency's international roles appear to be so advantageous for Britain. Rather, I do so because, of all the possible avenues of return to full 'domestication' of the pound, none appears to be anything but distinctly *dis*advantageous. This is certainly true of the various proposals to fund sterling or integrate it with another currency. Every one of these, over the relevant time horizon, would be more costly than the pound's present status as an international currency. Likewise, this is true of the various proposals to shift the cost of liquidation to others. In fact, it would not be so easy to pass on the burden of the sterling problem; moreover, attempts to do so could be seriously detrimental to British national interests. The idea is just not on.

The only role of the pound which I conclude should definitely be eliminated is the role of asset currency outside the sterling area – by far the most costly of any of sterling's present functions. By contrast, the role of transactions currency, both within the sterling area and (to the extent it remains today) extra-regionally, ought to be preserved: on balance, this brings more gains than losses to the British. Nothing at all need be done about the pound's role as quotation currency. At the level of official international transactions, all three functions should be retained within the sterling region. To minimise their costs, some reduction of use may be possible. Total elimination, however, would be inadvisable: that would cost more than the pound's official roles at present.

The basis for reform may be found in the three precedents established by the Basle arrangement of 1968: (1) the exchange guarantee; (2) the principle of limitation on the rate of withdrawal of sterling balances; and (3) the funding of sterling balances on a partial and self-qualifying basis. My own proposals build logically and organically from these.

To begin with, I propose two basic modifications of the Basle arrangement itself. First, parallel to the M.S.P. provision, I suggest that sterling-area countries be required, in addition, to maintain a Minimum Non-interest Sterling Proportion (M.N.S.P.). From the British point of view, this would be a fairer price than the overseas members currently pay for their exchange guarantee on reserve balances in London. And second, I suggest that the term of the stand-by credit facility provided through the B.I.S. be lengthened beyond the present six to ten years. This would ease any repayment obligations that the British might subsequently be obliged to assume. The facility should also be broadened to cover net withdrawals of private non-sterling-area as well as sterling-area balances. This would aid in liquidating the extra-regional asset-currency role of the pound. In order to maximise its effectiveness, the entire Basle scheme should be renegotiated on a permanent rather than an *ad hoc* basis.[1]

Second, I propose that the British resume active intervention in the forward-exchange market. This would provide private sterling users with an informal exchange guarantee in the form of a kind of officially subsidised insurance. Consequently, by resolving doubts about Britain's pledge of convertibility at a fixed rate of exchange, it would help to maintain the private transactions role of the pound within the sterling area as well as extra-regionally.

Finally, I propose that the British compel a liquidation of all non-sterling-area private investment balances in London. Liquidation would be on a self-qualifying basis. All balances remaining after a specified period would be treated as working balances and made subject to limitations on their rate of withdrawal outside the sterling area. This would effectively terminate sterling's extra-regional role as an asset currency without necessarily diminishing its convenience as a medium for transactions with sterling-area residents.

These proposals may not appear very dramatic. Indeed, after the glory of sterling's past they may seem rather squalid. However, they do at least have the advantage, I believe, of realism. They take into account not only the benefits and costs of sterling's present roles; they also consider the benefits and costs of all other conceivable reforms. As compared with the current situation, the reforms which I propose would bring the greatest possible net gain to the United Kingdom. What price glory, anyway?

[1] Subject to the same modifications, the B.I.S. stand-by might, alternatively, be replaced by a similar stand-by with the I.M.F., providing for supplementary issues of S.D.R.s when necessary to finance net withdrawals of balances from London (see above).

Postscript

In April 1969 General Charles de Gaulle suddenly resigned from the Presidency of France – and thus removed, at a single stroke, the most potent obstacle to British membership in the Common Market. Within a month the British Government formally requested a re-opening of the negotiations suspended after the General's veto in January 1963. Within six months the European Commission declared its support of the British initiative. And in December 1969 the six E.E.C. heads of government themselves, at a summit meeting in The Hague, officially committed the Community to renewed talks with the British. Formal discussions began on 1 July 1970. At the time hope was expressed that negotiations between Britain and the Six could be concluded by the summer of 1971, and the necessary ratification procedure by a year later. The transition period to formal British membership, it was anticipated, might then commence early in 1973.

As it has turned out, negotiations from the start have proceeded more slowly than was initially expected. Progress has been retarded on a number of issues, including especially such matters as the length of the transition period, the problems of New Zealand, Hong Kong and the Commonwealth Sugar Agreement, and the status of Britain's EFTA partners. Most difficult of all has proved to be the issue of agricultural finance. As this Postscript is written, the Six and Britain are still quite far apart over the size of Britain's contribution to the Community's common fund during the transition period, and over how quickly the contribution should rise before reaching the final, automatic annual contributions due at the end of the period. Even so, optimism remains high on both sides of the Channel that the talks will eventually end successfully – if not quickly.

What are the implications of these developments for the analysis and conclusions presented in this book? Specifically, will it be necessary to revise or modify the reform proposals recommended in Part Three if Britain does in fact eventually enter the Common Market?

As matters now stand, the answer to this question must, it seems, be in the negative. Even if Britain does enter the Common Market, it will make rather little difference to the future of sterling as an international currency – *unless the Six make much greater progress than they have until now towards some form of monetary integration.* As presently constituted, the Common Market is not much more than a unified trading bloc for industrial commodities, with the additional interesting features of a common agricultural policy and the beginnings of a common fiscal system. It has not yet got anything even faintly approximating a common monetary system. Capital markets in the Community are still sharply segregated, national banking systems are still fundamentally autonomous. The five currency areas (Belgium and Luxembourg have a long-standing monetary union) are still managed quite independently of one another. Moreover, the same rights still apply to new members as well. Accordingly, unless this situation changes, the British too can be expected, even after joining the Community, to continue managing their own currency area independently, just as they (and the Six) have been doing until now. In the event, the reform proposals recommended in Part Two retain their full logic and validity. These policies would be as appropriate for a Britain inside the E.E.C. of today as they were meant to be for a Britain inside EFTA.

But, of course, the situation could obviously change. Suppose the Six were in fact to make some significant progress towards monetary integration and a common currency. A genuine union of national money systems would imply central and undivided responsibility for a whole range of rather sensitive issues, including in particular central-bank policy, reserve management and exchange rates. And this would most certainly matter to the future of sterling as an international currency (as I have already suggested in Chapter 10). However, in the past most of the governments in the E.E.C. have been extremely reluctant to transfer such vital aspects of their sovereignty as these to any central Community institution. This was especially true of the Government of France under General de Gaulle. Consequently, apart from a few moves to liberalise intra-Community capital flows in the mid-1960s, no serious progress towards financial unification of the Six was even considered prior to the General's departure from the scene in April 1969.

Once the General did depart, on the other hand, some measure of progress did become possible, particularly after the new French President, Georges Pompidou, surprised his fellow heads of government at the December 1969 Hague summit conference by personally endorsing the objective of a monetary union for the Community. The effect of Pompidou's endorsement was striking. Within a month the Council of Ministers approved a first step towards effective monetary integration – a $2000 million short-term credit arrangement for mutual support of members' payments balances. In February the Ministers declared their aim to be a full monetary union within ten years. In October agreement was reached to begin, early the next year, an experimental reduction of the margins of fluctuations between the members' currencies. And in February 1971 more detailed agreement was reached on that move plus a whole range of additional steps, including a commitment to hold regular meetings of finance ministers and central-bank governors to co-ordinate national fiscal and monetary policies; creation of a $2000 million medium-term (two to five years) credit facility to supplement the earlier short-term arrangement; and initiation of a study, to be completed by mid-1972, of the possibility of setting up a common reserve fund of currencies which might lead eventually to an E.E.C. federal reserve system.

By this time, however, the French Government was having second thoughts. Throughout the autumn and winter traditional Gaullist resistance to any form of supranationalism had begun to reassert itself in Paris, to the extent that beginning in October, after the accord on exchange-rate margins, France refused to commit itself to any additional steps unless these could be adequately hedged about with safeguards of French sovereignty. As a result, the real significance of the February agreement, reached only after several months of hard bargaining, remains somewhat in question. Has the Community truly made a significant move towards currency unification? Or has it simply postponed the basic concessions of national power that will be required if that objective is ever to be achieved? In my opinion it is the latter. The agreement to hold regular meetings of finance ministers and central-bank governors, for instance, does not bind members' policies to common consent; it merely commits members to attendance. Likewise, no strings are attached to the earlier short-term credit arrangement for support of members' payments balances; and any commitments attached to the later medium- term facility can be easily circumvented by resort to financing through the International Monetary Fund instead. The one really significant move the Community might have taken was in the area of reserve pooling – and that, as indicated, was referred back to the technical experts for detailed study. The Six still cannot be said to have progressed very far towards their goal of monetary integration.

As this Postscript is written, the really hard decisions still lie somewhere in the future.

For better or for worse, therefore, over the near term at least developments between Britain and the E.E.C. are unlikely to make much difference as far as the analysis and conclusions of this book are concerned. Entering Europe would matter to the future of sterling, I have suggested, only if the Community were moving significantly close to a common currency. But the Six hardly seem on the verge of *that* kind of achievement – or even anything like it, for that matter – and Britain really cannot afford to wait. The British Government still has good reason to do something about the pound as quickly as possible; the most appropriate approach to reform, in my opinion, is still indicated by the set of proposals recommended in Part Three. Only one change might be in order. Once inside the Market, Britain might perhaps want to substitute a credit line from its Community partners for the 1968 Basle stand-by (or the I.M.F. alternative to it mentioned in Chapter 12). This would be consistent with the country's new European orientation; it could probably be worked out easily as an adjunct to the Community's newly devised arrangements for mutual support of the balance of payments. But otherwise there would be no reason to modify or revise any of the policy suggestions outlined on pp. 245–6. For the next few years at least, the burden of managing sterling's international activities will still continue to rest essentially on British shoulders.

March 1971

Index

Aldington, Lord, 134 n.
Aliber, Robert, 35 n., 38 n., 39 n., 43, 44 n., 46 n.
Arab countries, withdrawals of sterling during Middle East crisis (1967), 151
Argentina, 67, 69, 192, 193 n.
Asset currencies and purposes, 17, 18, 21, 26, 28, 29, 32, 33, 107, 114, 115, 143, 197, 198, 205: pounds held for private and official asset purposes, 62; decline of pound's importance, 74; proposed elimination outside sterling area, 242–3, 245
Attributes of money, 4
Australia, 67, 180, 194, 205: asymmetrical treatment of pound, 76–7
Austria, central bank credit to Britain, 97

Bagehot, Walter, 61
Bahamas, the, 194
Balance-of-payments data, 122: 'Pink Book' (1969), 122
Balancing item in balance of payments, 167–8
Balogh, Thomas, 80 n.
Baltic Exchange, 117, 127, 139 and n.
Bank for International Settlements (B.I.S.), 78, 204: credit facility, 97, 98, 148, 223, 236–9, 242, 246
Bank of England Quarterly Bulletin, 89, 122, 183
Banker, The, 146
Banking and ancillary earnings of international currency, 37–8, 48–9, 56, 57, 63: offsetting cost, 37–8
Banking in the City, 117: estimates of earnings, 122–6, 143; net earnings, 129–35; sources of invisible earnings,

124, 130; interest earnings, 130–3; extent of dependence on sterling, 130–5; services to foreign customers, 133–4; overseas branches and subsidiaries, 134–5
Bareau, Paul, 126 n., 229 n.
Barter and barter economy, 4–5, 9–10, 25
Basle facility (1968), 56, 78–9, 86, 149, 183–4, 222–33: stand-by credit, 78, 209, 223, 233, 236, 238, 244; exchange guarantee, 78–9, 147, 151, 183–4, 218–19, 223–4, 226, 228–30, 237, 240–2, 245; Minimum Sterling Proportion, 79, 147, 151, 183, 219, 223–4, 229–31, 236–8, 242–5; ambiguity of ultimate implications, 222–224; Treasury White Paper on scheme, 78, 224; and funding, 231–3; partial funding principle, 232–3, 243–5; as basis for reform, 236–7; desirability of renewal, 236–8; possibility of modifications, 236–7
Belgium: francs, 19; central bank credit to Britain, 97
Bell, Geoffrey, 238 n.
Bell, Philip W., 80 n.
Benefits and costs of international currency, 34–51: seignorage, 35–8, 47–8; banking and ancillary earnings, 37–8, 48–9; flexibility over payments imbalances, 38–9, 41, 49; constraint over full-employment policy, 39–41, 49; effect of increase of official reserves, 41–2; money as unit of account, 42

    attribution, 43–51: cost-benefit analyses, 43–5, 56 n.; analytical procedures, 44–9; separate roles,